THE MARSHALL CAVENDISH ILLUSTRATED

# Encyclopedia of Gardening

EDITOR: Peter Hunt

AMERICAN EDITOR: Edwin F. Steffek

ART CONSULTANT: Al Rockall

ART EDITOR: Brian Liddle

**VOLUME 4**

MARSHALL CAVENDISH CORPORATION / NEW YORK

# CONTENTS

THE MARSHALL CAVENDISH ILLUSTRATED

# Encyclopedia of Gardening

**PHOTOGRAPHS IN THIS VOLUME BY:** Alpine Garden Society; Aluminum Greenhouse Inc., Cleveland, Ohio; John Banks; Dr. Peterson Becker; K. A. Beckett; Blackmore and Langdon; A. Boarder; R. J. Corbin; Gordon Douglas; J. E. Downward; Dr. Elkan; Valerie Finnis; Paul Genereux; W. Grant; Miles Hadfield; Iris Hardwick; R. M. Hatfield; Humex Ltd. (by John Hovell at Syon Park); Peter Hunt; A. J. Huxley; G. E. Hyde; Leslie Johns; Reginald Kaye; John Markham; P. Minay; Alan Mitchell; Mondadoripress; Opera Mundi; Murphy's Chemical Company, Ltd.; National Botanic Gardens of South Africa; Maurice Nimmo; Orchid Society of Great Britain; R. Parrett; Plant Protection Ltd.; E. W. Putnam; G. A. Robinson; Gerald Rodway; Patricia Rosenwald; Royal Botanic Gardens, Kew; J. T. Salmon; Kay N. Sanecki; Shell Photography; Donald Smith; Harry Smith; Violet Stevenson; G. S. Thomas; C. Williams.

**ARTWORK:** Cynthia Newsome-Taylor; G. Kingbourn; Tudor Art.

## Cynorchis (si-nor-kis)

From the Greek *kynos*, a dog and *Orchis (Orchidaceae)*. A genus of about 30 species of terrestrial orchids, with fleshy tuberous roots, some with deciduous leaves. The usually bright coloured lip of the flower is the attractive feature and is flattened and curiously lobed. The sepals and petals are mostly greenish. Several species are well worth growing for the very vivid lip colouring.
**Species cultivated** *C. compacta,* white, spring, South Africa. *C. fastigiata,* with small pink flowers at various times, often appears as a casual in orchid pots, growing and seeding itself quite freely. *C. grandiflora,* green, lip rose-purple, winter, Madagascar. *C. lowiana,* purple-magenta, winter, Madagascar. *C. purpurascens,* branching spike of twenty flowers, greenish with purplish lip, summer, Madagascar. *C. villosa,* lilac-purple, lip white, late summer, Madagascar.
**Cultivation** These orchids should be provided with a mixture of loam fibre, leafmould, coarse sand and sphagnum moss in pots. Water when in growth but when the plants are resting, give them only enough to prevent shrinking of the tubers. Maintain a temperature of 50–55°F (10–13°C) in winter and 55–70°F (13–21°C) in summer. Propagation is by separating large tubers in spring.

## Cypella (si-pel-a)

From the Greek *kypellon*, a goblet, a reference to the flower shape *(Iridaceae)*. Bulbs from tropical and South America not wholly hardy except in the warmer climates. Beautiful when grown in pots for the conservatory. The leaves are long and narrow, wrinkled and from 1–4 feet in length.
**Species cultivated** *C. herbertii* (syn. *Tigridia herbertii*), 1 foot, flowers deep golden-yellow, summer, the best known species. *C. peruviana,* 1 foot, outer petals deep yellow, spotted at the base, inner petals smaller also spotted brown. *C. plumbea,* 2½ feet, flowers pale yellow in centre and outer petals bluish-mauve, late summer and autumn.
**Cultivation** In the greenhouse, pot the bulbs in November, five in a 5 inch pot, about 3 inches deep. The pots can be left in a cold greenhouse and protected by peat or matting until shoots appear, then kept at a minimum temperature of 40°F (4°C) and watered regularly until after flowering. Dry gradually through fall to ripen bulbs. Can be planted outside in spring, stored inside for winter. Pot offsets to increase stock.

## Cyperus (si-per-us)

From the Greek *kypeiros,* a sedge *(Cyperaceae)*. Greenhouse and hardy perennials belonging to the sedge family, grown for their foliage. The long, narrow, grass-like leaves are produced at the tops of the slender stems and

1 Cynorchis grandiflora, an orchid introduced from Madagascar in 1893. 2 Cypella peruviana, a bulbous plant that is not reliably hardy, prefers sandy soil. 3 Cyperus alternifolius, a good house plant for a moderately warm room.

radiate like the ribs of an umbrella, hence the common name of umbrella plant given to *C. alternifolius,* a good house plant in moderately warm rooms. **Species cultivated Greenhouse** *C. alternifolius,* umbrella plant, 2½ feet, spikelets brown; vars. *variegatus,* leaves striped white; *gracilis,* 1 foot, an elegant form with narrower leaves, *C. diffusus,* 2–3 feet, very long leaves, spikelets greenish to brown; var. *variegatus,* leaves variegated white. *C. papyrus* (syn. *Papyrus antiquorum),* Egyptian paper reed, papyrus, 8–10 feet, good dark green.
**Hardy** *C. esculentus,* chufa, 2–3 feet, producing edible underground tubers known as tiger nuts in southern Europe. *C. longus,* 4 feet, a good foliage foil for poolside planting.
**Cultivation** The plants are semi-aquatic in nature and require quantities of water, which is best given by standing the pots in a shallow vessel of water. A compost of equal parts of loam and leafmould maintains the moisture well. *C. alternifolius* can be divided each March and repotted to maintain a supply of young plants. Out of doors

the plants lend themselves to planting in boggy situations and on the margins of pools. Plant either in autumn or spring, climate permitting, and remove the dead stems when faded, otherwise the plant has an untidy appearance.

**Cyphomandra** (si-form-an-dra)
From the Greek *kyphoma,* a hump, *aner,* a man, referring to the way in which the anthers form a hump *(Solanaceae).* A genus of softwooded shrubs or small evergreen trees from South America. The only species cultivated is *C. betacea,* the tree tomato, a greenhouse perennial growing 8–12 feet tall, with fragrant purple and green flowers in spring, followed by egg-shaped pendulous fruits, red or reddish-orange, up to 2 or 3 inches long. These fruits are edible and are sweeter than those of the common tomato. Plants can be expected to produce fruit in their second year indoors.
**Cultivation** A light greenhouse where a winter temperature of 50°F (10°C) can be guaranteed is ideal. Tree tomatoes are also grown in borders or in large tubs or troughs in a rich compost of loam, rotted manure, leafmould and sand in equal proportions. Water moderately in winter and freely in summer. Prune plants in April to

restrict growth and prevent straggling.

**Cypress**—see Chamaecyparis and Cupressus

**Cypress Spurge**—see Euphorbia cyparissias

**Cypress, Summer**—see Kochia scoparia trichophila

**Cypress, Swamp**—see Taxodium

**Cypripedium** (si-pre-pee-de-um)
From the Greek *kypris,* one of the names of Venus, *podion,* a little slipper, Venus's slipper *(Orchidaceae).* Lady's slipper orchid. Formerly this generic name covered all the slipper orchids, but as treated here includes only hardy terrestrial species, which are mainly from temperate regions, having pleated deciduous foliage which more or less covers the stem (for the large group of warm house slipper orchids see Paphiopedilum).
**Species cultivated** *C. arietinum,* yellowish-green, brown and white, summer, N. America. *C. calceolus,* dark brown and yellow, summer, Europe (including Britain) and north Asia. *C. candidum,* a small white species from marly bogs, summer, North America. *C. japonicum,* greenish-white, spotted red, summer, Japan. *C. macranthum,* red, purple and pink, summer, north Asia. *C. reginae,* white flushed rose, summer, North America. *C. tibeticum,* greenish-yellow and purplish, summer. Also *C. pubescens, acaule, montanum,* North America.
**Cultivation** Most of these species can be grown outside in woody areas, especially *C. calceolus* and *C. reginae.* The mixture should contain 2 parts of peat, 1 part of leafmould, 1 part of fibrous loam, also some sand and chopped sphagnum moss. Mulch with leaves in winter. Great success can be had with these plants by growing them in an alpine house, in pots or pans in a compost similar to the above. Propagation is by division.

**Cyrilla** (se-ril-a)
Commemorating Dr Dominico Cyrillo, professor of botany at Naples in the eighteenth century *(Cyrillaceae).* A hardy deciduous flowering shrub (evergreen in the more southerly parts of its native habitat) giving good autumn colour. The only species is *C. racemiflora,* the leatherwood, from southern USA, Brazil and West Indies. It is not often grown though it succeeds well in a lime-free soil. The white flowers are borne in July or August in slender racemes on the ends of the old wood at the base of the current year's growth. In the north it requires the shelter of a warm place. Propagation is by 3–4 inch long cuttings taken in July and rooted in either a cold frame, cold greenhouse or under a cloche. Pruning merely

**Cyphomandra betacea, the Tree Tomato, grown under glass like the common tomato, will produce fruit 2 inches long.**

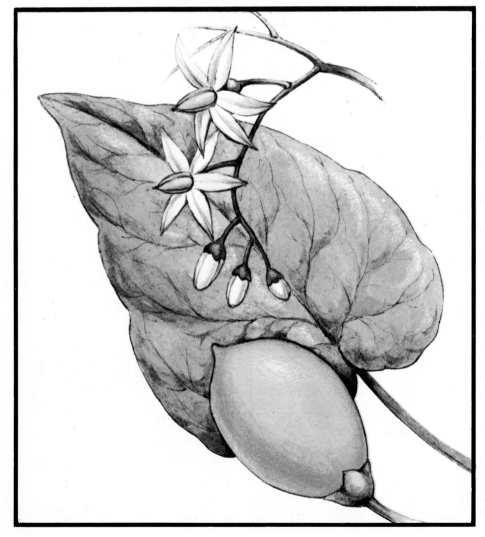

consists in removing unwanted and twiggy growth and shortening any long and disproportionate growth.

## Cyrtanthus (ser-tan-thus)
From the Greek *kyrtos*, curved, *anthos*, flower, referring to the way in which the flowers curve from the stem *(Amaryllidaceae)*. A genus of bulbous plants from South and East Africa, grown in greenhouses here. They are not often cultivated although they have been known in England for two hundred years.

**Species cultivated** *C. angustifolius*, 1 foot, with two or three orange flowers, tubular and horizontal or drooping about $1\frac{1}{2}$ inches long, July and August. *C. falcatus*, $1\frac{1}{2}$ feet, flowers pinkish-red flushed with greenish-yellow along the centres of the petals and the margins shaded crimson, March. The attractive flowers are up to $2\frac{1}{2}$ inches in length. The stem is spotted with purple. *C. flanaganii*, 1 foot, flowers yellow, trumpet-shaped, June. *C. obliquus*, 1–2 feet, with as many as a dozen flowers, nearly 3 inches long, yellow at the base,

shading to orange and then green at the tips of the petals, May and June.

**Cultivation** These plants may be grown in a greenhouse with a winter temperature of not less than 50°F (10°C), on shelves near the light. A compost of equal parts of sand and peat with double the quantity of loam is best and water is needed freely from March to October. Pot bulbs in November, 2 inches deep, and withhold water until growth starts.

## Cyrtomium (ser-to-me-um)
From the Greek *kyrtos*, curved, referring to the habit of growth *(Polypodiaceae)*. Greenhouse evergreen ferns that are almost hardy and make good room plants because of their arching, firm, glossy green, fronds. They have been known to have survived out of doors, but become deciduous under such circumstances.

**Species cultivated** *C. caryotideum*, 1–2 feet, fronds arch beautifully. *C. falcatum*, holly fern, 2–3 feet, tufted growth, the commonly grown species, with drooping fronds. Both have long pinnae, thick and stiff in texture.

1 Cypripedium pubescens, the hardy Lady's Slipper Orchid. 2 Cypripedium speciosum grows to 12 inches and is a native of Japan. 3 Cypripedium reginae is native to USA.

**Cultivation** A greenhouse from which frost can be excluded affords sufficient protection for these ferns but they are happier and entirely evergreen when the minimum temperature in winter is 45°F (7°C). Shade is needed from strong sun and water should be given frequently during the summer, and the pots kept dry during the winter. Out of doors a sheltered corner is best and when planting in April peat should be mixed into the soil. Propagation is effected by sowing spores on the surface of soil in a seed pan which should then be stood in water. Green leaf-like growths appear first and tiny ferns grow from these, which can be potted up when they are big enough. A suitable potting compost is made up of equal parts of peat and loam with a few pieces of charcoal to prevent sourness. Repot in March as soon as new fronds begin to uncurl.

423

## Cystopteris (sis-top-ter-is)

From the Greek *kystis*, a bladder and *pteris*, a fern, referring to the swollen growths on the fronds *(Polypodiaceae)*. Bladder fern. Hardy deciduous ferns, most of them suitable for a shaded rock garden, some of which are native American plants. All start growth very early and last late in the season.

**Species cultivated** *C. bulbifera*, 6–12 inches, North America. *C. fragilis*, 6–8 inches, found in Scotland, the most widely grown British species, variable, many authorities sub-dividing the species; var. *alpina*, 4 inches is a delicate form with finely cut fronds. *C. montana*, 6 inches is very similar, Scotland, Europe, North America.

**Cultivation** These like most ferns, delight in shade and they soon dry and become brown if grown in sunshine. They need a moisture-holding compost of peat and loam but good drainage is also essential. They can be grown in pots but the plants need to be divided from time to time to keep their shapes properly because the stems run along the surface of the soil. They are really better, therefore, in the open. Propagation is by sowing the spores on the surface of pans of regular seeding mixture and from the green leaf-like growth that appears, small ferns will later be produced. Alternatively the plants may be divided in March or April. The small bulbils produced on the fronds of *C. bulbifera* may be stripped from the plant and pressed into light soil in summer and new plants will arise from the green leaf-like growths that first appear.

---

## Cytisus (si-tis-us)

From the Greek *kytisos*, trefoil, a reference to the leaves of some species *(Leguminosae)*. Broom. A genus of deciduous and evergreen shrubs and small trees, some tender, all very colourful and decorative, natives of Europe, particularly the Mediterranean region, some from Asia Minor.

**Species cultivated: Greenhouse** *C. canariensis* (E), the florists' 'genista', up to 6 feet, fragrant yellow flowers, spring and summer; var. *ramosissimus*, smaller leaves, longer flower racemes. *C. fragrans* (D), Teneriffe broom, 2–3 feet, fragrant, yellow flowers, summer; var. *elegans*, 4 feet, taller but with similar yellow flowers. Both grown as florists' flowers. Both species are from the Canary Isles and not hardy even in Britain, except maybe in the most favoured spots where the pots can be stood out of doors in the summer.

**Hardy** *C. albus* (syn. *C. multiflorus)* (D), white Spanish broom, white Portugal broom, 6–10 feet, white, May and June. *C. ardoinii* (D), about 6 inches, mat-forming, bright yellow, April and May. *C. austriacus* (D), 2–3 feet, bright yellow, July to September. *C. battandieri* (D), Moroccan broom, 10 feet, bright yellow, pineapple scented flowers in

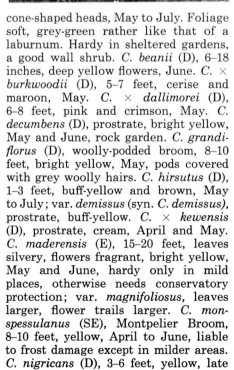

cone-shaped heads, May to July. Foliage soft, grey-green rather like that of a laburnum. Hardy in sheltered gardens, a good wall shrub. *C. beanii* (D), 6–18 inches, deep yellow flowers, June. *C. × burkwoodii* (D), 5–7 feet, cerise and maroon, May. *C. × dallimorei* (D), 6–8 feet, pink and crimson, May. *C. decumbens* (D), prostrate, bright yellow, May and June, rock garden. *C. grandiflorus* (D), woolly-podded broom, 8–10 feet, bright yellow, May, pods covered with grey woolly hairs. *C. hirsutus* (D), 1–3 feet, buff-yellow and brown, May to July; var. *demissus* (syn. *C. demissus),* prostrate, buff-yellow. *C. × kewensis* (D), prostrate, cream, April and May. *C. maderensis* (E), 15–20 feet, leaves silvery, flowers fragrant, bright yellow, May and June, hardy only in mild places, otherwise needs conservatory protection; var. *magnifoliosus*, leaves larger, flower trails larger. *C. monspessulanus* (SE), Montpelier Broom, 8–10 feet, yellow, April to June, liable to frost damage except in milder areas. *C. nigricans* (D), 3–6 feet, yellow, late

**1** Cystopteris bulbifera, a hardy deciduous Bladder Fern that produces small bulbs on the leaves. **2** Cytisus x kewensis, a deciduous shrub for the rock garden or dry wall. **3** Cytisus x praecox, the Warminster Broom, flowers in May. **4** Cytisus x burkwoodii needs acid soil.

---

summer. *C. × praecox* (D), 4–6 feet, cream, May. *C. procumbens* (D), 2 feet, yellow, May to July. *C. purgans* (D), 3–4 feet, usually leafless, flowers fragrant, yellow, April and May. *C. purpureus* (D), purple broom, 1½–2 feet, purple, May and June; var. *albus*, white. *C. ratisbonensis* (D), 3 feet, bright yellow, May and June. *C. scoparius* (D), common broom, Scots broom. 5–10 feet, bright yellow, May and June, native plant; vars. *andreanus* 6 feet, yellow and red; *fulgens,* 6–7 feet, orange and maroon; *prostratus,* 2 feet, yellow; *sulphureus (pallidus),* moonlight broom, dwarfer, deep cream. *C. sessilifolius* (D), 4–6 feet, bright yellow, June. *C. supinus* (D), 2½–3 feet, yellow, July and August. *C. × versicolor* (D), 2–3 feet, buff and

pinkish-purple, May and June.
**Named cultivars** All deciduous, include
'Cornish Cream', 6–7 feet, creamy-yellow;
'Donard Seedling', 6–8 feet, red, streaked
yellow; 'Dorothy Walpole', 6–7 feet,
rich crimson; 'Enchantress', 5–6 feet,
pink; 'Goldfinch', 4–5 feet, lemon-yellow
and cream; 'Hillieri', 2–3 feet, yellow
and bronze, fading to pink, May and
June. 'Johnson's Crimson', 5–6 feet,
carmine and red; 'Lady Moore', 6–7 feet,
red, buff and rose; 'Lord Lambourne',
6–7 feet, crimson and cream; 'C. E.
Pearson', 6–7 feet, apricot, yellow, red,
pink; 'Peter Pan', 1–1½ feet, crimson;
'Porlock', 6–8 feet, fragrant cream,
early-flowering, hardy in the south.
Cultivars of *C. scoparius* include
'Criterion', 6–7 feet, red and lemon-
yellow; 'Diana', 6–7 feet, yellow and
primrose; 'Firefly', 6–7 feet, crimson
and yellow; 'Golden Sunlight', 6–7 feet,
rich golden-yellow.
**Cultivation** Brooms are always grown
in pots until they are big enough to
plant in their permanent positions,
because they do not transplant easily.

They thrive best in a sunny, open,
well-drained position and do very well
in poor, stony, dry soils. The smaller
kinds are ideal for rock gardens and
the taller growing ones are elegant
enough to use as specimen shrubs.
Pruning consists in cutting back old
shoots immediately after flowering to
the base of promising new ones. Never
cut into old wood, as the broom does
not break readily to produce new
growth from the old wood. If shrubs
become leggy at the base it is often
better to replace the plant by a young
one than try to cut it back. The hardy
species can be propagated from seed
sown out of doors in April or May
but hybrids do not come true from seed
and stock of these is increased by
cuttings taken in July or August and
put into a sandy mixture and potted
up into sand and loam once they are
rooted. Grafting is possible and should
be done in March or April, when the
named varieties can be grafted on to
laburnum stocks and kept in a
temperature of 60°F (16°C) until the

**1** A seedling Cytisus scoparius, the
common yellow or Scots broom. **2**
Cytisus battandieri, from Morocco is
not very hardy. **3** Cytisus scoparius, the
influence of which is to be seen in many of
today's popular hybrids and cultivars.

union is complete.
The greenhouse kinds are grown in
pots in a medium of 2 parts of loam,
1 of peat, 1 of sharp sand. Pot in May or
June. Prune after flowering, cutting
flowered shoots to within 2 inches of
their bases. Keep pruned plants in a
temperature of 50–55°F (10–13°C) to
encourage new growth; after repotting
place pots out of doors in a sunny
place to ripen the growth. Bring them
into the greenhouse again in October.
Water freely June to November,
moderately at other times. Feed when in
flower. They are usually propagated by
cuttings taken in spring and put into
a propagating frame in a temperature
of 75–80°F (24–27°C). Seed of the species
can be sown in a temperature of 65–70°F
(18–21°C) in March.

# D

## Daboecia (dab-ee-se-a)

Commemorating St Dabeoc, an Irish saint *(Ericaceae)*. A small genus of low-growing evergreen shrubs resembling the heathers.

**Species cultivated** *D. azorica*, 6 inches, a compact cushion of spikes of rose-red flowers, June and July, Azores. *D. cantabrica* (syns. *D. polifolia, Menziesia polifolia*), St Dabeoc's heath, Irish heath, 1–3 feet, erect spreading shrub with rich dark green leaves, white on the lower surface, and spikes up to 4–5 inches long of purple-red flowers; vars. *alba*, white flowers; *bicolor* some flowers white, some purple, others mixed, all on the same plant, flowering all summer, as late as October or November in dry seasons, native of Ireland, south-west Europe, Azores.

**Cultivation** Like the heathers, daboecias need lime free soil with some moisture-holding peat in it. Plant during the winter. A good effect is made if the shrubs are put in groups of three or five, about 1½ feet between the plants. Pruning consists in removing the old flower spikes. Propagation is from short cuttings taken in August and put into a sandy mixture and protected throughout the first winter.

## Dacrydium (dak-rid-e-um)

From *dakrudion,* the dimutive of *dakru,* a tear, describing the way in which the resin drips from the tree *(Taxaceae).* Ornamental evergreen trees, rather tender and only the comparatively hardy kinds can be grown except in very warm and sheltered areas. Some are important timber trees in their native countries of New Zealand, Borneo, Malaya and Chile, the figured wood being used for cabinet work.

**Species cultivated** *D. cupressinum,* New Zealand rimu, 80–100 feet in its native habitat but probably less than half the size here. *D. franklinii,* Huon pine, 80–100 feet in Tasmania, elsewhere a small tree up to 30 feet, with long pendulous branches.

**Cultivation** A really sheltered spot is needed but the plants can be grown in a large greenhouse and restricted when the chief interest is the variation of leaf form between the seedling and the matured plant. Alkaline soil suits them, and they may be planted either in September, October, March or April. Propagation is by cuttings taken of ripened wood in the late summer and kept in a greenhouse until established and then gradually hardened off.

## Daddy Longlegs—see Leatherjackets

## Daffodil—see Narcissus

## Dahlborg Daisy—see Thymifolia tenuiloba

## Dahlia (day-le-a or dah-le-a)

Commemorating Andreas Dahl, a Swedish botanist who was a pupil of Linnaeus *(Compositae).* Half-hardy, tuberous-rooted perennials from Mexico, first introduced into Britain in 1789 by Lord Bute.

**Species cultivated** (Few of the following original species are available although they may occasionally be seen in botanic gardens and the like) *D. coccinea*, 4 feet, scarlet, September, the parent of the single dahlia. *D. coronata*, 4 feet, fragrant scarlet flowers on long stems, autumn. *D. excelsa*, 15–20 feet, purplish-pink flowers, summer. *D. gracilis*, 5 feet, scarlet-orange flowers, September. *D. juarezii*, 3 feet, parent of the cactus dahlias, flowers scarlet, late August and September. *D. merckii*, 3 feet, lilac and yellow flowers, October (together with

1 Daboecia cantabrica, the Irish or Connemara Heath, flowers from June to November. It won the Award of Garden Merit in 1930. 2 Dahlia 'Beauty of Baarn', 3½ feet, a medium Semi-Cactus that holds its blooms high above the foliage.

*D. variabilis* the parent of most modern double dahlias). *D. variabilis*, 4 feet, (syns. *D. pinnata, D. rosea, D. superflua*), variable flower colours, even a green form was suspected at the end of the nineteenth century. The parent of show, fancy and pompon dahlias.

**Cultivation** Nowadays dahlias are comparatively easy to grow. They tolerate all soils between the moderately acid and alkaline and for ordinary garden purposes need little or no specialised attention, yet will flower profusely. In their evolution they have produced multiple types and hundreds of thousands of varieties simply because they are a cross-pollinated plant. This means that it is possible to produce unusual and original cultivars by raising plants from seed, which is an additional asset. Furthermore, with correct culture, plants will flower continuously from July until the first autumn frosts, providing a colourful display over a range of several months.

**Soil Preparation** This begins in fall or early spring digging of the site, at the same time incorporating plenty of bulky organic materials such as peat, leafmould, spent hops, vegetable compost, or well-rotted horse, pig or cow manure, but not poultry manure which encourages too much growth at the expense of flowers. Put any of these into the top foot of soil, because dahlias make a mass of fibrous roots in this region. The organic materials can be mixed into the planting holes if a few tubers or plants only are grown, or if dahlias follow spring bedding plants, but generally it is better to dig them in the ground overall.

A fortnight before planting, topdress the ground with a general granular fertiliser containing a higher amount of potash in comparison with the nitrogen and phosphate content. Root crop fertilisers have this analysis, and potato fertilisers are very good for the purpose. This application will provide the extra plant food needed during growth, the organic materials previously supplied mainly providing humus for improving the soil conditions and water retention.

**Type of Stock** The choice of stock will depend on the purpose which the plants are to fulfil. Dormant tubers are best for a general garden display, for they flower earlier than dahlia plants and produce more flowers over the season as a whole. If you want extremely early flowers, for instance blooming in May, you can plant tubers in pots, or even in the greenhouse border, in February. If you have Hotkaps you can plant tubers out of doors in April and they will start to flower during early July. Remove the covers in mid-June. In both these instances the best flowers will be over before the growing season has finished. For the best results over the whole

**Dahlia 'Comet', an Anemone-flowered type which is becoming popular.**

season, plant dormant tubers during the month of May out of doors. They will not usually need protection, because by the time the shoots emerge above ground level it is likely that the threat of any late spring frosts will be past. Nevertheless keep sacks, pots, polythene bags or other materials handy in case of occasional night frost at this time. Flowering will start in late July and early August.

There are two types of tuber, one being the ground root, a large bulky root resulting from growing a dahlia out of doors without restricting the roots. If replanted from year to year, the number of tubers tends to increase to excess, too many poor quality flowers result, and vigour and tuber formation decrease. Division each year into at least several portions is advisable; each portion containing several growth buds, or eyes, and having at least one complete healthy tuber to start them into growth. (At this point, it may be noted that, unlike the potato, dahlia eyes are not on each individual tuber, but are congregated at the base of the old stems). An easy way to judge how many portions a root can be divided into is to put it in the greenhouse for a fortnight or three weeks. Spray overhead with water every second day until the shoots are about ½ inch long. Do not bury the tuber in any material as this will encourage unwanted root growth. With a small hacksaw cut the root into portions according to where the emerging shoots are grouped, or lever it apart with an old screwdriver.

The other type of dahlia tuber, the pot-grown or pot tuber, may be sold in general garden shops and nursery stores in the spring. It is produced from cuttings struck in early spring and grown in pots all through the season so that the roots are restricted and the tuber forms into a neat rounded mass. Although pot tubers are easy to store and transport, forming very good stock for the garden, they are not so good as ground roots for producing cuttings, generally having insufficient bulk to be divided. Pot tubers become ground roots after a season of growth out of doors and their planting times are the same as for ground roots. Before actual planting, chip away some of the wax coating if present to allow moisture to swell the tuber. All tubers can be planted until mid-June.

The dahlia plant itself, which provides a type of stock commonly sold by dahlia nurseries, is formed by rooting dahlia cuttings. Plants grown from cuttings may flower later than those grown from tubers, though if you need early flowers before mid-August, it is a good idea to specify on the order sheet 'Early Delivery'. If you have a greenhouse or frame, you can then pot the plants into 5 inch pots and they will grow into fine bushy specimens by planting out time. This is standard technique for large and giant-flowered varieties.

1

2

It is not difficult to keep dahlias from one year to the next, provided simple precautions are observed. The dahlia was introduced from Mexico in 1789 and, therefore, in cool climates the tubers have to be lifted in the autumn, and after drying, stored in a dry, frost-free place. 1 The foliage of the dahlia is very sensitive to frost and will be blackened by the first one experienced in the autumn. 2 Immediately after this occurs, the plants should be cut down to within 9 inches of ground level. 3 The tops are removed and the plants are lifted with a fork, care being taken to ensure that the tubers are not speared in the process. 4 The soil is shaken off and the tubers are stood upside-down in a dry, airy place so that surplus sap will drain away. 5 Once the tubers are thoroughly dry they can be stored in any dry, frost-free place. 6 A fibre-board box will suffice, but the addition of dry peat will help to exclude frost and absorb excess moisture. 7 The tubers can be stored close together in a deep frame, placed against a south wall, but frost must be excluded with leaves. Mats will also be needed on the outside of the frame, weighed down so that they remain in position in a gale. Dahlias are usually propagated by means of cuttings. These are made from the shoots that arise from the base of the old stems to which the tubers are attached. 8 The tubers are stood close together on a greenhouse bench and lightly covered with soil or peat to retain moisture. 9 A temperature of 60°F (16°C) is maintained and the cuttings are taken when the shoots are 2 to 3 inches long. 10 The lower leaves are removed with a sharp knife. 11 The basal cut is made below a joint and the prepared cuttings are inserted firmly with a dibber around the edge of a 3½ inch pot, in a sandy mixture. 13 Each pot should be clearly labelled with the name of the variety, and having been watered in should be stood in a close frame in the propagating house. The use of hormone rooting powders usually increases the number of cuttings that root and reduces the time taken. The inclusion of a fungicide reduces loss of cuttings.

6

10

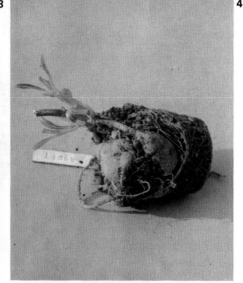

1 Pot-grown dahlias are sometimes sold for planting out. Raised from cuttings the previous spring, and grown in the open in pots throughout the season, the tubers develop into a neat rounded mass. 2 Cut down and, 3 and 4, dried off after the first frost, they are stored until required for planting in the spring.

Moreover, arranging the stakes in a desired pattern can be a useful guide to design.

**Summer Care** The main requirement is copious watering, not a lot of feeding. Provided that you have prepared the soil as suggested, all that will be needed during the growing period will be two topdressings of sulphate of potash, each at the rate of $\frac{1}{4}$ oz per square yard. One should be given at the first sign of the petal colour opening from the bud, to improve stem strength and flower colour; the other during early September to improve tuber formation. Monthly feeds of liquid manures made from fish emulsions are also very good and give excellent results even if used for foliar feeding. The dahlia makes a lot of leaves in August and even in very wet weather the soil may remain dry round the roots. The need to water very frequently can be largely avoided even in the hottest weather if a thick mulch of straw is provided at the roots in mid-July. This keeps down weeds as well as encouraging better root growth.

Tubers will need at least one strong stake, but dahlia plants are better if they are supported by a triangle of three canes or stakes. Such plants have to carry all the weight of stems, leaves and flowers on one main stem or 'leg', so are very prone to wind damage. Tubers on the other hand, push out rigid shoots from below soil level and are much less likely to be broken by the wind in the early stages of growth. These shoots should be tied to the stake every 18 inches, whereas the dahlia plant needs tying every 6 inches for additional protection. A good average length for dahlia supports is 5 feet; these are knocked in to the ground to a depth of 1 foot. Avoid having the stakes higher than the blooms because the wind will knock the flowers against them.

Ground tubers can be left to produce flowers on the tips of their main stems. Allow about eight main stems per division to emerge, and cut off any others below soil level carefully with a knife. Large and giant-flowered varieties should be allowed to produce about five stems only.

Pot tubers, unless they produce sufficient main shoots from below soil level, will have to be treated like green plants. The leading growth tip of the plant is pinched out, or 'stopped', about a month after planting out, usually when about six pairs of leaves have developed. This encourages sideshoots to be produced so plenty of flowers come into bloom as a start; otherwise, if not stopped in advance, dahlia plants produce one central flower only at first. Take notice which are the strongest emerging sideshoots after stopping, and when they are 3 inches long, remove the excess ones by snapping them out from their joints with the main stem. Retain five shoots only, however, with large and

You cannot plant unprotected dahlia plants out of doors until late May, or first ten days of June in the North. With Hotkaps or in sheltered places, free from late spring frosts, you can plant out in late April or early May. In the coldest areas, mid-June.

**Planting Out** This stage is best tackled by digging out a hole in the ground with a small spade. Stakes should be inserted at this time to avoid damage to the tubers which would occur if they were put in later. The hole should be wide enough to prevent cramping and deep enough to allow the upper surfaces of the tubers to be about 2 inches below ground level. Replace the earth on top, shaking the tuber to settle it round the root as you proceed, firming it in by gentle treading. This applies to both ground and pot tubers. Planting distances are 2 feet apart for pompons, $2\frac{1}{2}$ feet for ball dahlias and all others, except the large and giant decoratives, such as cactus and semi-cactus, which should be 3 feet apart.

Keep the soil watered periodically to swell the tubers and to start the shoots into growth. Shoots should emerge above the soil within five weeks; if not, dig up the tuber and inspect it for decay and slug damage. Slug pellets applied above soil level round the root when planting both tubers and plants are an advisable precaution. Dahlia plants are placed in a hole taken out with a trowel and their roots set so that the potting soil is just below ground level. Bituminised paper, or fibre pots, should be carefully removed from the plants before planting out. (With peat pots especially, make sure to keep the soil moist enough to encourage the roots to penetrate into the open ground, since failure to do this is a frequent cause of stunted, poorly growing plants). Again, it is important to plant to a stake, previously driven in, thus avoiding damage to the roots.

**Rooted cuttings are potted up singly into 3 inch pots. When these are full of roots, the plants are potted on into 5-inch pots as follows. 1 Place a crock over the** drainage hole. **2 Cover with leaves or roughage from the mixture. 3 Knock the plant out. 4 Place it so that the general level is about the same. 5 Leave enough** room in the pot for water. **6 Firm evenly with the fingers all round and level off. Until established, keep the plant in close conditions.**

giant-flowered varieties. The technique with the pot tuber is to select initially the strongest main shoot, similar to that of the dahlia plant as the central growing stem, removing the others. This main shoot will be stopped and the sideshoots selected in exactly the same way. A ground tuber is not usually stopped, the flowers being borne on the terminal, or crown buds of each stem. It can, however, be treated like a pot tuber or green plant as far as shoot growth is concerned, but by stopping and selecting one main stem, the flowers, through having to be produced on sideshoots, will be about three weeks later than on the tips of the main stems. Pompon varieties need no de-shooting or disbudding.

Disbudding should be done to all other types when the flower buds are about the size of a pea. Allow the main, centrally placed, largest bud to remain and flower on each shoot, removing the others, together with the fresh secondary

shoots which will emerge from each leaf joint on the stem as the flowers mature. Leave just one, fairly low down, on each stem to produce the successive flower, again disbudding and de-shooting. This technique is adopted throughout the flowering period and is the only way to achieve a long flowering season combined with good quality flowers with long stems for cutting.

Left to their own devices, dahlias produce a mass of buds and flowers and soon become uncontrollable, their very tiny, poor blossoms often becoming single by the end of the season. If you need small-flowered dahlias, grow special small-flowered varieties.

**Lifting and Storing** Ideally this is done once frost has blackened the foliage. If, however, the autumn continues without frost, it does no harm to lift dahlias in late October and early November. Only in the mildest of places, in very sheltered situations or during unusually gentle

winters can dahlias be left out of doors in the ground all winter. They can be put into a pit in the same way as potatoes, but the disadvantage here is that they may be killed if the weather becomes very severe. Furthermore, you cannot examine them for signs of rotting or put them in the greenhouse to take cuttings.

To lift dahlia roots, first cut off the stems just above soil level. Then lift by digging in a circle with a broad-tined fork, working well away from the stems. After lifting the roots clear of the soil, pick off as much adhering earth as possible. Then place the roots upside down in a well-ventilated greenhouse, frame or shed for at least a fortnight. During this period they will lose excess moisture and by the time the remaining soil becomes dust dry, they will be ready to be put into winter storage. There they should be covered with sacks or straw at night if frost threatens. Only in very wet autumns should artificial heat be used, never exceeding 70°F (21°C).

Before placing them in store, retrim the stems as low as possible, without actually cutting into the tubers. Retie the labels on one of the tubers, because in storage the stems become paper dry and will actually drop off. Most dahlia roots need no covering in storage. In fact, a frequent cause of loss during the winter is covering them up, putting them away in a cupboard and forgetting about them until the spring. Lay them on racks in a frost-proof shed, cellar, or in a greenhouse which can be kept frost free. Straw bales provide good frost protection.

Very tiny tubers, however, should be covered in boxes or pots with material such as garden soil or sand. During the winter, sprinkle the surface with water very occasionally if it gets dust dry, but avoid giving sufficient water to start the tubers into growth. A good temperature for any storage is 40–50°F (4–10°C); failing that, it should never fall below 34°F (1°C) nor exceed 50°F (10°C). If you have to store them in a warm place, shrivelling is likely, so all tubers must then be covered with sand or soil in boxes, but keep the boxes separated and put only one layer of tubers in each box. Avoid storage that is subject to drips or draughts, or is so airtight that it encourages fungus rot.

Every month inspect the tubers and if any parts are rotting, cut them out with a sharp knife. Dry the surfaces left with a rag and smear on captan or zineb to prevent further rot. Occasionally fumigate with smoke pellets to deal with aphids which may have hatched out in store or bulb flies which sometimes attack the roots.

**Pests and diseases** As a general precaution, always spray dahlias with insecticides every three weeks during the season of growth, including those growing in the greenhouse and frame.

Sometimes the soil becomes infected with verticillium wilt, when the stock must be burnt and a fresh growing site found. Cauliflower-like outgrowths, due to crown gall, also mean that affected stock must be destroyed, but it is slow to spread and healthy stock can still be grown in the same ground.

A common leaf disease, especially in humid summers, is dahlia leaf spot, causing light green ringed spots which later turn brown. In this event, treat the leaves with zineb.

Plants are sometimes attacked by virus diseases, of which light green patches or yellowing bands up the veins

Before planting dahlias in the open, water thoroughly. 1 Dig out a hole with a trowel, large enough to take the ball of roots. 2 Knock the plant out of its pot, and remove the crocks. 3 Position the root ball just below the level of the soil. 4 Fill in the hole, gradually firm evenly all round and leave a shallow depression for water.

and perhaps dark green blisters on the leaves are symptoms. A more certain sign is dwarfing of the plant, which becomes very close-jointed and bushy, producing small flowers. Burn stock affected in this way, for there is no cure at present.

Common pests are black aphids in early summer, often migrating from broad beans, green aphids during summer and autumn, thrips and capsid bugs (see Aphids and Pest control).

A difficult pest to control is the red spider mite which may attack some plants in dry seasons, causing yellow mottling. Frequent syringeing under the leaves with water and spraying with malathion every ten days is the control routine to follow (see Red spider mite).

Earwigs are often a nuisance, eating holes in leaves and flowers. These can be controlled if you provide upturned pots, loosely filled with woodwool, straw, hay, etc., and placed on top of the canes or stakes; these should be emptied into boiling water or kerosene. Also puff insecticides on flower buds (see Earwigs).

Wasps sometimes make damaging attacks on dahlia flower stems and it is usually necessary to destroy the nest (see Wasps).

**Propagation** The preparation for growing from seed is a simple matter. Remove the petals as they fade and take the seed pods indoors before the frost, later extracting the seed and placing it in envelopes. The seed is sown in boxes in mid-March, and the seedlings are potted off in May and planted out in June. The best breeding, however, is done by crossing selected varieties by hand, and covering the blooms with old nylon stockings to prevent chance pollination by bees and other insects. It should be remembered that dahlias do not come true to type or variety from seed, though dwarf bedding types, such as 'Coltness Gem' or 'Unwins Hybrids' are commonly grown in this way as they come reasonably true.

Years ago dahlia shoots were grafted on to tubers to produce plants, but only research into virus control now employs this technique. Nowadays dahlias are commonly propagated from cuttings. Tubers are packed close together in boxes of soil in February, put on the greenhouse bench with bottom heat of about 60°F (16°C) and watered. When the shoots, produced after some three weeks, are about 2½ inches long, they are cut off close to the tuber just below a leaf joint, and after removing the lower leaves, they are inserted into holes round the edge of 3 inch pots. The holes are made by inserting a pencil-sized dibber 1½ inches deep into the rooting medium in the pots, commonly sand or a mixture of equal parts of peat and sand. Five cuttings are placed in each pot. The pots are then placed over bottom heat from soil-warming wires, boiler pipes, or kerosene or electrical heating. The temp-

erature should be about 60°F (16°C) round the pots. Cover the pots by suspending polythene sheets above them in the daytime, plus brown paper if the sun shines, and spray them gently with water morning and night, removing the covers over night. Do not make the mistake of overwatering the pots during the rooting period, or rotting may take place. Add water to the pot only when the sand surface dries out and then dip it in a bucket of water with a finger over the drainage hole until bubbles cease to rise. Otherwise, rely on overhead spraying on the cuttings themselves.

After two or three weeks, when new tip growth is evident, the cuttings will have rooted and can be potted off individually in ordinary potting mixture. For the first ten days afterwards, keep them in a warm part of the greenhouse, but for the rest of the time until planting out they grow much better if kept cool. Certainly they should be ready to be put into a cold frame three weeks after potting off.

The division of tubers described earlier is the other method of propagation.

**Types of dahlias** On January 1st 1966, a new system of dahlia classification came into being. As far as Britain is concerned the National Dahlia Society is the authority: in the US, the American Dahlia Society. It issues a classified list of varieties showing the type or size to which any named variety belongs.

1 To encourage a bushy plant, the growing point is taken out when six pairs of leaves have developed. 2 This results in the appearance of three or four 'breaks' or side shoots. 3 Plants from old tubers planted out may produce too many shoots. Those not wanted can be removed. 4 Mulching with peat or compost retains moisture and controls weeds.

There are now ten main groups, some being subdivided into sizes according to flower diameter. These include single-flowered, anemone-flowered, collerette, paeony-flowered and miscellaneous (containing such types as orchid-flowered). As far as the gardener is concerned the most popular groups are the decorative dahlia, with flat broad petals; the cactus

433

dahlia with petals that roll backwards to form a quill; semi-cactus dahlias, which have part only of their petal length rolled; pompon dahlias, like drumsticks, their flowers having blunt, tubular petals, under 2 inches in diameter; and the new group of ball dahlias comprising all previously known groups of medium and large pompons,

---

**Dahlias require support from an early age. 1 A stout stake should be knocked in at the time of planting, to avoid root injury. 2 Canes can be used, connected up with string to enclose the plant as it grows. 3 An alternative system of staking for the biggest plants. 4 Cutting for exhibition in the early evening.**

larger double show varieties, and glove shapes (small or miniature decoratives).

Size groups are: pompons one size only; ball dahlias are divided into miniature balls, 2–4 inches, and balls over 4 inches, decorative, cactus and semi-cactus dahlias are each divided into five groups; miniature, under 4 inches, small, 4–6 inches, medium 6–8 inches, large-flowered 8–10 inches, giant-flowered over 10 inches. Bedding dahlias go by flower shape. US catalogues may list: anemone, ball, cactus, colarette, dwarf, formal dec., incurved cactus, informal dec., miniature, orchid, peony, pompon, single, semi-cactus.

**Exhibiting** Cultural technique varies little from that described. Cuttings are

mostly used for propagation purposes; they flower during late August and the first half of September when most dahlia shows are held. Tubers of the large-flowered and giant varieties are started into growth in the greenhouse in mid-January, cuttings being taken for rooting during early March; plants, when put in the frame, later on, should be put into 5 inch pots by early May. All other varieties are started off in mid-March, the best plants being obtained from cuttings rooted during the end of March and the first three weeks in April. Those taken before this period will usually flower much too early for the shows. For show work, it is much better to grow at least six plants of each good variety, so

restricting the number of varieties to the capacity of the outdoor space available to grow them in. When garden plants are grown for display, distances should be 2 feet apart for pompons, 2½ feet apart for ball dahlias and all others, except the large and giant decoratives cactus and semi-cactus which should be placed 3 feet apart. Many exhibitors mulch the giant varieties with manure in July; for the others, a straw mulch is used. During flowering it is common practice to protect the flowers of the large and giant varieties either with cones of builder's waterproofed brown paper, or even by erecting metal uprights to support a roof made of corrugated vinyl clear plastic sheeting, giving the effect of an open-sided greenhouse.

Always cut the flowers the evening before and stand them in a cool, dark place in water over night. Large and giant blooms must have a 2 foot cane tied along the stem when it is cut to prevent the bloom toppling over in transit. Common methods of transport include oil or fiber drums with holes drilled round the edge to which the individual blooms can be tied; milk crates with one bloom in each corner resting in a water-filled bottle, or old one gallon cans especially for pompons. It is always advisable to carry flowers to a show in water.

The best way to pick up showing technique is to join a dahlia society if there is one in the locality, or if not, to contact the American Dahlia Society.

**Recommended varieties** It is always unwise to be dogmatic about recommending varieties as they quickly pass out of favour, but those mentioned here are likely to remain attractive in the garden, as well as being suitable for exhibition, for years in Britain. Small flowered decoratives, medium and small cactus and semi-cactus, the ball dahlias and poms are the best to choose for cutting and flower arrangement.

**Giant decoratives** These do not necessarily grow tall and in fact some are dwarf growers. If you allow up to eight flowers per tuber or plant you will get quite small blooms which are preferred by those who object to a very large size: 'Black Monarch', deep maroon; 'Bonafide', yellow; 'Evelyn Rumbold', light purple; 'Go American', orange bronze; 'Grand Prix', very bright yellow tipped, white; 'Hamari Girl', a dwarf, pale rose pink; 'Holland Festival', popular orange and white; 'Jaconda', wine purple; 'Kelvin Floodlight', yellow; 'Kidd's Climax', pale lavender and cream; 'Lavengro', outstanding lavender; 'Liberator', deep crimson; 'Margaret Bowyer', white.

**Large decoratives** These are not so widely grown but very good varieties include: 'Color Sketch', two-tone pink; 'Hamari Boldness', a tall variety, glowing crimson; 'Moon Probe', very attractive golden variety with long stems; 'Ovation', a golden-bronze with pointed

1 Dahlia 'Lady Tweedsmuir', a Small-flowered Decorative with blooms over 4 inches in diameter, but not exceeding 6 inches. 2 Dahlia 'Coltness Gem'.

petals; 'Lois Walcher', violet purple.

**Medium decoratives** 'Betty Russell', bright yellow; 'Breckland Joy', orange-pink; 'Crossfield Standard', bright orange, an improvement on 'House of Orange'; and 'Pattern', bright lilac, tipped white.

**Small decoratives** 'Amethyst', pale bluish-lavender; 'Angora', white with split petal tips; 'Chinese Lantern', orange and gold; 'Dedham', deep lilac and white; 'Hamari Fiesta', very bright yellow and red; 'Marie Rust', bright orange; 'Mrs Silverstone', pale silvery-pink; 'Procyon', orange and red; 'Rosy Cloud', glowing cerise-pink; 'Snow Queen', white; 'Twiggy', a bright pink water-lily type; 'Worton Gold', golden-yellow; and 'White Princess', white with laciniated petals.

**Miniature decoratives** 'David Howard', golden-orange with purple foliage; 'Horn of Plenty', scarlet; 'Jo's Choice', deep crimson; and 'Funny Face', a red and white.

**Giant or large cactus or semi-cactus** 'Frontispiece', white with frilly petal tips; 'Hamari Dream', pale primrose; 'Nantenan', deep yellow; 'Miss Universe', bright burnt-orange; 'Bali Hai', a deep shocking pink incurved cactus; 'Desert Song', smoky rose, yellow, semi-cactus.

**Medium cactus or semi-cactus** 'Autumn Fire', orange-red; 'Exotica', deep pink and cream; 'Frigid Friend', white fimbriated; 'Hamari Bride', white; 'Hill's Delight', red tipped yellow; 'Homespun', buff-primrose and red; 'Lucky Fellow', deep pink; 'Piquant', red and white; 'Rotterdam', crimson; 'Sure Thing', scarlet with needle-like petals; 'Victory Maid', blood red.

**Small cactus or semi-cactus** 'Combo', pink and primrose; 'Doris Knight', deep purple sport of 'Doris Day', which is deep crimson; 'Goya's Venus', light orange-pink; 'Orange Nymph', golden-orange with finely-cut foliage; 'Pink Angel', a soft pink cactus; 'Temptress', cream and lilac; 'White Swallow', white; and 'Worton Sally Ann', lavender-pink.

**Ball dahlias** 'Gold Ball' yellow; 'Dr. John Grainger', burnt-orange; 'Florence Vernon', lavender, tipped white; 'Ian Patterson', lilac; 'Rothesay Superb', scarlet; 'Rev. Colwyn Vale', purple; and 'White Frost'.

**Pompons** 'Andrew Lockwood', lavender; 'Czar Willo', purple; 'Kym Willo', orange and yellow; 'Darkest of All', dark red; 'Whale's Rhonda', purple, tipped silver; 'Winnie', pink, tipped silver; 'Zonnegoud', golden yellow.

2

3

4

1 'Rotterdam', a Medium-flowered Semi-Cactus dahlia which has blooms over 6 inches in diameter but not usually exceeding 8 inches. Other dahlias in this category are 2 'Homespun' and, 3 'Hamari Bride'. 4 A typical Pompon dahlia which has blooms similar to those of Ball dahlias, but more globular and of miniature size. 5 'Worton Jane', a Small-flowered Decorative dahlia. 6 'Ruwenzori' a popular dahlia in the Collerette class. 7 Dahlia 'Worton Pride' has the fully double or slightly flattened blooms that are typical of the Ball class. 8 'Amethyst Piper', a Small-flowered Decorative dahlia, which has blooms over 4 inches in diameter but usually not exceeding 6 inches. 9 'Schweiz', a Medium Decorative dahlia. 10 'Hamari Girl' and 11 'Grand Prix', are both Giant Decorative dahlias.

5

8

9

10

6

7

11

437

1 Dais cotinifolia, flowering in the National Botanic Garden of South Africa, at Kirstenbosch. 2 The operation of damping down is carried out in the greenhouse when a humid atmosphere is required. 3 Antirrhinum seedlings 'damping off'. These are susceptible to soil-borne fungus diseases.

## Dais (di-is)

From the Greek *dais*, a torch, referring to the shape of the inflorescence *(Thymelaeaceae)*. A small genus of shrubs, natives of South Africa and Madagascar. The flowers appear in a flattened umbel on very slender stalks. The only species cultivated is *D. cotinifolia* (D) 8–10 feet, sometimes exceeding this, but rarely in this country. The shrub bears pale lilac flowers in June and July.

**Cultivation** Out of doors in the milder counties it may be planted in a sunny well-drained position, well sheltered from cold winds. Elsewhere it needs the protection of a cool greenhouse where it may be grown in large pots of fairly light potting mixture. Propagation is by cuttings of new wood taken in July and rooted in a propagating frame in sandy compost.

**Daisy**—see Bellis

**Daisy, Barberton**—see Gerbera jamesonii

**Daisy Bush**—see Olearia

**Daisy, Kingfisher**—see Felicia bergeriana

**Daisy, Swan River**—see Brachycome iberidifolia

**Daisy, Transvaal**—see Gerbera jamesonii

## Dalapon

This is a chemical selective weedkiller which kills couch and other grasses and most monocotyledons but is much less damaging on other weeds and plants. It is particularly useful for getting rid of grass around the bases of fruit trees and in soft fruit plantations, and in the ornamental garden among trees and shrubs. It is sold in powder form and dissolved in water according to the manufacturers' directions printed on the packet and is watered on to the infested areas with a watering can fitted with a dribble bar. It is slow acting and is, therefore, best applied in the winter when quick results are less important.

When couch and other grasses are the main weeds on uncropped land dalapon is perhaps the best weedkiller to use. Some regrowth will occur, especially if the ground is not cultivated and dug well after the first application. Buttercups, dandelions and docks are unaffected by dalapon and may well take over ground cleared of grass in this way unless cultivation is carried out, or unless another kind of weedkiller is used (see Weeds and Weed control).

**Dame's Rocket, Dame's Violet**—see Hesperis matronalis

## Damnacanthus (dam-nak-an-thus)

From the Greek *damnas*, to conquer, *akanthos*, a prickle, with reference to the spiny leaves *(Rubiaceae)*. A small genus of evergreen shrubs from Japan, China and the Himalayas. The only species cultivated is *D. indicus*, which grows 2–4 feet tall and bears small trumpet-shaped, fragrant, white flowers in summer, followed by coral red berries.
**Cultivation** This is a decorative shrub for

a cool greenhouse when grown in a pot containing a loamy compost. Maintain a minimum winter temperature of 45°F (7°C). Propagation is by cuttings, rooted in gentle bottom heat.

## Damping down

This operation is carried out in the greenhouse when a humid atmosphere is required. It is essential to maintain the correct amount of atmospheric moisture for many plants to survive, especially in high temperatures, and by keeping the surroundings damp this can be achieved. Moisture retaining material such as ash, gravel, peat are used as staging material rather than metal, concrete or wood for this reason and greenhouse floors are often ashed over where high temperatures and high humidity are to be maintained. Damping down is done up to four or five times daily when necessary, either with a watering can with a rose spray, or a syringe or even with a rotary sprinkler attachment to a hose in large greenhouses and staging, walls, floors, pots are all made wet rather than the plants themselves. High atmospheric humidity is not only essential for the survival of many plants but is the best condition to prevent the spread of red spider mite in greenhouses.

## Damping off

This is a term used to describe one of the best-known symptoms of plant disease in which young seedlings of almost any kind begin to collapse through a decay at soil level so that they are soon destroyed. The trouble may be the work of any of several fungus parasites which live in the soil but the common one in young seedlings is known as *Pythium de baryanum*. Other species of *Pythium* and of the genus *Phytophthora* are also concerned but usually the latter genus attacks slightly older seedlings. In forest nurseries young conifers are often affected by a damping off due to attack by the fungus *Rhizoctonia solani (Corticium solani)* which is a difficult fungus to control although the chemical TCNB (tetrachlornitrobenzene) is said to check it. Today we recognise two states of damping off, (1) pre-emergence damping which rots the seed before the seed leaves break through the soil, and (2) post-emergence damping off in which the seedlings wilt and rot soon after they appear. Although seed treatments are useful against the first named it is best to ensure against both types by using sterilised media at least for young seedlings. Also avoid overcrowding and overwatering and if necessary use Captan or Cheshunt compound.

**Damsons**—see Plums

## Danae (dan-ee)

Commemorating Danae, the daughter of King Acrisius of Argos *(Liliaceae)*. An evergreen shrub, graceful and berry

1 Daphne laureola, the Spurge Laurel, a British woodland shrub. 2 Daphne mezereum flowers in February and March.

bearing related to *Ruscus,* introduced into Britain from the Middle East more than two centuries ago. The only species is *D. racemosa* (syns. *Ruscus racemosus, Danae laurus),* the Alexandrian laurel, 2–3 feet, with greenish-white, inconspicuous flowers borne in early summer, followed by red berries in autumn which provide excellent cut material for floral arrangements.

**Cultivation** Plants are happiest in shade and need a moist loam and are useful for carpeting in large shrubberies or under trees, provided that there is sufficient moisture at the roots. Propagation is by division in spring or from seed sown out of doors in autumn as soon as it is ripe.

**Dandelion**—see Weeds and Weed control

## Daphne (daf-nee)

Named in commemoration of Daphne who in Greek mythology was pursued by Apollo and after praying for help was transformed into a laurel bush *(Thymelaeaceae).* A genus of deciduous and evergreen shrubs notable for their fragrant flowers, widely distributed, many of them wild in Europe and two of which are native plants.

**Species cultivated** *D. alpina* (D), 6–18 inches, flowers white, May and June. *D. arbuscula* (E), dwarf, almost prostrate, rosy-pink flowers, June. *D. aurantiaca* (E), 2–2½ feet, flowers yellow, May. *D. blagayana* (E), 9–12 inches, semi-

439

prostrate branches ending in clusters of richly scented cream flowers, March and April, good for the rock garden; spreads by its underground stems. *D.* × *burkwoodii* (syn. *D.* 'Somerset') (D), 3 feet, hybrid, quick-growing, flowers pale pink, May and June, very free flowering. *D. caucasica* (D), 4–5 feet, white flowers, May and June. *D. cneorum* (E), garland flower, 9–12 inches, fragrant pink flowers, May; vars. *album,* white; *eximia,* more prostrate; *pygmaea,* prostrate; *variegatum,* leaves cream-edged. *D. collina* (E), 15–18 inches, purplish-rose flowers, spring and early summer; var. *neopolitana,* 2–3 feet, rosy-pink. *D. genkwa* (D), 2–3 feet, lilac-blue, April and May, often difficult to establish. *D. giraldii* (D), 1½–2 feet, flowers yellow, June, berries bright red. *D. gnidium* (E), flax-leaved daphne, 2 feet, white, June to August. *D.* × *houtteana* (D or SE), leaves purplish, flowers reddish-purple, April, hybrid. *D. hybrida,* (syn. *D. dauphinii*) (E), 3–4 feet, pinkish-purple, almost continuously in flower, hybrid. *D. laureola* (E), spurge laurel, 3 feet, a British woodland species, slightly fragrant, green flowers, February and March. *D. mezereum* (D), the British mezereon, 4 feet, rich pinkish-purple flowers, February and March, scarlet autumn berries; vars. *alba,* white flowers, March, yellow berries; *grandiflora,* autumn-flowering; *rosea,* flowers rose-pink. *D. odora* (E), 2–3 feet, white, purple-marked flowers, January to March, rather tender, and frequently grown in a greenhouse where its blossoms escape the frost; var. *aureomarginata,* leaf margins variegated yellow, a hardier form. *D. oleoides* (E), 1½ feet, flowers variable, white to purplish, May and June. *D. pontica* (E), 2–3 feet, yellowish-green flowers, April. *D. retusa* (E), 1–1½ feet, slow-growing, dense habit, good for the rock garden, white flowers touched with purple, May. *D.* × *rossettii* (E), 1½–2 feet, flowers pink, but not often produced, hybrid. *D. sericea* (E), 1–2 feet, rosy-pink, May and June. *D. tangutica* (E), 4–5 feet, rosy-purple, March and April.

**Cultivation** Most daphnes like rich loam or sandy peat and fail in hot dry conditions; *D. mezereum* and *D.* × *neopolitana* like lime, the others need a lime-free soil. Some, e.g. *D. blagayana* and *D. retusa,* are at their best among stones in rock gardens. Propagation is by seed sown as soon as it is ripe for such easily grown species as *D. mezereum,* but *D. blagayana, D. cneorum, D. laureola, D. retusa* and *D. pontica* can be propagated by layering in autumn and the rarer species can be grafted on to stock of *D. mezereum* or *D. laureola,* depending

on whether they are deciduous or evergreen. Grafting needs to be done in a greenhouse where a temperature of 55°F (13°C) can be maintained, in March.

**Daphniphyllum** (daf-nee-fil-um)
From the Greek *Daphne* and *phyllon,* leaf *(Euphorbiaceae).* Hardy evergreen shrubs bearing large rhododendron-like leaves.
**Species cultivated** *D. humile,* 1½–2 feet, flowers inconspicuous, fruits blue-black, Japan. *D. macropodum* (syn. *D. glaucescens),* 8–10 feet, slow-growing, striking plant with pale green leaves, glaucous on the lower surface, giving a white effect, China, Japan, Korea.
**Cultivation** These plants will tolerate limy or chalky soils and shade and are grown mainly for their handsome foliage and berries. The flowers are unisexual, carried on different plants and thus it is necessary to plant both forms for good berries to be produced. Plant in November. Propagation is from cuttings of the ripened wood, rooted under cloches or in a frame in July.

**Dard**
A short lateral shoot not more than 3 inches long on an apple or pear tree. Usually a dard has a fruit bud at the tip, in which case it develops into a fruiting spur, but it may end in a wood bud and then grows in length and becomes a brindille.

**Darling River Pea**—see Swainsona coronilliflora

**Darlingtonia** (dar-ling-to-ne-a)
Commemorating Dr William Darlington,

1 **Daphniphyllum macropodum,** a hardy evergreen shrub that tolerates non-acid soil. 2 **Darlingtonia californica,** a hardy herbaceous insectivorous plant. 3 **Dasylirion acrotriche** at Tresco, England.

American botanist *(Sarraceniaceae)*. the western pitcher plant. A hardy herbaceous insectivorous plant, native of Northwest, brought to England about a century ago. Although fairly hardy, it is frequently grown under glass in unheated greenhouses. The leaves are funnel-shaped, up to 2 feet in length and form hoods and pitchers at the top, for the purpose of catching insects attracted to the plants by the honey glands. The only species is *D. californica,* 1–2 feet tall, with yellow and green, red-brown veined flowers in April and May.

**Cultivation** The plant does best in a damp position, such as in a bog garden or by the margin of a pool, well sheltered from winds. Plant out in May in soil containing peat and sphagnum moss. Propagation is effected by detaching the sideshoots in summer and potting them up under cloches or in a sunny cold frame until they are established. Under glass, pots should contain a compost of equal parts of peat, chopped sphagnum moss, sharp sand and sifted loam. Pot up in April, water freely at all times and syringe the plants daily during high summer heat.

## Dasylirion (das-ee-lir-e-on)
From the Greek *dasys,* thick, *lirion,* a lily, referring to the succulent leaves *(Liliaceae).* Greenhouse evergreen foliage plants, related to the yuccas. The leaves grow in a tuft from the short stem and are narrow, several feet in length, tough, leathery and with spines along the margins. They grow upright for more than 1½ feet, then the tops curve outwards. The small flowers are bell shaped.

**Species cultivated** *D. acrotriche,* 6–8 feet, flowers white. *D. glaucophyllum,* 10 feet, white. *D. hookeri,* 3 feet, purplish. *D. serratifolium,* 2 feet, white. All from Mexico.

**Cultivation** These plants are not hardy but the pots in which they are grown may be put out of doors in the summer, particularly for creating subtropical bedding effects, or they may be used as conservatory or house plants all the year round. Water is needed frequently during the summer but little should be given from October to March. Pot very firmly in February or March, in a mixture of 2 parts of loam and peat to 1 part of sand. Maintain a minimum winter temperature of 45°F (7°C). Propagation is by seed sown in March in a cold frame or greenhouse.

## Date Palm—see Phoenix dactylifera

## Date Plum—see Diospyros lotus

## Datisca (dat-is-ka)
Derivation of name unknown *(Datiscaceae).* Hardy perennial herbaceous perennial plants used for foliage effect.
**Species cultivated** *D. cannabina,* false hemp, 3–6 feet, leaves composed of slender leaflets, yellowish-white flowers, summer. Male and female flowers are carried on different plants, the latter being the more attractive. *D. glomerata,* 2½–4 feet, lighter clusters of similar cream-yellow flowers, summer.

**Cultivation** A rich deep soil in an open position where the plants catch as much sun as possible is most suitable. Propagation is from seed sown in March out of doors, the seedlings transplanted later in the summer to their permanent positions.

## Datura (dat-ur-a)
From *tatorah,* the Arabic name for one species *(Solanaceae).* Hardy and half-hardy annuals, perennials, trees and shrubs, with funnel-shaped or trumpet-shaped flowers, many of them large and beautiful, natives of warm and temperate regions of the world. The trees and shrubs are often known as Brugmansias.

**Species cultivated: Annuals** *D. ceratocaula,* 3 feet, white July, half-hardy. *D. metel* (syn. *D. fastuosa),* 2–5 feet, flowers varying from violet to yellow or creamy-white outside, whitish within, often double, July; var. *alba,* white, half-hardy. *D. stramonium,* thorn apple, stink-weed, jimson-weed, 2–3 feet, white, July, large, egg-shaped, prickly fruit, British plant, often exciting adverse comment when found, source of the drug stramonium used in the treatment of asthma, hardy.

**Perennials, shrubs and trees** *D. arborea,* (syn. *Brugmansia arborea),* angel's trumpet, to 10 feet, flowers white, up to 8 inches long, August. *D. chlorantha,*

yellow-flowered thorn-apple, 4 feet, flowers double, yellow, August to October; the cultivar 'Golden Queen', sometimes known as 'Trumpet in Trumpet', has deeper yellow flowers, sometimes with three trumpets, one inside the other; may be treated as a half-hardy annual. *D. cornigera,* horn of plenty, to 10 feet, flowers white or cream, single or double, the double form also known as *Brugmansia knightii.* *D. meteloides* (syn. *D. wrightii),* 2½–3 feet, pale rosy-lavender to white, fragrant, late summer, perennial which may be treated as half-hardy annual. *D. sanguinea* (syn. *Brugmansia sanguinea),*

**1 Datura suaveolens, the Angel's Trumpet, flowers in August. 2 Datura sanguinea.**

1

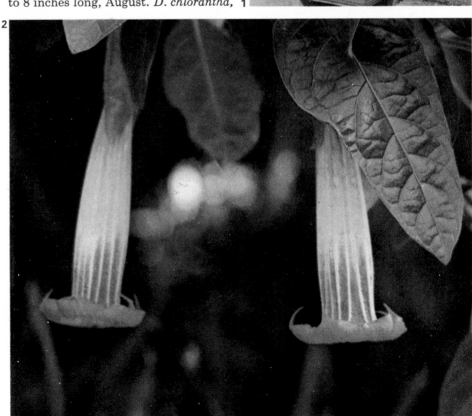

2

4–8 feet, flowers orange-red, up to 8 inches long, summer, *D. suaveolens*, angel's trumpet, 10–15 feet, flowers white, up to 1 foot long, August, more often seen in its double form and sometimes confused with *D. arborea*.

**Cultivation** The half-hardy annuals may be grown in pots from seed sown in a temperature of 55–65°F (13–18°C), in spring, and planted out of doors in May. *D. stramonium* is grown from seed sown out of doors in spring. The shrubs and tree-like species are fine plants for cool greenhouses and conservatories, where they may be grown in large pots or tubs or in the border. When grown in containers these may be moved out of doors in June and brought in again in September. They do well in a mixture consisting of equal parts of loam peat, rotted manure and silver sand, and should be potted in March. They make large specimens in time and may be pruned hard to keep them in bounds, either after they have finished flowering or in the autumn. They need a good deal of water in summer and weak liquid feeds as they come into flower, but should be given little water in winter. Propagation is by 6 inch long cuttings, rooted in heat in spring or autumn.

**Daucus**—see Carrots

## Davallia (da-val-e-a)

Commemorating Edmund Davall, a Swiss botanist *(Polypodiaceae)*. Ferns, deciduous and evergreen, some of them tropical, for the greenhouse, all beautiful, distinguished by their conspicuous rhizomes from which the fronds arise. The rhizomes are covered with silvery or brown hairy scales. Some species are particularly useful for hanging decorative baskets.

**Species cultivated** *D. bullata* (E), squirrel's foot fern, 6–8 inches, rhizomes creep and can be pegged down, rhizomes dark with light brown tips, hence the common name, fronds polished and rich green, useful for hanging baskets. *D. canariensis* (E), hare's foot fern, 1½ feet, rhizomes thick and stiff, almost erect, fronds of good substance, a good fern for growing in a pot in any frost-proof place. *D. mariessii cristata* (D), 6 inches, attractive crested form. *D. solida*, 1–2 feet.

**Cultivation** Davallias need partial shade and a mixture of 2 parts of loam, 1 part each of leafmould, peat, sand and powered charcoal. Pot the young plants in March or April and maintain a temperature of 50–60°F (10–16°C) during the summer and water freely. During the winter not so much water is needed and a minimum temperature of 40°F (4°C) is sufficient. Propagation is by division of the rhizomes in February or March, or by spores sown on the surface of sandy peat in a temperature of 60–75°F (16–24°C) at any time of the year.

1 Davallia solida, a fern for greenhouse hanging baskets. 2 and 3 Davidia involucrata, the handkerchief tree.

## Davidia (dav-id-e-a)

Commemorating Father J. P. A. David (1826–1900), French missionary and pioneer naturalist in China and Tibet *(Nyssaceae* or *Cornaceae)*. Dove tree, pocket-handkerchief tree, ghost tree. A genus of a single species, *D. involucrata*, a hardy deciduous tree to 50 feet, bearing in May small insignificant flowers carried between two white bracts, one 6 inches long, which gives it the popular names; var. *vilminiana* has shiny leaves which show off the flowers better than the downy underside of the leaves of the type, central and western China.

**Cultivation** This attractive tree requires a sheltered position in ordinary soils, including those containing lime. Propagation is by the large, nut-like seeds

442

which must be exposed to the winter weather, or by cutting from half-ripe wood in late summer, or by hardwood cuttings in October.

## David, J. P. A.

Père Jean Pierre Armand David (1826–1900) was one of a long line of French Jesuit priests who combined missionary work with plant hunting in China and was probably the one best equipped for his work. Not only was he a skilled botanist, but was equally at home as a geologist, mineralogist, zoologist, geographer, hydrographer and ethnologist.

He first went to China in 1860 as a member of the Mission Etrangères and carried out three great plant hunting expeditions, the first to Mongolia, the second, of more than two years' duration, to the borders of Tibet, and the third in the Central Provinces of China.

His second expedition, which took him to the Tibetan marshes and the great gorges and mountains of the Yangtze River, was worked from the missionary station at Mupin.

As a result of his painstaking field notes and the immense numbers of herbarium specimens sent to the Jardin des Plantes in Paris he laid the foundations for the study of the flora of China.

During his second expedition, climbing Hong-shantin, a mountain which reached 15,000 feet, he found at 6,000 feet the plant most connected with his name, *Davidia involucrata,* the dove tree or pocket handkerchief tree, so called because of the creamy-white bracts which flutter from the branches.

His introduction of plants in seed form were few, *Clematis davidiana,* being the best known, but according to E. H. M. Cox, the historian of Chinese plant collecting, he sent back to France more than 2,000 species of plants. Among these were *Cotoneaster salicifolia, Stranvaesia davidiana, Viburnum davidii, Rhododendron calophytum, R. davidii, R. decorum, R. moupinense* and *R. strigillosum, Primula heucherifolia,* and *Lilium davidii* and *L. duchartrei.*

M. A. Franchet, a French botanist, said of David that at least 1,000 of his specimens were lost when his boat was sunk on the Han River. Armand David's exertions in the mountainous areas of China sapped his health and, as a sick man he left China in 1874 for France, never to return.

**David's Harp**—see Polygonatum multiflorum

**Dawn Poppy**—see Eomecon

**Dawyck Beech**—see Fagus fastigiata

**1 Viburnum davidii, and 2 Rhododendron decorum, were introduced by J. David.**

**Day Lily**—see Hemerocallis

**DD**—see Insecticides

## DDT
A chlorinated hydrocarbon insecticide which controls leaf-eating insects by contact and as a stomach poison. It is also useful against thrips, adult whiteflies, capsids, leafhoppers etc. The Cook Report of February 1964 recommended that no restrictions should be placed on the current uses of DDT but that its use should be reviewed at a later date.

It is used in the form of dusts, wettable powders, emulsions, aerosols and smokes, sometimes combined with other insecticides. Crops should not be harvested within two weeks of spraying. DDT is currently banned in the United States because of its harmful effects on animal life.

## Dead-head
To dead-head plants means to remove the faded flower heads before seed is produced, not only to enhance the appearance of the plants but to divert the strength into making new flower buds rather than seed. Dead-heading is a common practice with rhododendrons to encourage free flowering. Lilacs require practically no pruning, but benefit from dead-heading. Among border plants the operation is carried out as a routine to preserve the appearance of the plant and general effect of the border. Among bedding plants, pansies, tagetes and petunias are commonly dead-headed to maintain a succession of flowers throughout the season, as also are most other annuals unless it is intended to gather seed.

## Dead Nettle—see Lamium

## Deblossoming
This is the removal of either individual flowers or complete flower trusses. In fruit growing the operation is sometimes necessary to prevent fruiting at too early an age: for instance, any blossom produced by top fruits in the first spring after planting should always be removed.

Partial deblossoming is also carried out as a first stage in fruit-thinning to prevent a glut crop in a year of prolific blossom following a resting year when the crop was abnormally light (probably as a result of frost damage). This action may help to prevent a habit of biennial cropping developing. Apples which are notoriously prone to this are: 'Cottenham Seedling', 'D'Arcy Spice', 'Dumelow's Seedling', 'Ellison's Orange', 'Laxton's Superb', 'Melba', 'Miller's Seedling', 'Newton Wonder', 'Ontario', 'Wagener' and 'Baldwin'.

Strawberries are sometimes deblossomed in their first spring because, although first-year berries are bigger and earlier, the total yield in the first

To 'dead head' is to remove faded flowers and prevent the production of seed.

two years is then less than that in the second year alone from deblossomed plants which have had a whole year and more in which to built up their strength.

### Debregeasia (de-breg-eas-e-a)
In honour of Prosper Justin de Bregeas, French explorer *(Urticaceae)*. A small genus of deciduous shrubs from mild areas of Asia and Africa. The only species likely to be found in cultivation is *D. longifolia*, from southeast Asia, which grows 4–6 feet tall. The long lance-shaped leaves and the yellow or red fruits as large as peas are the most striking features.

**Cultivation** This shrub requires cool greenhouse treatment except in the warmer districts where it may be grown without undue protection in a moist loamy soil. Under glass it should be grown in a mixture of loam and peat in equal parts. Maintain a minimum winter temperature of 45–50°F (7–10°C); water only moderately in winter, freely during spring and summer. Propagation is by seed or by soft-wood cuttings taken in spring and rooted in sandy soil in a warm propagating frame.

### Decaisnea (de-kaiz-ne-a)
Commemorating Joseph Decaisne, a French botanist *(Berberidaceae or Lardizabalaceae)*. A genus of two species of

which one only is likely to be found in cultivation. This is *D. fargesii*, a distinctive Chinese shrub introduced into France in 1895 and at about that time brought to England. It grows to 10 feet tall and has large pinnate leaves, 2–3 feet long and yellow-green flowers in June borne in racemes up to 18 inches long, followed in the autumn by distinctive metallic blue pods which look like those of broad beans. These pods are 3–4 inches long and contain many black seeds embedded in white pulp.

**Cultivation** Choose a sunny shrub border with a rich loamy soil, sheltered from early frosts and cold winds. Plant in late autumn and protect the plant during the first winter in hard weather. Propagation is from seed sown in February or March in pans under cloches or in a cold frame.

### Deciduous (bot.)
A term meaning leaf-losing applied to shrubs and trees that drop their leaves in the autumn and burst into fresh growth in the spring. The opposite of evergreen. When deciduous plants are without their leaves they are said to be dormant and this is the time at which they can be safely transplanted. A few normally deciduous plants, such as beech and oak, hold their brown withered

1 Decaisnea fargesii, a Chinese shrub. 2 Decumaria sinensis prefers a warm spot. 3 A woodland composed of deciduous trees. The leaves fall in the autumn.

leaves throughout the winter in their young state and, when used for hedging purposes, are said to be marcescent.

**Deciduous Cypress**—see Taxodium

### Decumaria (dek-u-mar-e-a)

Thought to be from the Latin *decuma*, a tenth, as certain parts of the flower are in tens *(Saxifragaceae)*. A genus of climbing shrubs, clinging by means of aerial roots, closely related to the hydrangea.

**Species cultivated** *D. barbara* (D or SE), up to 20 feet or more, flowers white, each small but in clusters 3–4 inches across, June and July, Florida to Virginia. *D. sinensis* (E), up to 20–25 feet, small cream flowers in clusters up to 4 inches across in June, faintly scented, central China.

**Cultivation** These climbers will grow in ordinary soil in a sunny position, with wall protection somewhat farther north and west than their usual rather limited range. Plant in late autumn and prune away dead or weak growing shoots in February before new growth begins. Propagation is from cuttings taken in summer and inserted in good garden

445

soil under a cloche or bell jar.

## Decumbent (bot.)
A term used to describe plants that lie on the ground, usually turning up at the tips. Hence the specific name *decumbens*.

## Deficiency diseases
In a naturally fertile soil the various food substances which plants require for healthy growth are present in an available form and in suitable quantity. This occurs in many types of soil and every gardener knows that in Great Britain soils vary very much in different localities. In nature the demands of wild plants are not so heavy as those of domestic ones as they do not produce such large crops or heavy seeds and with trees etc. the land remains fertile with ordinary leaf fall which provides humus and other foods as the debris rots in the moist soil. Where domestic crops are concerned the grower has to remember that heavy crops, especially fruit and vegetables, are a drain on the soil and fertility must be kept up by rotating the crops (different crops take different amounts of food elements out of the soil)

and by adding fertilisers and humus in suitable quantities.

It is possible that a soil is found to be lacking in one or more of the required plant foods, either because the soil is naturally a poor one, unsuitable for good root development, or because from being a good soil it has been cropped heavily without any thought of food replacement.

The result is seen in the general unhealthy appearance of the plants although the signs may not be as spectacular as those caused by infection with a parasite. Nevertheless, the plants show various symptoms (usually on their leaves) which are now referred to as deficiency diseases. Much research has been done on the identification of symptoms caused by shortage of various food substances and on the best methods of providing remedies for these troubles.

The elements required by plants for normal healthy growth have been divided into two groups the so-called major and minor (trace) elements. The names do not indicate the relative importance but only the quantities. In general plants require the first group

1 Manganese deficiency shown by the leaves of strawberries. 2 The tissue between the veins of cherry leaves dies prematurely when there is an acute deficiency of magnesium. 3 Coffee shoots compared show nitrogen deficiency.

(major) in greater quantity than the second group (minor) but they must have both kinds. Although the minor or trace elements are needed in very minute amounts their absence will cause ill-health, resulting in abnormal growth or even death (see Chlorosis and Whiptail).

Some plants are much more sensitive to shortage of a minor element than others and this is true to some extent with the major elements as well. The commonest cause of mineral deficiencies in plants is the presence of excessive lime causing extreme alkalinity and other unsuitable conditions. This occurs in some western soils. Plants often show by pale foliage a shortage of iron or even magnesium and manganese. These symptoms are referred to as common chlorosis owing to the food elements, e.g. iron, becoming combined with the calcium and so unavailable to plant roots. In some cases the addition of the fertiliser in the ordinary way results only in it becoming unavailable and special treatments need to be devised (see Chlorosis).

Crops are often short of the major elements which they need in fairly large quantities. Nitrogen shortage shows as small, pale coloured leaves and stunted plants with early autumn tinting. Phosphate shortage is similar with purplish tinting of the leaves and premature leaf-fall. Potash shortage is indicated by the colour becoming a dull bluish-green and a scorching (browning) of the leaf margins, while fruits such as tomatoes do not colour properly (see Greenback). Calcium is often short in acid soils and this leads to many unwanted conditions and in some instances encourages diseases (see Clubroot). Some plants seem to need magnesium more than others and two such are tomatoes and roses. It can be supplied in various forms and a convenient one is Epsom Salts which is best sprayed on young foliage at ½ lb in 2½ gallons of water with spreading agent. Other trace elements are iron, manganese, boron and copper, some of which can be supplied to plants in the form of special fertilizers.

### Defruiting
The removal of all the immature fruit from a tree, or part of a tree. This may be done when deblossoming was intended but left until the fruit had set (see also Fruit-thinning).

### Deherainia (deer-an-ia)
Commemorating Pierre Paul Deherain, a nineteenth century French naturalist *(Theophrastaceae)*. Evergreen greenhouse shrubs from Mexico and Cuba. A genus of two species, only one of which, *D. smaragdina*, from near Tabasco, Mexico, is encountered in cultivation. A somewhat bushy rhododendron-like shrub, rarely exceeding 3 feet in height, with matt-green lanceolate leaves aggregated towards the ends of each season's growths. Flowers almost 2 inches across, singly or in small clusters, jade-green fading to yellowish-green, borne from February to July.
**Cultivation** Warm greenhouse with a night temperature of 55–60°F (13–16°C), shading during the summer months and a humid atmosphere. An open, well-drained yet general potting mixture should be used. Repotting is best carried out after flowering and not later than September. Propagation by semi-hard cuttings with a heel in a peat and sand mixture in a propagating case with bottom heat.

### Dehiscent (bot.)
A term used to describe fruits or anthers which split open to release the seed or pollen. Seeds are dispersed in various ways and in plants which commonly dehisce, the fruit does not split until the

seeds are ripe. The seed capsules of the violet and iris slit longitudinally along each capsule. Those of the wallflower peel back away from the central placenta and the scarlet pimpernel releases the whole of the top of the capsule.

Occasionally this splitting is sudden and produces an explosive action, as in the gorse pod which flings its seeds out at the same time.

Similarly the anthers do not split open or dehisce until the pollen is ripe and it is usually when a flower is old that the fluffy pollen grains can be seen on the anther, e.g. in tulips that have been indoors for some time or open wide to the sun.

### Dehorning
Cutting main branches hard back. This is sometimes done to re-invigorate old fruit trees but such drastic pruning should be spread over five or six years. Always cut to a side branch so that no 'snag' remains and make a saw cut on the underside first so that the bark is cut through cleanly. Pare smooth any rough patches with a knife (see also Pruning).

1 The seed capsule of Datura stramonium which, when ripe, dehisces to allow the seeds to be dispersed. 2 Primula malacoides, and 3 Incarvillea delavayi, were discovered in China by J. M. Delavay.

### Delavay, J. M.
Père Jean Marie Delavay (1834–1895) who, it is claimed, collected more plants suitable for temperate zone gardens than any other collector, was a French Jesuit stationed in China.

He was stationed east of Canton and first collected for Harry Fletcher Hance, an Englishman and Vice-Consul at Whampoa. On holiday in France, however, Delavay met Armand David (see David, J. P. A.) who persuaded him to send his plants to Paris in future.

For ten years he assiduously collected in the hilly country of north west Yunnan, one of his hunting grounds being Tsemei-shan, a mountain near his station, which, it is said, he climbed sixty times during his ten years of plant hunting. In 1886 he caught bubonic plague in Yunnan which left his left arm paralysed and he left China for France in 1891 but returned in 1893, being stationed at Logki in a climate which only added to his ill health. He left there for Yunnan-fu, where he died in December 1895.

Adrien Franchet, a French botanist estimated that Delavay sent to Paris more than 200,000 plant specimens representing 4,000 species of which 1,500 were new and all were collected by Delavay personally without the help of native collectors.

The many seeds he sent home were unfortunately treated as hot house plants and were killed in the stove houses of the Jardin des Plantes, while his many thousands of specimens had not been sorted out fifty years after their collection.

But his discoveries were immense and among the plants he actually introduced were *Deutzia discolor, Aster delavayi, Rhododendron ciliicalyx, R. irroratum* and *R. racemosum, Primula forbesii* and *P. poissonii, Osmanthus delavayi* and *Incarvillea delavayi.*

Among his discoveries were *Paeonia delavayi, Magnolia delavayi, Thalictrum dipterocarpum, Rhododendron fastigiatum* and *R. yunnanense,* the ever popular *Primula malacoides,* the Blue Poppy, *Meconopsis betonicifolia, Primula nutans, Lilium ochraceum* and *Nomocharis pardanthina.*

### Delayed open-centre
A form or shape of fruit tree. Bushes, standards and half-standards are normally pruned so that an open or goblet-shaped centre is formed. The development of this open centre may be delayed, however, so that several branches radiate from the central stem (as in a pyramid) below the point where it is cut and the head thus opened out (see also Pyramid).

### Delonix (del-on-iks)
From the Greek *delos,* conspicuous, *onyx,* claw, a reference to the long-clawed petals *(Leguminosae).* African trees of which one, *D. regia* (syn. *Poinciana regia),* the peacock flower or flamboyant, is occasionally grown in stovehouses. It comes from Madagascar, has acacia-like foliage and grows to 40 feet or more in its native habitat, but can be restricted for greenhouse cultivation. The flowers, borne in summer, are bright scarlet, yellow and red, showy, with ten conspicuous stamens. These are followed by long, flat seed pods. Grows in south Florida and similar climates.

**Cultivation** Pot in February in a mixture of 2 parts of loam, 1 part of leafmould to half a part of silver sand. Water freely during the summer when temperatures in the sunny greenhouse may rise to 85°F (29°C) or more. During hot weather through July and August the pots may be stood out of doors. A minimum winter temperature of 55 or 60°F (13–16°C) is helpful and plants then need less water than in summer. It is always better to let

these plants dry out well before saturating the soil again. Syringe and damp down regularly during the summer. Propagate from cuttings taken in summer and inserted in pure sand in pots in a temperature of up to 85°F (29°C).

### Delosperma (del-o-sper-ma)
From the Greek *delos,* conspicuous, *sperma,* seed *(Aizoaceae).* Greenhouse succulents from South Africa, formerly included in the genus *Mesembryanthemum,* dwarf bushy shrubs, many branched, spreading and prostrate, a few semi-erect, some perennial and others biennial; flowering freely in summer, flowers white, yellow or red. Can be grown out of doors in summer in sunny beds or rock gardens.

**Species cultivated** *D. angustifolia,* forming a mat 2–3 inches high, leaves narrow, bluish-green, flowers white with pink tips, Cape Province. *D. brevisepalum,* compact shrub, flowers white, Cape Province. *D. cooperi,* prostrate growth,

**Delosperma echinatum, a greenhouse succulent plant from Cape Province.**

flowers purple, Orange Free State. *D. echinatum,* shrub to 1 foot high, thick egg-shaped leaves, white or yellowish flowers, Cape Province. *D. grandiflorum,* erect growth, stems up to 3 feet high, flowers large purple, Cape Province. *D. litorale,* creeping habit, leaves green, edged with white, flowers white, Cape Province. *D. luckhoffii,* dwarf shrub, with dainty branches, flowers pink-purple, Cape Province.

**Cultivation** These plants will grow well in soil made from light, friable potting mixture, with a fifth part of added roughage. Pot in spring for greenhouse culture, plant out of doors in June, water freely in hot weather but keep dry during winter. Temperatures: 65°F (18°C) in summer; 45°F (7°C) in winter. Plants may be raised from seed or increased by cuttings; the cuttings soon make roots and can flower soon after.

## Delphinium (del-fin-e-um)

From the Greek *delphin,* a dolphin, the flowerbuds having some resemblance to that sea creature *(Ranunculaceae).* Larkspur. The genus consists of annual, biennial and herbaceous perennial plants, mostly hardy and showy plants for border cultivation, with some dwarf species suitable for the rock garden.

**Species cultivated**: Annual *D. ajacis,* 1–2 feet, blue, violet, rose-pink or white, summer, Europe. *D. consolida,* branching larkspur, 2 feet, purple or deep violet, summer, Europe. *D. paniculatum,* Siberian larkspur, up to 3 feet, single, violet, July to September, also grown as a biennial. Seedsmen list many beautiful varieties of these annual larkspurs, mainly 2½–3 feet tall, derived mainly from *D. ajacis* and *D. consolida.* They include such strains as 'Giant Hyacinth-flowered'; 'Giant Imperial'; 'Regal', 4 feet; 'Supreme', 4 feet, and named cultivars such as 'Blue Spire', dark blue; 'Carmine King'; 'Dazzler', bright scarlet; 'Exquisite Pink'; 'Lilac Spire'; 'Los Angeles', rose and salmon; 'Miss California', salmon rose; 'Rosamond', bright rose and 'White Spire'.

**Perennial** *D. brunonianum,* 1–1½ feet, light purple, June and July, western China. *D. cardinale,* 2–3 feet, bright red, July and August, California, somewhat tender. *D. denudatum,* 2½ feet, yellow and blue, summer, Himalaya. *D. elatum,* 2–3 feet, blue, June, Alps, Pyrenees eastwards, the plant from which most garden delphiniums have been derived. *D. formosum,* 3 feet, purple-blue, August, Caucasus, Asia Minor. *D. grandiflorum* (syn. *D. chinense),* 1–3 feet, violet-blue or white, long spurred, summer, Siberia. *D. nudicaule,* 1–2 feet, red and yellow, April to June, California. *D. speciosum* (syn. *D. caucasicum),* 6 inches–2 feet, blue and purple, summer, Himalaya. *D. tatsienense,* 1½ feet, violet-blue, July, Szechwan. *D. vestitum,* 2 feet, pale and deep blue, summer, northern India. *D. zalil* (syn. *D. sulphureum),* 1–2½ feet, lemon-yellow, summer, Persia, requires a well-drained soil.

1 Delphinium brunonianum, which has musk-scented foliage. 2 Delphinium zalil, introduced from Persia in 1892.

1

2

3

4

Delphiniums are easily propagated by means of cuttings taken from the basal shoots. 1 A delphinium crown showing the emergence of basal shoots. 2 A shoot is removed with a sharp knife. 3 As many as six cuttings can be taken from one strong crown. The basal cut is made below a leaf joint and the lower leaves are removed. 4 The cuttings are inserted firmly into a sandy medium and placed in a cold frame or deep box covered with a sheet of glass. 5 Vermiculite is a good rooting medium because of its porous properties. 6 Once the cuttings have rooted they are planted out and protected with a small jar until established. 8 Top: caterpillars of the Tortrix Moth attacking the growing points. Below left: A close-up of the caterpillars. Below right: slugs and snails are partial to the new shoots of delphiniums; it is necessary to take precautions against damage by these pests.

Cultivation Sow annual varieties in a sunny border in April or May where they are to flower, or in boxes of light soil under glass in March in a temperature of 55°F (13°C). Prick out seedlings when large enough to handle and transplant in the open in May. Perennials should be planted out in the spring or autumn in beds of rich, deeply cultivated soil; dwarf varieties are suitable for rock gardens. Feed with liquid manure in the early summer. Lift and replant every third year. Propagation of perennial varieties is by means of cuttings of young shoots in early spring, inserted in sandy soil in pots in a shaded propagating frame, or by seeds sown in the open ground in late spring or under glass in spring.

Cultivation of modern hybrid delphiniums

Fast-growing plants, delphiniums require a deeply-dug, rich soil with adequate drainage. A medium loam is preferable to a light sandy soil. Where the soil is light dig in deeply plenty of compost or old farmyard manure before planting and during the summer a mulch of garden compost is excellent. Nitrogenous fertilisers should be used with care as they may only result in producing weak stems. If the stems are cut back immediately after flowering a second crop of spikes may be produced, but these should only be encouraged with strong-growing varieties. Adequate moisture will be required to produce this second crop during what may be hot, summer weather. Slugs can be a menace with the tender young delphinium shoots, especially in the early spring,

5

7

6

8

so precautions should be taken with slug pellets or various repellents. Varieties that grow to about 4–5 feet in height are more suitable for small gardens than those that tower to 7 feet or more, and they are less liable to damage by summer gales. Pea sticks, brushwood or twigs can be used to support the young growths but these should be put in position around the plants in good time so that the stems grow up through them. This is often left too late with the result that the tender stems get broken when the sticks are being pushed into the soil. Staking for exhibition spikes must be carefully done, using one stout cane to each spike. When growing the large flowering varieties it is usual to restrict one-year-old plants to one spike and two-year-old plants to two or three

spikes. Pea sticks, however, provide adequate support for the lighter, less tall graceful belladonna types of delphinium, with their branching stems, which are also so attractive for floral arrangement. Exhibition spikes should be straight, tapering and well filled with large circular florets but not overcrowded, and bearing few laterals. The foliage should be clean, healthy and undamaged. Immediately spikes are cut they should be placed in deep containers filled with water and stood in a cool, but not draughty place. There they should remain for some hours or overnight. Each stem should be wrapped in a large sheet of tissue paper (30×40 inches) before being taken to the show. A further step to ensure that the spike does not flag is to turn it upside down, immedi-

ately before final staging, fill the hollow stem with cold water and plug with cotton wool.

As they are easily raised from seed the delphinium has been of much interest to the plant breeder who has produced many stately varieties. The era of immense spikes has passed its zenith and the trend is to develop a range of hybrids not exceeding about 4½ feet in height. These are of much more general use in gardens which are ever becoming smaller, but more numerous. From the glorious shades of blue the colour range has been extended from white and cream through pink, carmine, mauve, lavender, purple and violet. Now, thanks to the work done by Dr Legro, the celebrated Dutch hybridist, the range includes shades of cerise, orange,

1 Delphiniums in Regent's Park, London. 2, 3, 4 Some of the new range of delphiniums raised in England by Dr R. A. H. Legro and Blackmore and Langdon, Bath.

peach and tomato-red. Our garden hybrids have been mainly derived from *Delphinium elatum,* a natural tetraploid species, but Dr Legro succeeded in overcoming the sterility barrier when he made a number of species crosses at diploid level, tetraploided the resulting plants and then successfully married them to hybrid elatums (see Plant breeding). The rediscovery of the white African species, *D. leroyi,* which has a freesia-like fragrance, also opens up pleasing possiblities. First crosses at diploid level have shown that this quality is not recessive, so hopes are high, but this work takes time. In Great Britain Dr B. J. Langdon has also been working on these problems and during the next

few years we should see a truly remarkable range of hybrid delphiniums.

**Recommended tall varieties** 'Alice Artindale', light blue, 6 feet; 'Ann Page', deep cornflower blue, 5½ feet; 'Bridesmaid', silvery-mauve, white eye, 7 feet; 'Charles F. Langdon', mid-blue, black eye, 6½ feet; 'Daily Express', bright sky-blue, black eye, 6 feet; 'Janet Wort', pure white, 6½ feet; 'Jennifer Langdon', pale blue and mauve, 5½ feet; 'Mogul', rosy-purple, 6½ feet; 'Purple Ruffles', deep purple, overlaid royal blue, 5 feet; 'Royalist', deep blue, 6 feet; 'Silver

Moon', silvery-mauve, white eye, 5½ feet; 'Swanlake', pure white, black eye, 5 feet.

**Shorter-growing varieties** 'Blue Bees', pale blue, 4 feet; 'Blue Tit', indigo blue, black eye, 3½ feet; 'Blue Jade', pastel blue, dark brown eye, 4 feet; 'Cliveden Beauty', pale blue, 4 feet; 'Naples', bright blue, 4 feet; 'Peter Pan', deep blue, 3½ feet; 'Wendy', gentian-blue, 4–5 feet, the most popular of the belladonna type.

The Pacific Hybrids raised in America, growing 4–6 feet tall, include 'Astolat', lilac and pink; 'Black Knight' series, shades of violet; 'Blue Jay', mid-blue; 'Camelot' series, lavender shades; 'Elaine', rose-pink; 'Galahad' series, whites; 'Guinevere' series, shades of

1 Delphinium 'Daily Express', a fine garden plant. 2 Delphinium 'Silver Moon', one of the finest cultivars ever raised.

lavender-pink; 'King Arthur' series, shades of violet-purple; 'Lancelot' series, shades of lilac; 'Percival', white with a black eye; 'Round Table', including various colours as above; 'Summer Skies', good true blues.

**Demeton-methyl**—see Insecticides

## Dendrobium (den-dro-be-um)

From the Greek *dendron*, a tree, *bios*, life, the plants growing on trees in their native habitats *(Orchidaceae)*. A very large genus of approximately 1100 species of epiphytic orchids, which are widely distributed throughout eastern regions and the Southern Hemisphere. Considerable variation is found in flower and plant habit, from small tufted plants to stout pseudobulbed plants, several feet tall. Many hybrids have been produced particularly in the *D. nobile* and *D. phalaenopsis* sections.

**Species cultivated** (A selection only) *D. aggregatum*, yellow, spring, requires a decided rest, Burma. *D. atroviolaceum*, creamy white, purple spotted, spring, New Guinea. *D. aureum*, amber-yellow and brown, very fragrant, autumn, India, etc. *D. bigibbum*, magenta-purple, winter, Australia. *D. brymerianum*, bright yellow with densely fringed lip, spring, Burma. *D. chrysanthum*, orange-yellow, maroon blotched, autumn, India. *D. chrysotoxum*, orange-yellow, spring, requires a decided rest, Burma. *D. dearei*, white, summer, Philippines. *D. densiflorum*, clusters of orange-yellow flowers, spring, Burma. *D. fimbriatum*, orange-yellow, various, Burma. *D. findlayanum*, white, yellow and magenta, winter, Burma. *D. formosum*, large, white and yellow, fragrant, autumn, Burma, etc. *D. jamesianum*, large, white, spring, Burma. *D. kingianum*, small purplish flowers, spring, Australia. *D. moschatum*, yellow, flushed rose, black blotches, spring, Burma. *D. parishii*, purplish-rose, spring, Burma. *D. phalaenopsis*, rose-red to magenta-purple, autumn and various, Australia and New Guinea. *D. regium*, large, rose, spring, India. *D. superbum*, large, rose-purple, spring, Philippines. *D. thyrsiflorum*, white and yellow, spring, Burma. *D. victoriareginae*, whitish approaching blue, one of the very few orchids having a near blue colour. *D. wardianum*, white, purplish-yellow and rose-red, winter, Burma.

Named cultivars run into many thousands. A few are given here from the *nobile* section, all having fine large, strongly coloured flowers derived mainly from *D. nobile, D. findlayanum* and their early hybrids. 'Fort Noble', 'Fort Alan', 'Winifred Fortescue', 'Montrose', 'Margaret Illingworth', 'Sunburst', 'Ann-Marie', 'Gatton Monarch'.

**Cultivation** General directions only can

1

2

**1 Dendrobium thyrsiflorum. 2 Dendrobium 'Lady Coleman'.**

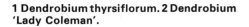

be given for this large and varied genus. The plants require a general mixture of 3 parts of osmunda fibre and 1 part of sphagnum moss, in well-drained pots or pans. An important factor with most types is maximum light in autumn to ripen the growths. Water freely in summer and rest carefully in winter. The *nobile* types, especially, require cooler conditions in winter to initiate flower buds; temperatures should be about 50–55°F (10–13°C). For other types they should be 55–60°F (13–16°C). Summer temperatures can for most species rise to 80–85°F (27–29°C) and moist conditions should prevail. Propagation is by division at potting time; *nobile* types and some others produce adventitious growths from the stems; these can be potted up in small pots. The stems of some species can be cut up into small pieces of about one node (joint) and placed in warm conditions; these will produce small plants.

### Dendrochilum (den-dro-ki-lum)
From the Greek *dendron*, a tree, *cheilon*, a lip, the flowers are lipped and grow on trees in their native habitats *(Orchidaceae)*. A large genus of epiphytic orchids, having small clustered pseudobulbs. The flowers though small are numerous, on semi-erect to pendent spikes, which are usually produced in abundance on large plants. They are of easy cultivation and are very attractive.
**Species cultivated** (A selection only) *D. cobbianum*, creamy-white, autumn. *D. filiforme*, golden chain orchid, dainty spikes with yellow flowers, very fragrant, spring. *D. glumaceum*, creamy-white, very fragrant, spring. *D. latifolium*, creamy-white and green, spring. All these species are from the Philippines.
**Cultivation** These orchids should be provided with a medium of 3 parts of osmunda fibre and 1 part of sphagnum moss, in pans hung near the glass. In summer, plants should have a temperature of up to 80°F (27°C), and abundant water; winter temperature 60–65°F (13–16°C), and reduced watering but not a severe drying. Propagation is by division at potting time in spring.

### Dendromecon (den-drom-e-kon or den-dro-mee-kon)
From the Greek *dendron*, a tree, *mecon*, a poppy *(Papaveraceae)*. Tree poppy or poppy bush. A small genus of tender, semi-woody deciduous shrubs related to *Romneya*, with yellow, poppy-like flowers. The only species cultivated is *D. rigidum*, usually about 5 feet tall but in warm, humid regions it will grow up to 10 or 12 feet. The poppy-like flowers are bright yellow, fragrant, 2–3 inches across and start to appear about May and bloom continuously until September, individual flowers lasting well. California.
**Cultivation** Plant in a sheltered position, or in a warm climate. Plants are liable to be damaged by frosts, but new growth

1 Dendrochilum filiforme produces up to 100 fragrant blooms on each raceme. 2 Dendromecon rigidum from California.

will often break from the base. Good drainage is essential and it is advantageous to put leafmould, peat and mortar rubble in the hole at planting time. Cut back shoots when they are bare at the base. Propagation is from cuttings taken in May or August, by layering or from root cuttings, 1 inch long, taken in autumn.

### Denmoza (den-mo-za)
An anagram of Mendoza, a city in Argentina, the home of these plants *(Cactaceae)*. Two species of greenhouse cacti with globular to cylindrical stems with many undulating ribs and many spines, curved and strong.
**Species cultivated** *D. erythrocephala*, stem always simple or solitary, round when young, becoming cylindrical, 20–30 ribs, well covered with spines, flowers

1 Dentaria digitata. 2 and 3 Rufford Old Hall garden before and after renovation.

red. *D. rhodacantha,* about 15 ribs, well covered with spines, reddish coloured when young later becoming rusty-red, flowers red.

**Cultivation** Provide a porous soil made up from light, porous potting mixture with a sixth part added of coarse sand or grit; repot only every three years in March or April. Keep plants in a sunny place in the greenhouse and water sparingly during the growing period, April to September. Keep plants dry during the winter. They can stand high temperatures in summer and down to 40°F (4°C) in winter provided the soil is quite dry. Propagation is by seed sown on sandy compost. Keep the seedlings moist and warm at a temperature of 70°F (21°C), shade them from sun for a year and prick out when they are large enough to handle.

**Dentaria** (den-tar-e-a)
From the Latin, *dens,* a tooth, an allusion to the tooth-like scales on the roots *(Cruciferae).* Coral root, toothwort. Hardy herbaceous perennials, useful because they flower early and tolerate shade well.
**Species cultivated** *D. bulbifera* (syn. *Cardamine bulbifera*), 1½–2 feet, British plant, quite rare, growing in light woodland, producing tiny bulbils on the stem which fall off when ripe. Flowers pale mauve, April. *D. digitata,* 1–1½ feet, purple-rose flowers, April, southern Europe. *D. laciniata,* 1 foot, leaves deeply cut, flowers almost white, larger than those of the other species, April, North America. *D. polyphylla,* 1 foot, purple flowers, May and June.
**Cultivation** These are excellent little plants for moist, shaded positions, in peaty loam. Plant in October or March in groups for good effect. Propagation is by division of roots in spring or by sowing the small bulbils of *D. bulbifera* in summer. Seed is not produced well.

**Dentate**—see Toothed

**Deodar**—see Cedrus deodara

### Derelict gardens and their renovation

At a first glance, a derelict garden seems a most depressing problem and one which would appear to be insurmountable. Certainly its renovation and reclamation will require a great deal of hard work but it is a task which can be made much easier and pleasanter if a plan of campaign is worked out beforehand.

There are, of course, degrees of neglect. Some gardens may have been unoccupied for a few months only, a few will have been neglected for years. Whatever the condition, the work of reclamation should be tackled in easy, logical stages. A garden is as good as its initial soil preparation and any hurried or glossed over soil cultivation will repay in poor growth and even more problems later on.

**Examining the site** The first thing which will have to be done will be to examine the site carefully to see where original beds and borders are and to identify these with long stakes. In extreme instances, it may even be difficult to trace paths, but these must be given priority as, if they are in reasonable condition, they will be most useful when the wheelbarrow is required.

The extent of the site examination must depend on the time of the year the garden is taken over. The work will be difficult at the height of the season when most of the garden's occupants are in full growth, but it will prove to be a most useful time as it will be possible to assess the quality of these plants. Those which are obviously weak and of very poor quality should be suitably marked or noted so that they can be removed. It might be possible to salvage some if they are cut back hard at the end of the season to encourage sturdier growth the following year.

If the garden is occupied in the autumn or winter, most of the plants will have died down and may be rather difficult to find and examine. It will, however, be an easier time to tackle the clearance problem, as much of the growth, including that of the weeds will have died down.

**Clearance** Once main features and plants have been located, the task of clearance or renovation can start. The first part will consist of weed removal. This can be done manually, by chemical means or a combination of both. In a seriously neglected garden where few established plants are worth keeping, the site can be cleared by the application of a powerful weedkiller such as sodium chlorate.

This must be used with extreme caution since it is so powerful that ground treated cannot be used for at least six to seven months afterwards. It must be applied away from neighbours' boundaries, too, otherwise many of their plants growing close by will be seriously affected and even destroyed.

A safer method is to use weedkillers based on dalapon or paraquat. The former is especially useful for the control of grasses, especially that particularly troublesome weed, couch grass. Paraquat is a most remarkable weedkiller as it kills all plants but is completely inert as soon as it touches the soil. It enables the gardener to control and deal with weeds round established plants such as shrubs, roses and fruit trees. It deals most effectively with annual broad-leaved weeds and the tops of perennial weeds. It is reasonably economical to use as a 4 oz pack makes up 4 gallons of liquid which is sufficient to deal with 30 square yards of ground.

Another useful chemical aid is found in the form of the brushwood killers. Tough weeds such as docks, brambles, briars, nettles and many other common weeds are controlled by applications of the diluted chemical. A 10 oz can makes up sufficient liquid to cover 600–1200

1 The derelict garden at Farnborough Hall before renovation. 2 After renovation was completed. 3 The garden at Wallington with beds and borders demanding labour for maintenance. 4 After renovation with the simplified labour-saving design. The regularly shaped lawn creates an impression of space, is easy to maintain.

square yards with some sorts.

Weeds can be dealt with by the more laborious method of hand weeding. Annual weeds such as chickweed can be killed if they are buried well beneath the soil surface during the cultivation of the soil. Perennial weeds such as dandelions, docks, thistles, plantains, couch grass, ground elder and bindweed must *never* be buried otherwise they will quickly take root again and grow even more vigorously. As many of these perennial weeds are deep rooted, care must be taken to see that they are dug or forked out as carefully as possible. Throw them into a heap as they are collected and allow them to dry out as much as possible. As there will be a lot of general rubbish being burnt during cleaning up operations, the best place for these dried weeds is on the bonfire; they will quickly burn if a good fierce fire is maintained.

The clearance of a neglected garden must never be hurried. It is a good idea to tackle small areas at a time. This will ensure that the work does not become too tiring, and it will also mean that it is carried out more thoroughly. Once most of the weeds and unwanted growth have been cleared, the soil itself will require attention. One of the first things to do is to gather any rubble which may be on the surface. This need not be discarded as it may come in useful for the foundations of new paths.

Cultivation The depth of cultivation must depend on the type of soil. If it is heavy, it will require deep digging in order to improve drainage. Light soils, on the other hand, will not need such thorough treatment. The heavy types should be double dug. That means that the top spit or 10 inches of soil is turned over and the bottom of each trench is broken up to the full depth of the fork. This will provide about 20 inches of well-worked soil.

The sticky types of soil can be opened up still further if sharp sand or well weathered gritty ashes are incorporated as the work proceeds. Small rubble can also be worked into the bottom spit to ensure adequate drainage. Organic matter is essential for neglected soils. It can

457

be supplied in several ways. A neglected garden can always supply quite a lot of its own in the form of grass clippings, annual weeds and other waste vegetation. These can be incorporated fresh or stacked to rot down in a compost heap.

Horticultural peat is an ideal form of humus which can be dug in large quantities. It can be bought fairly cheaply in bulk. Moss peat is often particularly suitable as it is extremely fibrous and has such a low degree of decomposition that it will last in the soil for several seasons. A six bushel bale will cover about 100 square feet to a depth of about 1 inch.

Spent hops can sometimes be purchased from local breweries and are very useful for digging into the soil at about 1 barrowload to 6 square yards. Where the gardener is lucky enough to be able to purchase some farmyard manure, this can be applied at the rate of a barrowload to 8 to 10 square yards.

There are many other products available from nurserymen which take the form of composted or concentrated preparations for digging into the soil. Most are very useful, but some are rather expensive to use on a large scale and it is important to read the application rate carefully before buying, so that the economics can be assessed. The lighter types of soil require much more organic matter than others. Humus or organic matter is essential, as it acts as a sponge and retains valable moisture, as well as providing food for the plants.

The heavy soils can be lightened by the application of hydrated lime or gypsum. The former is used at the rate of approximately ½ lb per square yard. The latter is particularly good for neglected, heavy soils. It, too, is applied at the rate of ½ lb per square yard and is worked into the surface immediately.

Ideally all soil cultivation should be carried out during the winter except for the light soils. During the preparation of the soil, a dressing of bonemeal should be applied and worked in at the rate of 4 oz per square yard. This is a slow acting fertiliser which supplies nitrogen and phosphate.

**Establishing plants** The busiest time in the newly reclaimed garden is the spring when new seeds and plants are established. It will be a problem time, too, as many seedling weeds will be appearing. The reason for this is that many weed seeds will have fallen to the soil the previous year. Regular use of the hoe is one way of killing most of these, especially if the work can be carried out during dry weather.

The chemical paraquat will be useful at this time of the year for keeping seed beds or rows free from weeds. If it is applied prior to germination, weeds will be killed and the soil will be clear so that the young seedlings can grow without competition from the weeds.

Before the main sowings or plantings are carried out, the soil must be sup-

Dermatobotrys saundersii, a winter-flowering shrub for the dry, airy greenhouse. It was introduced from Natal.

plied with sufficient foods to ensure sturdy, healthy growth. Neglected soils will be short of basic fertilisers such as potash, nitrogen and phosphates. These can be supplied individually or in a compound form. Sulphate of ammonia at 1 oz per square yard, sulphate of potash at 2 oz per square yard and superphosphate of lime at 2 oz per square yard will supply these essentials. A balanced or general fertiliser such as is widely available at 1 lb per 10 square yards will supply all three essentials at one application.

There are some proprietary complete foods or dressings which can be used instead. All have been specially blended, many with extras such as trace elements. Maker's directions should always be carefully followed.

It will be necessary to provide extra feeds at frequent intervals during the growing seasons. Again individual fertilisers can be applied or proprietary ones which have been specially formulated for particular plants. If the weather is

dry during the summer it will be necessary to provide plenty of water by means of sprinklers so that the various plants can become established as quickly as possible to transform what was once a neglected garden, into a place of beauty and charm.

**Dermatobotrys** (der-mat-o-bot-ris)
Name derived from *derma*, skin or bark, and *botrys*, a cluster, referring to the positioning and arrangement of the flowers *(Scrophulariaceae)*. A monotypic genus, the only species, *D. saundersii*, a deciduous epiphytic shrub from South Africa, where it is sometimes found on arborescent succulents. In cultivation a somewhat straggly shrub rarely exceeding 2 to 3 feet, with stout square branchlets, and 2 to 4 inches long ovate, toothed leaves somewhat reminiscent of forsythia. Flowers borne at the tips of the previous season's growths at the base of the new shoots and while the leaves are still immature; tubular and somewhat curved, 1¼ inches long with five flared lobes, pale or pinkish red. Borne November to spring, with sometimes odd clusters into summer.
**Cultivation** Cool greenhouse with plenty

of light and air; a house with a collection of succulents is ideal. Although an epiphyte in nature, when cultivated it thrives in fertile and friable potting mixture. Watering should be gradually withheld during the late summer, and after the leaves have fallen withheld all together until the new growth commences. Repot during October. Propagation is readily effected by cuttings of semi-ripe growths in a propagating case during late spring.

## Derris
Derris is an insecticide containing rotenone compounds. It is used against many pests including caterpillars, sawflies, aphids, beetles, wasps and red spider mites. It is made up as dusts, wettable powders and liquid formulations, sometimes with other insecticides, especially pyrethrum. It is not toxic to most warm-blooded animals but is a fish poison.

## Deschampsia flexuosa—see Aira flexuosa

## Desfontainea (des-fon-tain-e-a)
Commemorating a French botanist, René Louiche Desfontaines *(Loganiaceae)*. An evergreen flowering shrub, somewhat tender, first introduced in the middle of the nineteenth century. A good plant for west Scotland, Ireland and the mild parts of the USA. The only species is *D. spinosa*, 6–10 feet. The leaves are holly-like and the general habit of the shrub is stiff; the flowers are tubular in shape, scarlet and yellow, and are borne in late summer over a long period. This is a striking and magnificent shrub when established.
**Cultivation** *Desfontainea spinosa* dislikes lime and needs a good loam. It does particularly well on gritty granite soil. Plant in October, November or April. The only pruning needed is to take out dead or unwanted pieces of wood. The plant can be grown under glass in tubs or borders, in a compost of equal parts of loam, peat and sand with some charcoal. Pot or plant in March or April and water moderately during the summer, reducing water in the winter. Propagation is by cuttings in spring in a temperature of 55–65°F (13–18°C).

## Deshooting
The complete removal of young shoots on fruit trees, often performed with the nails of the finger and thumb. This is frequently necessary with wall-trained trees to prevent shoots growing directly towards the wall or at right-angles away from it and to concentrate the tree's growth into laterals in the desired position and direction. Fruit-growers now consider that this is a

459

1 Desmodium spicatum, a hardy deciduous shrub reaching 6 to 8 feet, flowering in September and October. It was introduced from China in 1896. 2 Deutzia gracilis, a shrub that reaches 3 to 4 feet and flowers in June.

preferable term to 'disbudding' which has been used in the past, particularly in the case of peaches, because 'disbudding' might also refer to the removal of blossom buds (see also Disbudding).

## Desmodium (dez-mo-de-um)

From the Greek *desmos*, a bond, a reference to the united stamens (*Leguminosae*). Hardy and greenhouse shrubby perennials and sub-shrubs, one greenhouse kind, (*D. motorium*), displaying a curious example of animated leaves.

**Species cultivated: Greenhouse** *D. motorium* (syn. *D. gyrans*), telegraph plant, 2–3 feet, flowers violet or mauve, summer. In sunshine, particularly, when the temperature is above 72°F (22°C), the leaflets move round in all directions. At night they droop.

**Hardy** *D. canadense*, tick trefoil, 8 feet, purple flowers, July and August, a hardy perennial dying down each year and breaking again from ground level. *D. tiliaefolium*, shrubby, 3–5 feet, pale lilac flowers, August and September.

**Cultivation** The tender species needs a winter temperature of 55–65°F (13–18°C), and a mixture of equal parts of good loam, peat and sand. The hardy kinds should be planted in March in sunny borders; they are propagated by division in March. *D. motorium* is raised from seed sown in a temperature of 75–80°F (24–27°C) in early spring, or by cuttings rooted in sandy peat in a propagating case in spring.

## Deutzia (doyt-se-a)

In honour of Johann van der Deutz, a Burgomaster of Amsterdam, a patron of botany (*Saxifragaceae*). Deciduous, hardy, free-flowering shrubs, useful out of doors and for forcing for conservatory decoration. They come mainly from China and other Far Eastern countries.

**Species cultivated** *D. × candelabrum*, 4–5 feet, white flowers, June, similar to *D. gracilis*, but hardier, hybrid. *D. chunii*, 5 feet, flowers pink outside, white within, July. *D. compacta*, 5–6 feet, fragrant white flowers, July. *D. discolor*, 4–6 feet, large flowers, white, pink flushed on the outside; var. *major*, larger flowers. *D. × elegantissima*, 4–6 feet, rose-pink, June, hybrid; var. *fasciculata*, flowers bright pink. *D. glomeruliflora*, 5–6 feet, flowers large, white, May and June. *D. gracilis*, 4–6 feet, Japanese snowflower, white flowers, June. This is the species usually grown under glass, when it flowers in April and May. *D. hookeriana*, 4–6 feet, flowers white, late June. *D. hypoglauca*, 5–6 feet, leaves white below, flowers white, June. *D. × kalmiaeflora*, 5–6 feet, flowers white, carmine flushed, June. *D. longifolia*, 4–6 feet, large clusters of lilac-pink flowers, June; var. *veitchii*, 4–6 feet, probably the most popular pink-flowered kind. *D. × magnifica*, 8 feet, a hybrid, vigorous in growth, double white flowers, June; vars. *eburnea*, flowers single, white; *latiflora*, large single flowers; *longipetala*, single flowers with long narrow petals. *D. monbeigii*, 4–6 feet, leaves white underneath, flowers white, starry, June. *D. ningpoensis*, 6–7 flowers white, July. *D. pulchra*, 7–8 feet, flowers white in long trails, May and June. *D. × rosea*, 4 feet, pinkish flowers, June, hybrid; vars. *campanulata*, white; *carminea*, 4 feet, rose-carmine flowers; *grandiflora*, flowers large white, flushed pink; *venusta*, flowers large, white. *D. scabra* (syn. *D. crenata*), 7 feet, white flowers, June; vars. *candidissima*, pure white, double; *macrocephala*, larger flowers, July; *plena* ('Pride of Rochester') double, flushed rosy-purple outside; *watereri*, single white flowers tinted carmine. *D. setchuenensis*, 6 feet, slow-growing, white flowers, June to August; var. *corymbiflora*, larger leaves and flowers. *D. sieboldiana*, 4–6 feet, starry

white fragrant flowers, June. *D. staminea,* 4–5 feet, flowers white, June. *D. vilmoriniae,* 4–6 feet, quick growing, flowers white, June.

Named cultivars include 'Contraste', 4–6 feet, starry, mauve pink, purple outside; 'Mont Rose', 4–6 feet, rose-pink; 'Perle Rose', 6–7 feet, rose pink.

**Cultivation** Deutzias prefer a good loam soil but will grow in most soils. It is essential to encourage well-ripened wood each year to ensure free flowering. Remove old worn-out wood once flowering is over, to a point where young shoots are developing, but do not shorten shoots generally as this results in loss of flower. Feeding with a mulch of old manure helps to ripen the wood and enrich the soil. Propagation is from cuttings in May or June or in July when the wood is firmer. Pinch out the tips of growth the following season to encourage bushy growth.

When *D. gracilis* is to be forced, pot up rooted cuttings into a medium of 2 parts of loam, 1 part of decayed manure and sand, in October or November. Keep in a cold greenhouse or frame throughout the winter, giving the plants little water. Start watering more in March when the plants respond to a minimum temperature of 55–60°F (13–16°C), and will flower in April and May. After three years or so plants should either be discarded or planted out of doors for a year before repotting.

---

**Devil's coach horse**—see Predators

---

**Devil's Fig**—see Argemone grandiflora

---

**Devil-in-a-bush**—see Nigella damascena

## Dew and dewpoint

Dew consists of the drops of moisture deposited on any cool surface by condensation of the water vapour in the air. In plants the leaves are usually cooler than the surrounding air because of evaporation from the leaf surface and so moisture condenses on the leaf as dew. The dead parts of a plant are often the first parts to be covered with dew.

The formation of dew is usually associated with the drop in temperature in the evening after a warm day. Water vapour is always present in the air, and the relative humidity is the amount of water present at the same temperature, usually expressed as a percentage (see Humidity). When air which is not saturated, as on a dry sunny afternoon, is cooled down (as at dusk) a temperature is reached at which it becomes saturated because the air cannot hold any more moisture. This temperature is the 'dew-

1 Deutzia 'Magician', a hybrid of Deutzia longifolia. 2 Drops of water, poised on the leaves of plants, that are unable to evaporate in a water-charged atmosphere, are called dew drops.

point'. Further cooling brings about the formation of dew, as moisture in excess of that which the air can hold at that temperature.

During the normal functions of the plant water is taken in from the soil by the root system and eventually given off by the plant as water vapour through stomata or specially adapted pores of the leaf surface. If dew has been deposited on the leaves and the plant has taken in the required amount of water from the soil, evaporation is hindered, thus 'safety-valve pores' known as water pores come into action. Drops of water are forced from the plant and if the surrounding air is not saturated they evaporate, but if the air can hold no more moisture the drops of water are poised on the leaf and make what we recognise as dew drops.

**Dewberry**—see Rubus caesius

## Diacrium
From the Greek *dia,* through, and *akris,* a point, referring to the sheaths round the stalks *(Orchidaceae)*. A small genus of epiphytic orchids with hollow pseudo-bulbs and thick leathery leaves. The spikes are borne at the ends of the stems and have up to twenty flowers of great beauty. The only species cultivated, *D. bicornutum,* has 2 inch wide flowers of creamy white, spotted purple, lip with yellow crest, summer, Central America.
**Cultivation** Provide this orchid with a compost of osmunda fibre and sphagnum moss. It needs warm moist conditions with ample light when growing. In winter suspend it near the glass giving maximum light and a decided rest. Maintain a minimum temperature of 60°F (16°C). It objects to sour compost so adjust watering accordingly.

## Diamond-back moth
Small, narrow-winged moths *(Plutella maculipennis)* with pale and dark markings that form a rough diamond-shape when the wings are at rest. Eggs are laid in early summer on brassicas. The caterpillars, which are light green in colour, pupate in cocoons on the leaves and give rise to adult moths. There may be several generations a year and influxes of migrants from the Continent, cause large-scale infestations in some seasons. Control is by DDT, trichlorphon, or derris and pyrethrum.

## Dianella (di-an-ella)
A diminutive of Diana *(Liliaceae)*. Flax lily, Paroo lily. Fibrous-rooted perennials, slightly tender, natives of south east Asia, Australia and Polynesia. They may be grown out of doors in the south and in sheltered areas, but also make

**1**
**2**

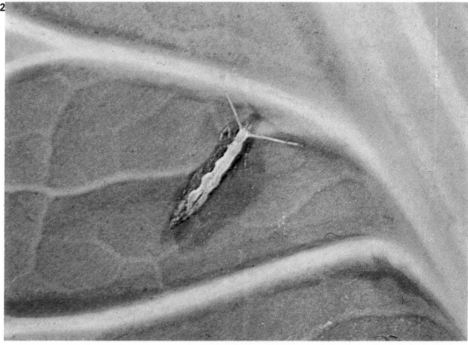

1 Diacrium bicornatum, a fragrant orchid grown in a greenhouse kept at a minimum winter temperature of 60°F (16°C). 2 The Diamond-Back Moth (Platella maculipennis) a pest of cabbages in Britain.

attractive pot plants for the conservatory. The blue berries are the most interesting features of the plants.

**Species cultivated** *D. caerulea,* 2 feet, blue flowers, May. *D. ensifolia* (syn. *D. nemorosa),* 2–6 feet, blue or white flowers, April and May. *D. laevis* (syn. *D. strumosa),* 2 feet, blue flowers, spring.

**Cultivation** In conservatories or cold greenhouses a mixture of equal proportions of sand, loam, peat and leaf-mould is required. Good drainage is essential and plants require fairly free watering in summer. Propagation is by seed sown in heat in spring or summer or by division in autumn or spring.

## Dianthus (di-an-thus)

From the Greek *dios,* a god or divine, *anthos,* a flower, divine flower, flower of Jupiter or Zeus *(Caryophyllaceae).* A large genus of hardy annual, biennial and perennial plants, which falls into three main groups: pinks, carnations and dianthus proper (see Carnation cultivation and Pinks). The greatest number of species come from the Balkans and Asia Minor, some from the Iberian Peninsula and North Africa, a few from China and Japan and two are natives of the British Isles. Many plants in the genus are very fragrant, with a unique perfume, predominantly clove, strongest among the pinks and carnations. Many of the dwarf kinds are excellent rock garden plants; the taller kinds are suitable for the front of sunny borders, banks or other places.

**Species cultivated** (All are perennials unless otherwise stated) *D. × allwoodii,* 6 inches–2½ feet, very variable in colour, single and double, summer, hybrid. *D. alpinus,* 3 inches, rose-red, May and June. *D. arvernensis,* 4–6 inches, clear pink, May and June. *D. barbatus,* Sweet William, 8 inches to 1½ feet, perennial usually grown as a biennial, variable in colour, summer. *D. × boydii,* 3–6 inches, rose-pink, May and July. *D. carthusianorum,* 1–1½ feet, rose-purple, June to August. *D. caryophyllus,* carnation, clove pink, picotee, 9 inches–3 feet, red, but very variable in cultivation, parent, with *D. chinensis,* of annual carnations and Chinese and Indian pinks (see Carnation cultivation and Pinks). *D. chinensis* (syn. *D. sinensis),* Chinese or Indian pink, 9–18 ins., annual, variable in colour, summer. *D. deltoides,* maiden pink, 6 inches, purple to crimson, spotted and striped, summer, native; vars. *albus,* white; *erectus,* rich red. *D. fragrans,* 1–1½ feet, white, summer. *D. gratianopolitanus* (syn. *D. caesius),* Cheddar pink, 1 foot, pink, May and June; vars. *albus,* white; *flore-pleno,* double or semi-double. *D. haematocalyx,* 4–9 inches, bright pink, July. *D. knappii,* 1 foot, pure

**1 Dianella intermedia,** the Turutu of New Zealand, is successful when planted out in the border of a conservatory or cool greenhouse, but it can be grown outside in the South. **2 Dianthus 'Shrimp'.**

1 Dianthus 'La Bourboulle', a low growing plant for the rock garden: the flowers are on 3 inch stems. 2 Dianthus 'Martinhoe' at home in a limey soil and when exposed to full sun.

yellow, July and August. *D. microlepis*, 2–3 inches, pink, flowers small, spring, scree plant. *D. monspessulanus*, 6–12 inches, pink, summer. *D. musalae*, 2 inches, bright pink, spring, scree. *D. myrtinervis*, 2–3 inches, pink, small, spring. *D. neglectus*, 3 inches, rose-red, June, dislikes lime. *D. nitidus*, 6 inches–2 feet, rose-pink, July and August. *D. noeanus*, 6–8 inches, white, July and August. *D. petraeus* (syn. *D. kitaibelii*), 8–12 inches, pink, June; var. *albus*, 6 inches, double white. *D. pindicola*, 2 inches, deep pink, summer, scree. *D. plumarius*, pink, Scotch pink, 1 foot, variable in colour, May to July. Parent of the garden pinks (see Pinks). *D. squarrosus*, 1–2 feet, white, summer. *D. sternbergii*, 6 inches, rose-red, June. *D. strictus*, 6 inches, white, June and July. *D. subacaulis*, 3 inches, rose-pink, June to August.

Cultivars are numerous (for those of carnations and pinks see Carnations and Pinks). Those of species described above include 'Ariel' ('Crossways'), 4–6 inches, cherry-red, July and

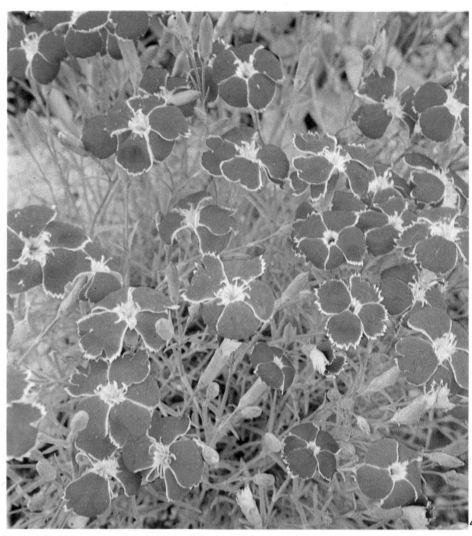

1 Dianthus alpinus, a grass-green, mat forming plant that will tolerate a slightly acid soil and a position in very light shade. The flowers are produced from July to August. 2 Dianthus neglectus forms a dense mat and flowers in July and August. Unlike most dianthus it dislikes lime in the soil. 3 Dianthus 'Charles Musgrave', and 4, Dianthus 'Red Robin' both flower in summer.

August; 'Baker's Variety', 6 inches, large, deep pink, June and July; *D. deltoides* 'Brilliant', 6 inches, crimson, summer, and 'Huntsman', 6 inches, bright red, June and July; 'Charles Musgrave', 9 inches, white with green eye, summer; 'Cherry Ripe', 6–9 inches, rose-red, summer; *D. gratianopolitanus* 'Prichard's Variety', 4–6 inches, rose pink; 'La Bourboulle', 3 inches, deep pink, summer, and 'Double Ruby', 9 inches, summer; 'F. C. Stern', 6 inches, rosy-red, June to September; 'Fusilier', 3 inches, shining crimson, summer; 'F. W. Millward', 9 inches, double pink, summer; 'Highland Queen', 1 foot, deep rose, summer; 'Holmsted', 6 inches, soft pink, summer; 'Inchmery', 1 foot, soft pink, double, summer; 'Isolde', 9 inches, pink and white, double, summer; 'Len Hutton', 1 foot, claret-red, edge laced white, summer; 'Little Jock', 4 inches, rose-pink with darker eye, semi-double,

summer; 'Little Jock Hybrids', various colours; 'Margaret Curtis', 1 foot, white, crimson zone, summer; 'Mars', 4 inches, rich red, double; 'Spencer Bickham', 4 inches, deep pink, summer; 'Sweet Wivelsfield' (*D.* × *allwoodii* × *D. barbatus*), 18 inches, half-hardy annuals in many bright colours, summer; 'Windward Rose', 6 inches, light rose, summer.

**Cultivation** Sharp drainage and preferably a limy soil in a sunny position is needed for most dianthus, except perhaps *D. alpinus* which likes less sun and tolerates an acid soil fairly well, and *D. neglectus* which dislikes lime. All do well in sandy loam. When the alpine species are grown in pots in the alpine house a mixture ensuring brisk drainage but at the same time sufficiently retentive of moisture is needed. Make it up of 2 parts of coarse sand or crushed gravel, 2 parts of leafmould or spent hops, 1 part of loam and a scattering of bonemeal. Cover the surface of the pots with limestone chippings for attractiveness, to present the plant as a perfect cushion and to guarantee surface drainage. Propagation is from seed for annual and biennial kinds and those species that set seed, or by pipings and cuttings taken immediately flowering ends, and inserted in pure sand round the edges of a pot and protected until rooting has taken place.

465

## Diapensia (di-ap-en-se-a)

From the Greek *di*, double, *pente*, five, referring to the five sepals and five stamens *(Diapensiaceae)*. A small genus of sub-shrubby alpine plants native of Alpine and Arctic regions and, therefore, in cultivation may miss the long dormant season and thus may not always succeed. The only species cultivated is *D. lapponica*, 2–5 inches high, which forms a mat of shining green foliage with white flowers in July; var. *obovata* differs in having shorter leaves but is easier to grow in this country.

**Cultivation** A peaty soil that never dries out suits this plant best. It should be planted in a well-drained pocket of the rock garden. Stones or scree gravel can be mixed into the compost to ensure sharp summer drainage when water is required quite freely. Propagation is by division of plants in March or April.

## Diascia (di-as-ke-a)

From the Greek *diaskeo*, to adorn, because of the highly decorative flowers *(Scrophulariaceae)*. A small genus of annual or perennial herbs, natives of South Africa. One species only is likely to be found in cultivation. This is *D. barberae*, 1 foot, a half-hardy annual with rose-pink flowers, from July onwards.

**Cultivation** Seeds sown in March in the warm greenhouse can be pricked off, hardened off and planted out of doors at the end of May or early in June where the plants make a good effect if put in groups. Alternatively seedlings can be potted up singly into a 4 or 5 inch pot, grown near the glass to prevent them from becoming drawn, watered freely and sprayed over in hot weather. Shading may be necessary during the middle of the day and small, twiggy stakes provide all the support necessary.

## Diazinon

An organophosphorus insecticide and acaricide, used in aerosol, wettable powder, granular and liquid spray form. Pests controlled include aphids, root aphids, leaf miners, symphilids, capsids, root flies and red spider mites. Crops should not be harvested within two weeks of spraying. Manufacturer's instructions should be followed strictly.

## Dibber or dibble

A simple hand tool used for making planting holes. Dibbers vary in size according to their use, from small twiggy sticks like pencils, useful for pricking out seedlings, to cut down spade or fork handles or similar sized implements with metal caps which are pushed into the soil to plant out brassica

**1 Diapensia lapponica, a tufted, evergreen sub-shrub that is difficult to cultivate. 2 A sharp metal-tipped dibber. 3 A blunt wooden dibber in use. 4 Diascia barberae, a South African half-hardy annual that requires fertile soil.**

crops, bulbs, and potatoes.

Ideally the dibber is suitable for use when planting small plants when it can be used to make a hole deep enough and, after the plant has been dropped in, the dibber can be pushed into the soil alongside the hole with a slight lever action to firm the soil the entire depth of the planting hole and not just round the collar of the plant. The main objection to the use of a dibber as a planting tool comes when it is used for making planting holes for bulbs and potatoes. It tends to consolidate the soil and even after firming the bulb may be suspended in air with the result that roots do not form and the plant fails. (The trowel is a better tool for planting bulbs.)

### Dicentra (di-sen-tra)

From the Greek *di,* two, *kentron,* a spur, referring to the two spurs on the petals *(Fumariaceae).* Hardy herbaceous perennials formerly known as *Dielytra.* Fibrous and tuberous rooted, they generally transplant badly because the roots are as brittle as glass. The flowers are pendent from arching stems, like lanterns hung along a cord.

**Species cultivated** *D. cucullaria,* Dutchman's breeches, 6 inches, very divided pale green foliage, flowers pearl white, tipped yellow, April and May. *D. eximia,* 1–1½ feet, reddish-purple flowers, May and September and intermittently between; var. *alba,* white flowers. *D. formosa,* 1–1½ feet, pink or light red, long flowering period; 'Bountiful' is a larger-flowered cultivar, with deep pink flowers. *D. oregana,* 6 inches, flowers creamy-pink, tipped purple, May and June. *D. peregrina* (syn. *D. pusilla),* 3 inches, rose-pink flowers in June and July, a good plant for a scree in the rock garden. *D. spectabilis,* Chinaman's breeches, bleeding heart, lyre flower, 1½–3 feet, flowers rose-red, May and June; var. *alba,* white. A garden hybrid *(D. eximia* × *D. formosa),* 9–12 inches, has deep red flowers.

**Cultivation** Dicentras will grow in light shade or full sun provided the soil does not dry out at the roots. A rich loam is best with shelter from cold winds. Some protection may be needed in winter. Propagation is by root cuttings in March or April raised in a temperature of about 55°F (13°C). Division of plants is possible in spring, but difficult because the roots are very brittle. *D. spectabilis* is sometimes grown in pots and forced in a mixture of equal parts of loam, peat and sand. The plants are kept frost free all winter and taken into a temperature of 55–65°F (13–18°C) during February and started into growth. Water, and feed moderately with a liquid feed once the buds begin to show. Forced plants should be planted out in the open ground after they have flowered.

## Dichaea (dik-e-a)
From the Greek *dicha*, two-ranked, as the leaves are borne in two rows *(Orchidaceae)*. A genus of epiphytic orchids, with slender, tufted stems, which are erect or pendent and are covered with small leaves. Well-grown plants can be very attractive.

**Species cultivated** *D. picta*, green and purple, winter, Trinidad. *D. bradeorum*, greenish, spotted red, summer, Costa Rica. *D. glauca*, whitish, autumn, West Indies. *D. vaginatum*, white, summer, Mexico.

**Cultivation** Plant in a mixture of 2 parts of osmunda fibre and 1 part of sphagnum moss, in small pans, in a shaded position in the greenhouse. Water freely in summer, less in winter. Temperatures should be from 60°F (16°C) in winter to 80°F (27°C) in summer. Propagation is by division at potting time.

## Dichorisandra (di-kore-iss-and-ra)
From the Greek *dis*, twice, *chorizo*, to part, *aner*, anther, referring to the 2-valved anthers *(Commelinaceae)*. A genus of herbaceous perennial plants from tropical America, grown mainly for their ornamental foliage, though some also have showy flowers. They need warm greenhouse treatment in cool climates.

**Species cultivated** *D. mosaica*, 2 feet, leaves green with white veins and other marks, reddish-purple on the undersides, flowers bright blue, autumn, Peru. *D. pubescens*, 2 feet, flowers blue; var. *taeniensis*, leaves striped with white, flowers blue and white, Brazil. *D. thyrsiflora*, 4 feet or more, leaves dark green, flowers dark blue in a 6 inch long spike, summer to autumn, Brazil. *D. vittata* 6–12 inches, leaves purplish-green with white stripes, Brazil.

**Cultivation** These plants are potted up in March in a mixture consisting of loam, leafmould and peat in equal parts, plus a little silver sand. The pots should be in the warmest part of the greenhouse, where a winter temperature of 55–65°F (13–18°C) can be maintained, rising in summer to 75–85°F (24–29°C), when shading from sunlight should be provided. Water freely from spring to autumn, moderately only in winter and avoid draughts at all times. Propagation is by seeds sown in heat in spring, by division of the plants in March or by cuttings taken at almost any time, rooted in a propagating case with bottom heat.

## Dichotomanthes (dik-o-toe-man-thus)
From the Greek *dichotomes*, to cut asunder, and *anthos*, flower *(Rosaceae)*. A genus of one species, *D. tristaniicarpa*, an evergreen, cotoneaster-like shrub

1 Dichorisandra thyrsiflora, a handsome plant from Brazil that reaches 4 feet and flowers in late summer. 2 Dicksonia squarrosa, a tree-fern from New Zealand that needs greenhouse protection.

from China, 15–20 feet tall, with white flowers in terminal corymbs in June. The alternate, oval leaves are attractively tinted in the spring. The oblong fruit is almost entirely enclosed by the calyx which becomes fleshy.

**Cultivation** This is not hardy enough to be grown in exposed gardens or in the colder parts of the country, but does well in ordinary garden soil when given a warm place. Propagate by cuttings of half-ripened wood inserted in sandy soil or by layering in spring.

## Dicksonia (dik-so-ne-a)
Commemorating James Dickson (1738–1822), nurseryman and botanist, one of the founders of the Royal Horticultural Society *(Dicksoniaceae)*. Greenhouse tree ferns.

**Species cultivated** *D. antarctica*, Australian tree fern, 18–20 feet, Tasmania. *D.*

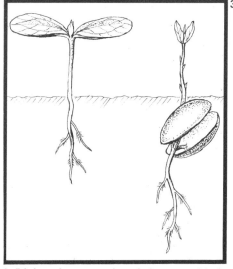

*squamosa,* New Zealand tree fern, 15–20 feet, length of frond nearly equalling height of plant, New Zealand.

**Cultivation** The medium should consist of peat and loam and an abundance of sand. Plant in large, well-drained pots or tubs in shady greenhouse or conservatory. Repot in February or March. Water moderately from October to March, freely afterwards. Syringe trunks daily from March to September. Temperature: September to March 45–50°F (7–10°C), March to September 55–65°F (13–18°C), or more from sun heat provided there is adequate shade and ventilation. Shade in summer is essential. Propagation is by spores sown at any time on the surface of finely sifted loam and peat in well-drained pots covered with a sheet of glass and kept moist. *D. antarctica* may be grown out of doors in sheltered places in the mild and warm parts of the country.

## Dicotyledon

A term denoting that a plant produces seedlings with two cotyledons, or seed leaves, as opposed to those that have only one cotyledon, viz. monocotyledons. These differences in seed leaf are associated with other differences in the structure of the plant and so provide a primary method of classification.

Dicotyledonous plants always have an internal root and stem structure differing from that of monocotyledonous plants but the visual differences are that the

**1 Dicksonia antarctica thrives outside in warmer parts of the country. 2 Dictamnus albus, the gas plant or Dittany, gives off a volatile oil from the upper part of its stem. 3 Dicotyledonous seedlings with two seed leaves. Left: above ground. Right: below ground.**

dicotyledons have veins on the leaves which radiate from a central vein and the flowers are composed of distinguishable parts in the great majority of cases, thus having corolla and calyx, a notable exception being the clematis. The parts of the flowers are generally arranged in fours or fives, whereas parts in threes or multiples of threes denotes that a plant may be a monocotyledon.

## Dictamnus (dik-tam-nus)

From *diktamnos,* the ancient Greek name; the plant was once common on Mount Dicte *(Rutaceae).* A genus of a single species, a herbaceous perennial, very long lived once established, with tall flower spikes and deeply divided leaves. Gas plant and burning bush, two of the English names, have been given to the plant on account of its curious ability to give off from glands on the upper part of the stem a volatile oil which on still, sultry days can be ignited above and around the plant. The flame does not harm the plant and thus it is regarded as sacred by the fire-worshippers in India. The only species is *D. albus* (syn. *D. fraxinella*), gas plant, burning bush, dittany, fraxinella, which grows 3 feet tall and has spikes of large fragrant white flowers in June and July, good for cutting; vars. are *caucasicus* (syn. *giganteus*), 5 feet, purple flowers; *purpureus*, 2½ feet, mauvish striped flowers; *rubra*, 2½ feet, rosy-red flowers.

**Cultivation** Well-drained garden soil in a sunny position is best, though the plants will tolerate light shade. Plant in autumn or spring and leave undisturbed once established. Propagation is reliable from root cuttings put into a cold frame or under a cloche in spring or from division of the crowns in autumn or spring. Seed can be sown in light soil out of doors in spring, but it is slow to germinate, and seedlings may take about three years to produce flowers.

**Didymella** (did-ee-mel-a)
A genus of fungi in which one or two of the species cause fairly serious diseases of plants. Perhaps the best known is that called stem rot of tomato in which the stem base develops a cankered area and is often girdled so that the plant dies. The fruit can be attacked so that it develops blackish brown sunken areas on which the fungus forms its spores. Spraying the bases of the stems with captan is recommended but in severe cases the greenhouse also should be sterilised in winter after the old stems have been disposed of by burning.

**Die back**
This is a general term used to describe the condition where a plant begins to die back from the tips of its shoots or branches. It can be seen not only in herbaceous plants with soft tissues but also in woody shrubs and trees but naturally the herbaceous type is quicker in its effects. It is difficult to separate the condition called wilt from that of die back because wilting of the leaves often precedes the dying of the shoot but usually wilting occurs all over the shoot or plant whereas die back proceeds slowly, beginning with the tip leaves and going downwards gradually.

Many plants show the condition and some important diseases begin with it. For example gooseberry branches show die back in summer due to injury lower down by the fungus *Botrytis cinerea* which enters through dead buds, wounds etc. Currants and cherries, roses and lilacs are all liable to the same trouble especially if they are old. Rhododendrons can show one whole branch dying back due to entry by the silver leaf fungus *(Stereum)*. Carnations under glass are subject to a serious die back disease due to the fungus *Fusarium culmorum* but this is often a result of injury to the roots or stem base and is better called stem rot. Some plants die back suddenly for no apparent reason and this can be seen in *Daphne mezereum* when it gets old and also the smoke bush, *Cotinus coggygria*.

**Dieffenbachia** (dee-fen-bak-e-a)
Commemorating J. F. Dieffenbach, early nineteenth century German physician and botanist *(Araceae)*. Dumb cane. Tender evergreen perennials from tropical America, grown for their foliage and used for greenhouse and room decoration. The large oval leaves spread outwards and downwards from the central stem and are spotted or lined with white or cream. The plants are poisonous in

**1 'Die Back' of the branches of pear. 2 Dieffenbachia picta, introduced from Brazil in 1820, and grown in a warm greenhouse for its ornamental foliage. All parts of the plant are poisonous.**

all their parts and are said to have been fed to slaves to render them dumb for several days.

**Species cultivated** *D. amoena,* laeves 1–2 feet long, 6–10 inches wide, heavily marked with cream. *D. bowmannii,* leaves to 2½ feet long, 1 foot wide (smaller when grown as a house plant), mottled with dark and light green. *D. imperialis,* leaves 1–2 feet long, 3–4 inches wide, blotched with cream. *D. oerstedii,* leaves 9–10 inches long, 4½ inches wide, dark green with ivory-striped mid-rib. *D. picta,* leaves 9 inches long, 3 inches wide, heavily marked with cream, but very variable in size and markings; vars. *bausei,* leaves bright green, blotched and spotted with dark green and silver (possibly a hybrid); *jenmanii,* leaves narrower; *memoria,* leaves silvery-grey, margins dark green; *roehrsii,* leaves wider, pale yellow-green, dark green midrib and margins, ivory veins.

**Cultivation** A rich mixture of equal parts of peat, loam and a quarter part of sand and well-rotted manure is needed. Pot in February or March and water freely until September, then water moderately only during the winter. Syringe daily during the height of summer and shade from strong sun. Indoors the plants should not be kept in a bright window. A winter temperature of not less than 50–55°F (10–13°C) is needed. Propagation is by stem cuttings 1–2 inches long taken in spring or summer and inserted in sandy mixture in a propagating case. There is a tendency to drop the lower leaves and if the top is treated as a stem

1 Dieffenbachia picta bausei is propagated by suckers that arise from the base. 2 Dieramas are in the Iris family and come from South Africa. They are commonly called Wand Flowers because of the flowers produced on drooping stems.

cutting in a propagating case roots will soon be formed.

---

## Dielytra—see Dicentra

---

## Diellia (di-el-e-a)

Name of doubtful origin *(Polypodiaceae).* A genus of six species of ferns, mostly tropical. The only species likely to be found in cultivation is *D. falcata,* from Hawaii, with sickle-shaped fronds up to 1½ feet long and 2–4 inches broad, with marginal spore pustules.

**Cultivation** This fern requires a humid, moist greenhouse atmosphere and partial shade. While needing ample moisture the plant requires good drainage and the pot should be half filled with crocks over which is placed a mixture consisting of 2 parts of turfy loam, 1 of fibrous peat and a little sharp sand. It is not an easy fern to grow but is well worth a little trouble. Propagate by division in the spring.

---

## Dierama (di-er-am-a)

From the Greek *dierama,* a funnel, a reference to the flower shape *(Iridaceae).* Wand flower. South African plants with a swollen rootstock resembling a corm, long, sword-like leaves and graceful flowers. They are hardier than is sometimes supposed but dislike a combination of winter wet and cold.

**Species cultivated** *D. pendulum,* 3–4 feet, lilac flowers, August. *D. pulcherrimum* (syn. *Sparaxis pulcherrima),* 4 feet, nodding rose-purple flowers, September and October; var. *album,* white. Many named varieties, ranging in colour from white to crimson have mostly been raised in Northern Ireland and some are named after birds, including 'Heron', wine-red; 'Skylark', violet; 'Kingfisher', mauve-pink. Will grow in California.

**Cultivation** The best position is in a rich well-drained loam where there is shelter from cold winds. Plant in November, 3 inches deep and 3 inches apart. When cultivated in pots they make attractive decoration for a conservatory or sun lounge. Put five or six corms in a 10 inch pot. Propagation is from offsets planted separately in October or spring.

---

## Diervilla (di-er-vil-a)

Commemorating N. Dierville, French surgeon and traveller in Canada, who introduced *D. lonicera* to Europe *(Caprifoliaceae).* Bush honeysuckle. A small genus of hardy deciduous flowering shrubs. Many of the plants long known as diervillas have been transferred to the genus *Weigela* (see Weigela).

**Species cultivated** *D. lonicera* (syn. *D canadensis),* 3 feet, flowers pale yellow, resembling those of the honeysuckle, June and July, good autumn leaf colour. *D. rivularis,* 4 feet, lemon-yellow, July and August, good autumn foliage tints. *D. sessifolia,* 2–4 feet, flowers sulphur-yellow, June to August. *D.* × *splendens,* 3–4 feet, flowers sulphur-yellow, summer, hybrid.

**Cultivation** Open positions in good garden soil, in sun or light shade are suitable. Some moisture-holding material at the roots provides better flowers, and the bushes benefit from an occasional mulch of humus material. Prune lightly by cutting back flowering shoots after flowering as far as a non-flowering sideshoot. Propagation is from cuttings with frame protection.

**Dietes**—see Moraea

## Digging

The various operations carried out on the soil by the use of a spade are all known as digging. The general purpose is to break up the soil to improve its physical nature, rendering it more suitable for supporting plant life.

Digging is generally carried out in the autumn and winter, when a solidly compact soil can be broken up and left rough throughout the winter. The more surface that can be exposed to the weather the better, and the action of frosts, drying winds and rain break up the surface into small crumbs or tilth, generally increase aeration, and render the soil more open in texture. Rain and snow drain from the surface more quickly, leaving the surface dry and, therefore, the soil absorbs warmth from the spring sunshine more easily. Drainage is improved and the air that exists between the soil particles supports the beneficial bacteria (see Bacteria).

The term digging means turning over the top soil one spit deep or the depth of the spade's blade, i.e. 10 inches. Surface weeds are buried, the level of the land remains the same and the clods of earth are left unbroken.

It is important that the spade is thrust into the soil to its full depth and in a vertical position. If this is not done, the land is dug quicker but cultivation is not deep enough or thorough enough and the weeds will not be properly buried.

**Single digging** To dig over a plot of land, a trench a spade's width and a spade's depth is dug out across one end and the soil removed and taken in a wheelbarrow to the other end of the plot and left in a heap so that when the plot has been dug there will be soil ready to put into the last trench. Alongside the first trench mark out with a line another strip and by standing facing the open trench and working along the line soil can be dug out and thrown well forward into the open trench, at the same time making a

In double digging the soil is cultivated to the depth of two spades (spits), but the position of the layers of soil remains unchanged. 1 A 2-foot wide trench is taken out down to the subsoil. 2 The subsoil is forked over and broken up to a fork's depth. 3 Organic matter, such as compost or well-rotted manure, is incorporated in the soil at this stage. 4 The last trench is filled with soil taken from the first, a common British practise.

new trench. The importance of throwing each spadeful of soil well forward cannot be emphasised too much because a slight discrepancy will after several trenches result in there not being sufficient space in which to work properly. Repeat the method of filling the last trench while making a new one and when the last strip is dug at the other end of the plot the soil heaped there from the first trench is ready to fill the last one.

Manure or compost can be put on the land at the same time and is scattered along the trench and the soil is thrown on to it.

**Double digging** This is a method of breaking up the soil to a greater depth than in single digging but retaining the topsoil in its relative position. As the name suggests the soil is disturbed to the depth of two spits. Alternative names are half trenching or bastard trenching. The method though difficult to describe is quite straightforward to execute and is really an extension of the process described for digging.

A trench 2 feet wide and a spade's depth is taken out across one end of the plot and the soil carried to the far end of the plot and put in a heap. The bottom of the open trench is then forked as deeply as possible and the surface left level. Mark out another area 2 feet wide alongside the open trench and dig soil out of this to a full spade's depth and throw the soil into the open trench and on top of the forked or broken up surface. Thus topsoil remains topsoil but the land is aerated to twice the depth that it is in single digging. If manure is added, and it is a usual practice to do this during double digging, it should be scattered over the forked surface before the topsoil is thrown on thus getting it down a good depth.

**Double digging on grassland** Where land that has not been cultivated before is being broken up and prepared for crops by hand rather than by mechanical means, double digging is the method recommended. The turf is first skimmed off with a spade over the area of the first strip or trench position, taken to the far end of the plot and left there. Then the topsoil is dug out of the trench to a spade's depth and also taken to the other end of the plot. The bottom of the trench is forked to a spit's depth and then the line moved back 2 feet to mark out the second trench. Skim off the turf from this second trench area, putting it upside down over the forked area of the first trench so that eventually the bottom of the whole trench is lined with inverted turf. Chop up the turf roughly into 4 inch squares with the spade. No manure is added as the turf itself will rot and provide plant food but a general artificial fertiliser may be scattered at this level if required. Then the top spit of soil from the first trench is thrown over the inverted turf, the bottom spit of the second trench forked and turf taken from

1

3

2

4

the third area inverted over that, and so on until the whole area has been broken up. When the last trench to be opened has been forked, put in the turf taken from the first trench, then cover it with the soil from the same trench.

**Trenching** This is an extension of the method used in half or bastard trenching and if the principle of half trenching has been mastered it is not difficult. Full trenching is heavy work and is often spread over three or four seasons by dealing with a portion of the land only

each winter. It is justified in exceptional circumstances only. It can increase the depth of fertility quite quickly but naturally cannot be carried out on some clay or stony soils where the subsoil would be impenetrable with a spade.

The trenches are cut 3 feet wide for full trenching, to allow better working space. As for half trenching the topsoil from the first trench is removed to the other end of the plot and left there.

There are two methods of dealing with the soil in this opened trench, equally

**In trenching the soil is cultivated to a depth of three spits. 1 Measure out two 2-foot trenches. 2 Take the top soil to the far end of the plot. 3 Remove the second spit also to the far end of the plot, but keep it separate from the top soil. 4 Fork over the bottom of the first trench adding strawy manure. 5 Place the subsoil from the second trench into the first and cover with top soil from the third. 6 The work finishes at the far end of the plot. The last trench is filled with soil from the first trenches. Take care to replace subsoil and topsoil in their correct order.**

5

6

into the narrow trench thus cut out and fork the base to a full fork's depth. The work proceeds in 18 inch strips along the plot and the smaller heap of topsoil is used to fill in the bottom of the last trench and the larger heap of topsoil goes over the last two 18 inch strips.

The Second Method is a version of full trenching which has exactly the same result but allows more working space and is probably, therefore, quicker. In this method not only the first but every subsequent trench opened is 2 feet in width. The topsoil and the second spit of soil are carried away from the first trench and kept separately at the far end of the plot. The base or third spit is then forked and broken up. The first spit from the second trench is then taken to the other end of the plot and left apart from the larger heap of soil from the third trench. The second spit of the second trench is thrown on to the forked subsoil and the base of the second trench forked to break it up. The top spit of the third trench is taken right over to the top of the first trench; the second spit of the third trench turned over on to the forked surface at the bottom of the second trench and the base of the third trench broken up. Thus the pattern is repeated until at the far end of the plot the next to last trench has one of the heaps of topsoil put on to it and the last trench has the second spit pile put in on top of the broken up base of the trench and the top spit soil put on the top.

**Deep trenching** is a variation of full trenching in which the subsoil is brought on top of topsoil but this practice is drastic and could be disastrous under many circumstances and could only be justified on expert advice.

**Ridging** As an alternative on heavy land to ordinary digging, where the surface is left level, the soil can be thrown up in ridges and furrows resembling ploughed land in a method known as ridging, in which a greater surface of soil is exposed to the action of the weather.

The plot to be dug is divided into 3 foot strips running across it, starting at one corner of the plot. At one end of the first strip take out soil to a depth of 10 inches (one spade's depth) and two spade widths and take the soil in a wheelbarrow to the other end of the strip. Then working backwards stand on the soil and dig three spadesful of soil side by side throwing each forward onto the space from which topsoil has been taken. The right-hand spadeful goes forward and slightly towards the centre, the next spadeful to the left and slightly towards the centre and the third spadeful goes on top of these two. Step backwards and repeat the process and a ridge of soil will be made the length of the strip, the hollow at the end being filled in with the soil taken and reserved from the beginning of the strip. Continue digging in this way forming parallel ridges until the whole area has been dug.

advantageous to cultivation. In the first method, stretch a line along the middle of the opened trench and remove all the soil on one side of it and put this soil in a heap at the side of the plot quite distinct from the topsoil already removed. The base of the trench is now in the form of a step, the trench depth at one side being two spits deep (about 20 inches) and at the other side one spit deep, 10 inches. Get down into the lower part of the trench and fork the subsoil, as in half trenching. Stand then on the

upper part of the step and working backwards turn this soil over onto the lower half of the step that has just been forked. The fresh strip of subsoil thus exposed is then forked to the full depth of the fork.

Mark out another strip at ground level alongside the original trench and only 18 inches in width. Dig the top spit out, throwing it right forward on to the raised step of the open trench. Turn the second spit on to the forked surface of subsoil in the first trench, then get down

**Digitalis** (dij-it-ay-lis)
From the Latin *digitus*, a finger, refer-ring to the resemblance of the flower to the finger of a glove *(Scrophulariaceae)*. Foxglove. A genus of hardy biennial and perennial plants, the common foxglove growing wild extensively in Britain. They are excellent woodland plants, useful both for borders and informal gardens where they will seed them-selves profusely.

**Species cultivated** *D. davisiana,* 2 feet, bronze flowers, summer, perennial. *D. ferruginea,* 4–6 feet, rust-red flowers, July, biennial. *D. grandiflora* (syn. *D. ambigua*), 2–3 feet, pale yellow blotched brown, July and August, a poor peren-nial, best grown as a biennial. *D. laevigata,* 3 feet, bronze-yellow, white-lipped flowers, July, perennial. *D. lanata,*

Foxgloves are known botanically as Digi-talis. They are excellent woodland plants, useful for borders and flower gardens.

2–3 feet, cream-yellow with deeper markings, July and August, a good biennial. *D. lutea,* 3 feet, yellow, July, perennial. *D.* × *mertonensis,* 3 feet, large attractive crushed strawberry-coloured flowers, summer, perennial, hybrid which comes true from seed. *D. orientalis,* 1 foot, pale cream, July and August. *D. purpurea,* common foxglove, 3–5 feet, flowers purple with deeper spots, July to September; var. *gloxinae-flora* (gloxinia-flowered or *gloxinoides* of the nurserymen's catalogues), flowers more open than the type. Many good strains and varieties are available now, including the 'Shirley Strains' and 'Ex-

celsior Hybrids', in which the flowers are borne all round the stem and do not droop. Beautiful 'art shades' are avail-able, ranging through cream and yellow to pink and purple.
**Cultivation** Rich moist soil is ideal for foxgloves and they are most effective when planted in drifts. The perennials are planted in spring or autumn and none are long lived so replacements may be necessary to maintain an effect. The biennials, and those perennials treated as biennials are raised from seed sown in April or May, the seedlings being trans-planted to a shady reserve bed in July and to their final positions in October. Propagation of the perennial kinds is from seed treated as for biennials or by division of the crowns into separate rosettes in autumn after flowering.

## Digitate (bot.)

A term used to describe leaves that are arranged in the form of a hand, being united to a common stalk, such as those of the horse chestnut or lupin.

## Dill

This is the common name for *Anethum graveolens* (syn. *Peucedanum graveolens*), an annual from the Mediterranean regions grown in our gardens for several hundred years for its aromatic seed and foliage *(Umbelliferae)*. It does not enjoy the popularity it used to enjoy as a culinary herb, probably because it needs to be used with restraint. The seeds contain an essential oil with carminative and stimulant properties, which is especially associated with dill water, given to babies to settle minor digestive disorders and relieve flatulence. Seed should be collected by cutting the stems when the fruits on the lower inflorescence are ripe and spreading them on paper in an airy room or shed away from sunshine and threshing them when they are completely dry. Seed can be purchased whole or ground. The foliage is sometimes used for flavouring salads

**1 The leaf of the horse-chestnut is digitate or hand shaped. 2 Dill, botanically known as Peucedanum graveolens, the seeds of which are used for flavouring. 3 Dimorphotheca barberiae will do well out of doors in sheltered gardens.**

and sauces but should be used with restraint and always finely chopped.

Seed, which serves in many ways as a substitute for caraway, can be soaked in vinegar for several days to make dill vinegar and used with vinegar in the pickling or preserving of gherkins and baby cucumbers. In Scandinavia the leaves are added to sauces and glazings served with cold meats especially on the cold tables. Generally here dill sauce is served with fish, preferably turbot or salmon.

In eastern Europe, particularly in Poland, the seed is scattered on boiled potatoes or mixed with cream potatoes, and is a delicious variation with sausage and mash.

## Dimethoate

A systemic organo-phosphorus insecticide and acaricide used against aphids

and red spider mites. It is available in liquid formulations (formerly with DDT). Crops should not be harvested within 1 week of spraying. The spraying may cause damage to chrysanthemums and manufacturer's instructions should always be followed carefully.

## Dimorphotheca (di-mor-foth-e-ka)

From the Greek *di*, two, *morphe*, shape, *theca*, seed, because the flower produces two different shapes of seed, one from the disk florets and another from the ray florets *(Compositae)*. Cape marigold, star of the veldt, Namaqualand daisy. A genus of half-hardy annual, herbaceous perennial and sub-shrubby plants from South Africa, grown for their long-lasting daisy-like flowers in bright colours. Considerable confusion in naming exists in many books and catalogues and according to some authorities those plants known as dimorphothecas should be split up between the genera *Castalis*, *Chrysanthemoides*, *Dimorphotheca* and *Osteospermum*. Here, for the sake of convenience, they are all treated as belonging to the genus *Dimorphotheca*.
**Species cultivated** D. *aurantiaca* (syn.

477

*Castalis tragus, D. flaccida* and apparently the true name for many of the plants grown in gardens under the names of *D. calendulacea* and *D. sinuata*), 1–1½ feet, bright orange flowers with a dark brown disk, edged with metallic blue, June to September, a perennial usually treated as a half-hardy annual. This species has given rise to several garden hybrids (listed in catalogues) such as 'Buff Beauty'; 'Goliath', extra large, mainly orange flowers; 'Lemon Queen'; 'Orange Glory'; 'Glistening White' and 'White Beauty'. *D. barberiae* (syn. *Osteospermum barberiae*), 1½ feet, aromatic foliage, long stemmed rosy-lilac flowers, summer to autumn, with occasional flowers appearing at almost any time, sub-shrubby. This plant is hardier than is generally supposed and will often survive out of doors in the South and far West, making large spreading clumps. There is a dwarf form, *compacta*, which is said to be hardier still. *D. calendulacea* see *D. aurantiaca*. *D. ecklonis*, 2–3 feet, flowers white with reverse of petals purple and a deep purple zone on the petals, perennial treated as annual. *D. pluvialis* (syn. *D. annua*), 1 foot, almost hardy, white above, purple below; var. *ringens*, violet ring round disk, June onwards. *D. sinuata* see *D. aurantiaca*.

**Cultivation** Sun is essential for all species and in a poor, cloudy summer nothing can be done to improve the results since the flowers of most kinds open only in sunny weather, closing or failing to open when the sky is overcast, or in late afternoon. Out of doors they do best in the lighter soils, although *D. barberiae* will thrive on any kind of soil, even heavy clay. In the sunny greenhouse dimorphothecas are grown in pots containing a mixture of 3 parts of sandy loam, 1 part of leafmould, plus silver sand. The minimum temperature in winter, when they need moderate watering only, should be 40°F (4°C). Propagation is by seed sown in March in pans or boxes in heat and, after hardening off, the seedlings may be put out in the border in late May or early June. The plants grow quickly and will start flowering in June. Perennial species may be propagated by cuttings taken in late summer and rooted in a greenhouse or frame. *D. pluvialis* is probably the hardiest of those grown as annuals and seed of this species may be sown out of doors in early April in fine soil, the seedlings later thinned, to start flowering at the end of June.

## Dimple

This word is not much used nowadays. At one time the term dimple pear was

1 Dimorphotheca ecklonis, a half-hardy South African plant, growing to 2 feet. The flowers open only in bright sunlight. 2 Dimorphotheca 'Giant Goliath' produces extra large flowers.

used to describe the condition where the fruits developed sunken pits in the surface with the flesh underneath spoiled by pockets· of gritty cells. This is a disease caused by a virus which is now known by the name stony pit (see Stony pit).

### Dioecious (bot.)
A term describing plants which bear flowers of one sex only on any one plant of the species. Flowers on one plant will have stamens and no pistil and will thus be male flowers and on another pistils and no stamens and thus be female flowers.

If such female plants are to bear fruit a male form needs to be grown nearby in order that the flowers can be fertilised on the fruit-bearing plant. Examples are *Skimmia japonica*, Taxus, Humulus, Juniperus and Hippophaë.

### Dionaea (di-o-ne-a)
From the Greek *Dione*, one of the names given to Venus *(Droseraceae)*. Venus's fly trap. A genus of a single species, a greenhouse plant grown as a curiosity because of its insect-catching habit. The

1 The flowers of the Sea Buckthorn, Hippophaë, are dioecious. 2 Dionaea muscipula, the Venus's Fly Trap. 3 Dionysia demarendica, a cushion-like plant for the alpine greenhouse.

English name refers to the twin-lobed leaves which bear sensitive hairs on the upper surface and teeth round the edges. When an insect touches these the lobes fold together, thus trapping the insect, which is later digested. *D. muscipula*, a Carolina native, grows 6–12 inches tall and produces spikes of white flowers in July and August, rising above the rosette of leaves. It is usual to remove the flowering spike as it weakens the plant when it is allowed to flower.
**Cultivation** Venus's fly trap should be grown in a sunny greenhouse where a winter temperature of over 45°F (7°C) can be guaranteed. The plants are potted in a mixture of equal parts of peat and sphagnum moss in spring and set so that the rosettes rest on the surface of the soil. Plants need to be kept moist all through the year. Propagation is by division in spring (see also Insectivorous Plants).

### Dionysia (di-on-iz-e-a)
From *Dionysos*, the Greek Bacchus *(Primulaceae)*. Evergreen alpine plants from Persia, forming dense, low cushions, usually with stemless flowers.
**Species cultivated** *D. bryoides*, mauve-pink flowers, spring. *D. curviflora*, reddish-lilac flowers, April. *D. oreodoxa*, yellow flowers, April.
**Cultivation** Plant out of doors in well-drained pockets in the rock garden or in

479

the alpine house in pans with medium in both instances made up of leafmould, grit, sharp sand and good loam in equal proportions. In the alpine house or cold frame the plants are at their best, as they will not be splashed by rain and, like most tiny plants, their true beauty can be seen when one can look down upon them. Watering must be done very carefully at all times. Propagation is by seed sown in the cold greenhouse or frame in spring, and covered only very lightly with fine soil. Careful division may be attempted in spring.

## Dioscorea (di-os-kor-ee-a)

Commemorating Pedanios Dioscorides, first century Greek physician and author of a book on medicinal herbs *(Dioscoreaceae)*. Yam, cinnamon vine. One of the quickest growing of all hardy twining plants, even reputed to grow three or four inches in twenty-four hours. The plants are cut down to ground level each autumn, the enormous amount of top growth being produced each season. The juicy tubers are eaten in the east and in many tropical countries, cooked like potatoes. Of the 200 or more species the only one likely to be found in cultivaiton is *D. batatas,* the Chinese yam, which grows 12–20 feet, and produces tiny, white, cinnamon-scented flowers in late summer or autumn before the top growth dies down.

**Cultivation** The Chinese yam is quite hardy in warm districts and warm soils, but it is often advisable to treat the tubers the same way as dahlias, lifting them and storing through the winter and planting them out again in spring about 3 inches deep. Supports will be necessary for the plants to climb up. They are best grown in rich soil which has been prepared by digging and adding leafmould or decayed manure. Water freely and give liberal dressings of liquid feed during the summer. Propagation is by division of tubers in spring in the same way as a dahlia tuber is divided, or by stem cuttings, with a leaf, taken in summer and dibbled into a sandy compost in a temperature of 55°F (13°C).

## Diosma (di-oz-ma)

From the Greek *dios*, divine, *osme*, odour, referring to the fragrance of the flowers *(Rutaceae)*. A small genus of evergreen, flowering South African shrubs, with heath-like leaves, needing greenhouse protection in this country.

**Species cultivated** *D. ericoides*, 2 feet, white flowers in terminal clusters in spring. *D. pulchella* (syn. *Barosma pulchella*), 3 feet, mauve, spring. *D. uniflora* (syn. *Adenandra uniflora*), 1½ feet, pink and white flowers, June.

**Cultivation** A winter temperature of 40–45°F (4–7°C) is required and a mixture of equal proportions of sand, peat and fibrous loam. Potting is done in April and after flowering the shoots are cut back to about one third of their length to

**1** Dionysia curviflora comes from Persia and flowers in April. **2** Dioscorea alata requires a warm greenhouse. The tubers are edible and in India can be up to 8 feet long and weigh up to 100 lb. **3** Diospyros kaki, the Chinese Persimmon, that requires rather gentle climate to ripen its fruit. It can be grown in the open in warm places.

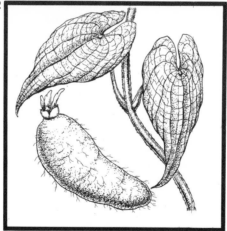
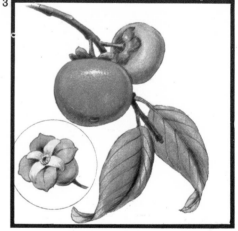

encourage new growth. Syringe at this time and repot firmly into larger pots and once the plants are established they can be stood outside during the day and given full sunshine to ripen the new shoots. Propagation is by cuttings taken with a heel in spring and rooted in a

cold house or frame. Pot up singly once roots have formed.

## Diospyros (di-os-pe-ros)

From the Greek *dios*, divine, *puros*, wheat, meaning 'the wheat of Zeus', referring to the pulpy, edible fruit of some species *(Ebenaceae)*. A large genus of deciduous and evergreen trees and shrubs, mostly from warm climates, including the timber trees producing ebony and those bearing fruits such as the persimmon and date plum.

**Species cultivated** *D. armata* (SE), bush to 20 feet, yellow fruits, central China. *D. kaki* (D), kakee, Chinese persimmon, tree to 40 feet, fruits yellow, tomato-like,

**Dipelta floribunda produces fragrant flowers in May and June. It will grow to 12 feet and was given the Award of Merit by the RHS in 1927. 2 Diplacus glutinosus, the Californian Shrubby Mimulus.**

China, much cultivated in Japan. *D. lotus* (D), date plum, tree to 40 feet, fruits small, purple or yellowish, west Asia to Himalaya, China and Japan. *D. virginiana* (D), persimmon, tree to 50 feet, flowers yellow, July, fruits red or yellow North America.

**Cultivation** Plant in either fall or spring in ordinary soil in open, sunny positions, *D. armata* and *D. kaki* preferably in warmer areas. The fruit needs a hot summer to ripen. Prune as for apples. Propagation is by seeds sown deeply out of doors in early autumn.

**Diostea juncea**—see Baillonia juncea

### Dipelta (di-pel-ta)

From the Greek *di,* two, *pelta,* a shield, referring to the opposite, shield-like flower bracts *(Caprifoliaceae).* A genus of four species of hardy deciduous shrubs closely resembling *Diervilla,* introduced to Britain early this century from China.

**Species cultivated** *D. floribunda,* 10–12 feet, a first-class shrub, fragrant, goblet-shaped flowers, pink with yellow at the throat, May, produced in great profusion. *D. ventricosa,* 8–14 feet, variable deep rose flowers, shaded coral or orange, May. *D. yunnanensis,* 10 feet, flowers cream with orange markings, May.

**Cultivation** Well-drained loam, with some moisture-holding material is best. Plant in autumn in sunny, sheltered positions

where they will escape damage from cold winds early in the spring. Pruning consists merely in cutting out dead wood or unwanted shoots. Propagation is from cuttings of ripened wood in autumn inserted in a cold frame or under a cloche until the spring.

### Diphylleia (di-phil-e-a)

From the Greek *dis,* two, and *phyllos,* leaf, the plant having deeply two-lobed leaves *(Berberidaceae).* A genus of two species of herbaceous perennials, one from North America and one from Japan, of which the former, is in cultivation. This is *D. cymosa,* the umbrella leaf, 1–3 feet tall with a basal leaf up to 2 feet across and small white flowers in terminal clusters in early summer, followed by bluish-black berries.

**Cultivation** *D. cymosa* does best in a peaty moist soil and partial shade. Plant from October . to March. Propagate by division of the rootstock in spring.

### Diplacus (dip-la-kus)

From the Greek *di,* two, *plakos,* placenta, referring to the two placentas of the seed capsule *(Scrophulariaceae).* A sub-

shrubby plant from California with sticky leaves and large handsome flowers, related to *Mimulus* and sometimes placed in that genus as *M. glutinosus.* It is barely hardy but may be used for bedding out in warm areas, when it makes an elaborate effect, or may be grown in pots for decorative work. It will survive out of doors in warmer gardens, particularly if planted in a rather warm location or area, although its growths may be cut by frost. The only species is *D. glutinosus.* The flowers, borne in summer, are large and vary in colour from buff to orange-salmon and mahogany red. The height varies according to cultivation. By pinching, the plants can be kept bushy and dwarf or by pruning the shoots in February to one third their length the plants can be shaped into good compact form. Alternatively plants can be grown at the base of a screen or trellis and trained to it or used to clothe a conservatory pillar, when they may reach 4–5 feet in height. If the pots are stood above eye level and no support is provided for the growths an attractive curtain can be made by using a sufficient number of plants.

**Cultivation** The plant will grow satisfactorily in ordinary potting mixture, especially if some old manure is added. Water regularly and feed during the summer at flowering time. Stakes or supports are required if the plants are not restricted in growth. Out of doors the plants will grow in any kind of soil. Protection in winter will prevent loss or damage. Propagation is by seed sown in the greenhouse in spring or by late summer cuttings 3–4 inches long, rooted in the greenhouse in sandy medium.

## Dipladenia (dip-la-dee-ne-a)
From the Greek *diploos,* double, *aden,* gland, referring to a pair of glands on the ovary *(Apocynaceae).* Greenhouse, evergreen twining plants, first grown here in the mid nineteenth century, natives of tropical America, bearing racemes of beautiful periwinkle-like flowers opening in long succession. They are slender plants suitable for training up stakes or wires fixed to the structure of the greenhouse, when they flower very freely.

**Species cultivated** *D. atropurpurea,* 10 feet, maroon-purple flowers, in summer. *D. boliviensis,* 8–10 feet, white and creamy-yellow flowers, summer. *D. sanderi,* 10 feet, rose-red flowers, summer. *D. splendens,* 8–12 feet, white, mauve and rose flowers, summer; vars. *amabilis,* rose pink; *brearleyana,* pink turning to crimson; *profusa,* large carmine flowers, up to 5 inches across.

**Cultivation** Pot in a mixture of rough fibrous peat with a quarter of its bulk of silver sand added. Young plants are repotted in February and brisk drainage is essential, especially if plants are put into a greenhouse border. Plants in large pots or in borders need a top-dressing of fresh compost annually. Summer care against attack from red spider mite is necessary and daily syringeing is helpful. Water frequently and give liquid feeds throughout the summer, then give only very little water during the winter. Propagation is by cuttings taken in March inserted in sand in a propagating case in a temperature of 70–80°F (21–27°C). These cuttings are best taken from the new shoots formed after pruning, when growth is cut back to within two or three buds of the previous year's growth in February.

## Diplarrhena (dip-la-ree-na)
From the Greek *diploos,* double, *arrhena,* male, referring to the two perfect stamens of the flowers, the third stamen being without an anther *(Iridaceae).* A genus of two species of slightly tender rhizomatous plants with sword-like leaves, closely related to *Libertia.*

**Species cultivated** *D. latifolia,* 3 feet, flowers lilac and yellow, five or six on a stem, Tasmania. *D. moraea,* 1½–2 feet, flowers white, two or three together, the outer segments reflexed, the inner ones erect and shorter, southern Australia. Both flower in summer.

**Cultivation** A sunny, sheltered situation and well drained sandy loam are essential and frost protection in the form of a mulch will be needed in winter.

**Dipladenia sanderi, one of the finest of climbing plants for the warm greenhouse. It came from Brazil in 1896.**

The colder and more exposed districts are unsuitable for these plants. Plant in spring or autumn, preferably spring to encourage the plants to establish themselves before the first winter. Propagation is by division of the roots at planting time or from seed sown in cold frames or cold houses in summer, the seedlings pricked off and planted out in their permanent quarters the following April.

## Diplocaulobium
(dip-lo-cow-lo-be-um)
From the Greek *diploos,* double, *kanlon,* stem and *lobos* lobe *(Orchidaceae).* A genus of thirty epiphytic orchids mainly from New Guinea. The flowers are attractive but short lived. The floral segments are narrow, giving a spidery appearance to the blooms. The only species likely to be found in cultivation is *D. fariniferum,* with flowers 3 inches across, white on the first day, red on the second day and then withering. They are produced at various times throughout the year.

**Cultivation** A mixture of osmunda fibre and sphagnum moss is suitable. Maintain a minimum temperature of 60°F (16°C). The plant requires much less water in winter.

## Diploid
A plant in which the number of chromosomes has neither increased nor decreased in the species during breeding or through other causes, in contrast

1 Dipsacus sylvestris, the native Common Teasel, will grow to 6 feet. 2 Disas, terrestrial orchids from Africa. Disa uniflora has bright red flowers; Disa racemosa, purple-pink.

to a polyploid plant which has more than the normal number of chromosomes for its species.

**Diplopappus**—see Cassinia

**Dipsacus** (dip-sa-kus)
From the Greek *dipsao,* to thirst, a reference to the water-holding cavity formed by the leaves united round the stem *(Dipsaceae).* Teasel. Biennial or perennial herbs, stiff, erect, rough plants with spiny, prickly stems and fruits, some of which can be found naturalized in places. The heads have been used to tease wool and raise the pile on cloth. They are also useful for use in dried flower arrangements for winter decoration.
**Species cultivated** *D. fullonum,* fuller's teasel, 3–6 feet, flowers delicate mauve in conical heads from June to August, biennial. *D. sylvestris,* common teasel, 5–6 feet, flowers pale lilac, summer, a native biennial plant.
**Cultivation** Limey, well-drained soils in open sunny situations are best. Propagation is from seed sown in the open in May or June, the seedlings thinned and later transplanted to their

permanent positions in September for flowering the following year. No staking is required, but the plants need plenty of room and should be set not less than 2 feet apart. The flower heads should be cut with long stems any time in the late autumn and stored, wrapped in paper or polythene to keep them dust free, in a dry place until required. They can be gilded or silvered for indoor or Christmas decoration. Left unpainted they dry to a pleasant autumnal brown.

**Dipteronia** (dip-ter-o-ne-a)
From the Greek *dis,* two, *pteros,* winged, referring to the form of the winged seeds *(Aceraceae).* A genus of two deciduous trees from China, of which one, *D. sinensis,* is in cultivation. This is hardy and it makes a large bush or tree up to 25 feet tall, with handsome,

opposite, pinnate leaves and conspicuous clusters of winged fruits in the autumn.
**Cultivation** It will grow in any ordinary garden soil and is propagated by layers or by cuttings of half-ripened wood inserted in sandy soil in a cold frame.

**Disa** (di-sa)
The native name *(Orchidaceae).* A large genus of terrestrial orchids, mainly natives of Africa. The single species in cultivation has fine large flowers with the upper sepal as the dominant segment. The plants form a rosette of leaves. The species cultivated is *D. uniflora,* an African plant which has three to seven large, crimson, yellow-shaded flowers on tall stems in summer. Two other species have occasionally been in cultivation, *D. racemosa* and *D. tripetaloides,* with whitish to rose flowers.

Cultivation Recent reports indicate that the best mixture for this somewhat difficult plant is equal parts of sphagnum moss, sphagnum peat, leafmould and sand. A cool moist atmosphere is essential and the compost should not be allowed to become dry at any time. The minimum winter temperature should be 45–50°F (7–10°C). Give plenty of air but avoid draughts. Propagation is by separation of offsets and, with varying success, by sowing seed on pots containing established plants.

## Disanthus (dis-an-thus)

From the Greek *dis*, twice, *anthos*, flower, referring to the flowers borne in pairs (Hamamelidaceae). A genus of but one species, *D. cercidifolia*, a deciduous shrub from Japan, growing 10–15 feet tall. The leaves, which are rounded, resembling those of the Judas tree (*Cercis siliquastrum*), turn brilliant crimson and dark red in autumn before falling. The tiny purplish flowers, with strap-shaped petals, are borne in October.

**1 Disanthus cercidifolia, a deciduous shrub from Japan, grows about 10 feet tall. It is grown for its foliage colour in autumn. 2 Disbudding dahlias, leaving the central bud. 3 The bud selected grows to perfection.**

Cultivation This shrub needs a peaty, lime-free soil. Plant in autumn or spring. Propagation is by cuttings either of half-ripe wood rooted in summer in a mixture of sand and peat in a propagating frame or by hardwood cuttings taken in autumn and rooted in a cold frame.

## Disbudding

This is an operation in which buds or young shoots are removed from a plant. It is generally carried out to direct the strength of the plant into a few selected flowers or fruits to ensure good results rather than allow more shoots to develop than the plant can conveniently carry. It is also designed to shape the framework of the plant and allow space for development.

Usually it is the central or terminal bud that is retained and sideshoots or axillary buds are removed and it is good practice to do this as soon as possible before the buds are allowed to swell. By delaying the operation the development of the terminal bud is slightly arrested, and by delaying it even more a small flower will result from the remaining terminal bud.

Disbudding is done by rubbing the bud away with the thumb, rarely by pinching, or with a knife as for example when the axillary lower trusses of tomato flowers are taken away.

The operation is a routine one in the cultivation of dahlias, carnations, chrysanthemums and roses for exhibition and is described in the articles on these plants. The buds or eyes on vine rods are 'rubbed out' (or disbudded), leaving only a few laterals to develop. The routine work of removing surplus sideshoots on an established fan-trained peach tree is often accompanied by disbudding or de-shooting as the older generation more correctly call it; the

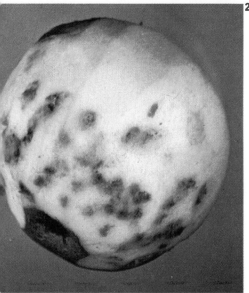

tight, pointed buds being the shoot buds. Those that are required to grow into position as replacement shoots are left and the others removed (see De-shooting).

## Disc or disk floret

This is one of the small tubular flowers that form the disk or centre of daisy-like flowers, members of the *Compositae*. Sometimes these disk florets are surrounded by ray florets, like a ruffle round the disk, as in the daisy. Disk florets alone sometimes constitute a whole flower head, as in thistles.

## Discaria (dis-car-e-a)

From the Greek *diskos*, the flower disk being large and fleshy *(Rhamnaceae)*. A small genus of spiny deciduous shrubs with tiny leaves, related to *Colletia*.
**Species cultivated** *D. discolor*, 4–6 feet and up to 8 feet in diameter, the lower branches arching almost to the ground, clusters of small white flowers, lacking petals, in May and June, the Andes and Patagonia. *D. serratifolia*, 10–15 feet,

1 The disc florets together comprise the compact centre (known as the disc or disk) of flowers in the Daisy family, Compositae. 2 Diseases of plants, Bitter Pit of apples. 3 Powdery Mildew of roses, Sphaerotheca pannosa.

with greenish-white, fragrant flowers on pendulous, spiny, branches in June, Chile, Patagonia. *D. toumatou*, wild Irishman, a shrub or small tree, 2–25 feet tall in its native habitat, with formidable spines up to 1½ inches long, leaves sometimes lacking, clusters of greenish-white flowers in May, New Zealand.
**Cultivation** Ordinary well-drained garden soil is sufficient but the plants need a sunny sheltered position, preferably in a milder climate. Propagation by cuttings taken in July and inserted in sandy soil in a frame with gentle bottom heat.

## Disease

The word disease in connexion with plants is considered to refer to any

disturbance in the normal life processes which results in such things as (a) abnormal growth (b) temporary or permanent check to the development or (c) premature death of part or all of the plant. Plant diseases can be divided into two sorts (i) Parasitic, where the trouble is due to attacks of parasites such as fungi, bacteria or viruses and (ii) Non-parasitic in which the trouble is a result of faults in the environment (soil, temperature, moisture etc). The biggest group of diseases is that caused by fungus parasites (including bacteria) which are spread about by spores produced in the fruiting bodies (equivalent to seeds of higher plants but, of course, microscopic in size). Viruses are incredibly small in size and in nature are carried from infected to healthy plants by insects, mainly aphids, and also by trimming knives and hands (in glasshouses), by knives etc., (in propagating houses) and in a very few instances by seed transmission. It will be noticed that the great difference between parasitic and non-

1 Watering damping off prevention on a seed box before sowing seeds, to prevent attack by damping-off disease. 2 Watering seedlings with the same material. 3 A chrysanthemum plant attacked by the disease powdery mildew.

parasitic disease is that the former is infectious while the latter is not. Despite this, where a non-parasitic trouble begins, there is likely to be great loss unless the fault in environment is quickly corrected. The symptoms in either kind of trouble can be very similar and even almost identical so that to judge the cause it is often necessary to consult an expert to get microscopic examination and sound advice (see Disease control).

## Disease control

The control of plant disease depends on an accurate estimate of the symptoms shown by the affected plant so as to arrive at the exact cause of the trouble. Even with parasitic diseases the cause is usually microscopic, requiring a careful examination and often laboratory tests on the diseased tissues. Similarly with non-parasitic troubles the environment must be studied as well as the plants and the details of cultivation carefully considered. There may have to be a careful soil analysis as well as a study of the drainage and soil texture and there may also be an analytical test of some of the foliage or fruits which could reveal a shortage of some essential plant food.

**Precautionary measures** Before considering measures which have to be taken to check diseases in plant crops we may

3

Wounded tissues are susceptible to invasion by disease spores which are always present in the atmosphere. Where large cuts have to be made protect them at once with a tree wound dressing.

healthy shoots and buds with good circulation of air among the branches.

Rotation of crops is intended to avoid growing the same kind of plant on the same spot year after year. If crops are grown on the same site year after year any disease of that crop is encouraged to build up and the soil can become heavily infected, addition to which the same plant foods are taken out of the soil. A different crop takes different amounts of the various chemical elements so that a balance can be easily kept. In glasshouses the same crop is very often grown each year but the disease build-up is checked by suitable methods of soil sterilisation. Other precautionary measures are weed eradication (e.g. wild celery harbours celery leaf spot disease and the common plantain can carry the virus of spotted wilt). Careful spacing is also helpful so that diseases are not provided with the humid and moist conditions between plants which they need to germinate their spores and infect the leaves.

The protection of large wounds is another obvious precaution and one which is very important where large specimen trees or even expensive fruit trees and shrubs are concerned. It is not suggested that small pruning cuts need to be treated but where a large branch is broken down by wind or snow or cracked during severe frosts it is wise to try to protect the broken or cut places. After any branch is removed the cut should be painted over with a suitable protective paint such as are generally sold in US to prevent the entry of fungus parasites. Not only are plum trees likely to be infected by the silver leaf fungus but many fine ornamental trees and shrubs can be lost by neglecting this simple precaution. Even after cutting out a canker from apple trees the wound should be painted.

**Resistant plants** An important method of avoiding plant disease is to use resistant plants. A plant immune to a particular disease is highly valued by the grower if its quality is so good as good as those which are susceptible to the disease. Growing immune varieties is the simplest way of avoiding disease and it is a pity that such varieties are so limited in number (see Immune).

**Soil sterilisation** One of the most important precautions taken to avoid disease in horticultural crops is the practice of soil sterilisation. In this the soil in a greenhouse intended for tomatoes, cucumbers, lettuces etc., is treated by passing hot steam through it (a commercial practice) or by watering with chemicals (e.g. formaldehyde or cresylic acid) before the crop is planted

look at some of the things which can be done to guard against disease ever appearing. These can best be termed precautionary measures. They aim at building up the vigour of the plants to help them to resist any possible attack by a parasitic disease and they also include various precautions which can be taken to eliminate the possibility of disease being in the neighbourhood of the crop, more especially in the soil.

It is of the utmost importance to study the special requirements of any particular plant so that the soil can be prepared in order to ensure good drain age and also that it contains sufficient organic matter (humus) and the necessary plant foods. Where some plants are concerned, for instance camellias and rhododendrons it is important to ensure that there is no lime present in the soil. Everything should be done to get vigorous plants with robust stems and foliage. In glasshouses, proper light and ventilation must be arranged and in fruit trees skilful pruning helps to build up strong,

1 Potato foliage attacked by Potato Blight, Phytophthora infestans. 2 Grey Mould, Botrytis cinerea, attacking lettuce at ground level. 3 Close-up of Chrysanthemum Powdery Mildew.

so that any dormant spores of disease are killed. However, at the temperature used, the spores of beneficial bacteria (see Bacteria and Nitrogen) are not killed, so that after the process is completed these can begin to enrich the soil without any immediate competition from other organisms. For use in small pots and seed boxes sterilised soil made after the John Innes formulae can be bought for use by gardeners. Similarly, sterile soilless composts are now available. Small glasshouses can be washed down inside with formalin or other disinfectants and the same sort of treatment can be given to garden frames, pots, boxes, seed trays and tools. Cresylic acid is one substance used for this purpose and in some instances also for sterilising the surface of the soil, but there are several other good disinfectants available for the gardener.

**Preventing the spread of disease** When, despite the precautions referred to, a disease makes its appearance it is necessary to act quickly and to take direct action measures. The chief of these is to cover the plant with a protective film of a chemical which will kill the fungus or at least prevent the germination of its spores. Diseased parts can be removed before treatment, but it must be remembered that in most diseases an affected plant is often doomed (except where the disease is superficial or where affected parts can be cut away). The object of the treatment is to protect still healthy tissues, so that it is wise to spray or dust early.

Various chemicals, known as Fungicides, which will deal with all types of diseases, are on the market (see Fungicides). These are applied as a fine misty spray or as dust (most people hold that spraying is more efficient than dusting). Many types of spraying and dusting machines are in use. There are also smokes which are lit to fumigate glasshouses, which have previously been cleared of all plant life. Seeds, bulbs and corms are also treated by dusting or by immersion in a liquid fungicide to give them protection from soil-borne diseases, etc., after planting.

### Disporum (dis-por-um)
Derived from *dispermus*, with two seeds, as the fruits are two-seeded *(Liliaceae)*. Hardy and tender perennials, related to *Tricyrtis*, from North America and tropical Asia.
**Species cultivated** *D. hookeri*, 1–2 feet, with erect stems, bearing small greenish flowers in May, followed by attractive red berries, hardy, California. *D. lanuginosum*, about 1 foot, yellow and green flowers, May, hardy, South Carolina.

**Cultivation** These plants require a light, moist soil and a cool shady position. They are propagated by division in early spring, while they are still dormant, or by seed.

### Dissotis (diss-o-tis)
From the Greek *dissoi*, of two kinds, referring to the anthers *(Melastomataceae)*. Perennial and annual herbs or small shrubs, usually with hairy leaves, from tropical and South Africa.
**Species cultivated** *D. grandiflora*, up to 2 feet, with terminal racemes of purplish flowers in summer, up to 3 inches across, perennial. *D. incana*, 2–3 feet, with rosy-purple flowers up to 1½ inches across in panicles, in June, perennial.

**Cultivation** Dissotis require a minimum winter temperature of about 70°F (21°C) and light shading from the sun in summer, with a humid atmosphere. In winter the atmosphere should be considerably drier. Pot in a mixture of equal parts of loam and peat with about one-third sharp sand and a little charcoal. Propagation is by cuttings, taken in spring and rooted in a propagating case with bottom heat.

### Distaff Thistle—see Carthamus

### Distylium (dis-tie-le-um)
Derived from the Greek *dis*, two, *stylos*, style; the flowers have two styles *(Hamamelidaceae)*. A small genus of

a good dark green with a prominent reddish mid-rib, the species most often seen and offered as house plant. *D. kerchoveana,* 2½ feet, glossy leaves with paler mid-ribs. *D. veitchii,* 2½ feet, dark green leaflets with white mid-ribs, reddish on the under surface.

**Cultivation** Interesting though they are, these are not very easy plants with which to succeed, particularly in the living room. They need a winter temperature of 60–70°F (16–21°C) and a mixture of equal parts of loam, peat, sand, leafmould and charcoal. Pot up in February or March and water freely throughout the summer with temperatures up to 80°F (27°C). Propagation is by cuttings in summer, put in a propagating case with bottom heat or by root cuttings taken in spring when the plants are being repotted. In the house they must be kept away from draughts and in an even, warm atmosphere. Unfortunately the air in our living rooms is too dry, a condition which is disliked *D. elegantissima,* the species usually offered as a houseplant.

## DNC (DNOC)

Dinitro-ortho-cresol is an insecticide and acaricide used on dormant trees against the egg stage of such pests as aphids, suckers, red spider mite etc., and is also used as a herbicide. It is usually combined with petroleum oil to form DNC winter washes and as proprietary preparations may differ in strength, manufacturer's instructions on application rates should be followed.

## Dobrowskya (dob-rows-ke-a)

Commemorating Joseph Dobrowsky (1753–1829) Hungarian philologist *(Lobeliaceae).* A small genus of half-hardy annuals and half-hardy perennials, closely related to *Lobelia.* The only species likely to be available is *D. tenella* (syn. *Monopsis unidentata),* which grows 6 inches tall with a spreading habit, and bears masses of purple flowers with a deep purple throat in summer. A half-hardy perennial.

**Cultivation** *D. tenella* is usually treated as a half-hardy annual. Seeds are sown under glass in early spring in a well-drained leafy soil and the seedlings are planted out in the open in May.

## Docynia (doc-e-ne-a)

The name is an anagram of *Cydonia* to which this small genus is closely related *(Rosaceae).* Oriental trees resembling the wild pear, from India, China and Assam, evergreen in the mildest districts.

**Species cultivated** *D. delavayi,* up to 30 feet bearing white flowers, rose-tinted without, in April and May, followed by yellow, apple-like fruit.

evergreen shrubs from China, Japan and north India. The only species in cultivation, *D. racemosum,* rarely exceeds 5–6 feet (although it is a slow-growing tree in Japan), with conspicuous red anthers to the blood-red flowers, in March and April. The branches are wide spreading and the leaves glossy.

**Cultivation** *D. racemosum* is suitable only for gardens in the milder districts in a light, sandy soil. It is propagated by cuttings of half-ripened wood inserted in sandy soil in a frame with gentle bottom heat.

**Dittany**—see Dictamnus albus

**Divi-divi**—see Caesalpinia coriaria

**Division**—see Propagation

## Dizygotheca (diz-ee-goth-ee-ka)

From the Greek *di,* two, *zygos,* yoke, *theka,* case, referring to the anthers which have double the usual number of cells *(Araliaceae).* False aralia. Tender shrubs for growing under glass or, in recent years in the house, cultivated particularly for their attractive leaves in their juvenile state. The long stems are tipped by narrow, toothed leaves, arranged like the spokes of a wheel. The plants were formerly included in the genus *Aralia.*

**Species cultivated** *D. elegantissima,* 2–3 feet, thread-like drooping leaflets, brownish-red when young, later turning

The leaves are up to 3 inches long, white-felted beneath, persisting into the winter, China. *D. rufifolia,* similar, but with less persistent leaves.
**Cultivation** These trees are suitable only for mild districts in well-drained soil. They may be propagated by cuttings of half-ripened wood inserted in sandy soil in a frame with gentle bottom heat.

### Dodecatheon (do-dek-a-thee-on)

From the Greek *dodeka,* twelve, and *theos,* god, an ancient name signifying Flower of the Twelve Gods *(Primulaceae).* American cowslip, shooting star. A genus of North American hardy herbaceous perennials, the flowers much reflexed like those of cyclamen. They are related to *Primula* and *Soldanella,* and are suitable for moist or semi-shady places in the rock garden.
**Species cultivated** *D. clevelandii,* 1 foot, violet-purple, May, California. *D. hen-dersonii,* 1 foot, violet, yellow base, April and May, California. *D. jeffreyi,* 1–2 feet, reddish-purple, large, slightly sticky leaves, May and June, California. *D. latifolium,* 1 foot, bright pink, May and June, north west America. *D. meadia,* shooting star, 1–2 feet, rosy-purple with white base and prominent yellow anthers, May and June, eastern North America. *D. pauciflorum,* 8–9 inches, pale lilac and yellow, May and June, western North America.
**Cultivation** Plant in March, April, May in partial shade and in a leafy soil. Top-dress annually in the spring with leaf-mould and old manure. Dodecatheons are useful cold greenhouse plants. For this purpose lift plants and pot them up in November, using a mixture consisting of equal parts of loam, leafmould and sharp sand. Keep the potted plants in a cold frame until March; do not force them. Plunge the pots after flowering. Propagation is by seed (somewhat slow to germinate) sown in pots containing light sandy soil in September or March and placed in a cold frame, or by division of the crowns in October or March.

### Dodonaea (doe-don-e-a)

In honour of Rembert Dodaens, sixteenth century botanical writer *(Sapindaceae).* A genus of tender trees and shrubs mainly of Australian origin, although a few species are found in New Zealand, North America, Africa and Hawaii.
**Species cultivated** *D. cuneata,* wedge-leaf hop bush, 5–6 feet, with small greenish flowers in winter, but more effective are the bronze-red winged seed pods, Australia. *D. viscosa,* giant hop bush, 12–20 feet, with greenish flowers borne in short terminal racemes and attractive brown winged seed pods, used for roadside planting in arid areas, Australia, New Zealand, South Africa. *D. viscosa purpurea,* the purple ake ake of New Zealand, 8–10 feet, a splendid ornamental foliage plant, with willow-like, deep bronze leaves in summer, becoming rich violet-crimson in winter. The flowers are insignificant but the reddish winged seed pods are attractive, New Zealand.
**Cultivation** These tender plants require a warm greenhouse and a light well-drained soil. Maintain a minimum winter temperature of 45°F (7°C), rising in summer to a maximum of around 65°F (18°C), when plenty of ventilation will be needed to help to keep the temperature down in hot, sunny weather Propagate by seed sown in the spring.

### Dogwood—see Cornus

### Dog's Tooth Violet—see Erythronium dens-canis

### Dolichos (dol-e-koss)

From the Greek *dolikos,* long, referring to the long shoots *(Leguminosae).* A small genus of evergreen or annual twining plants from tropical areas of the world, suitable for the greenhouse, grown for their pea-like flowers.
**Species cultivated** *D. lablab* (syn. *D. giganteus),* bonavist, hyacinth bean, half-hardy annual, 1–2 feet, rosy-purple or white flowers, July to September, followed by seed pods 3 inches long. Pods and seeds are eaten in the tropics. *D. lignosus,* Australian pea, evergreen twiner, rose-coloured flowers, July.
**Cultivation** These climbers are grown in pots containing a well-drained mixture of equal parts of loam and peat, with a little sharp sand. Water freely during the summer. Propagation is by seed sown in March in a light garden

soil after frost danger is past. The perennial species may be increased by cuttings in the spring, rooted in sandy soil in a warm propagating frame.

---

## Dolichothele (dol-e-koth-ee-lee)
From the Greek *dolikos*, long, *thele*, nipple, referring to the long tubercles *(Cactaceae)*. Greenhouse cactus plants, recognisable by their large fleshy tubercles; all have large yellow flowers followed by greenish fruits. The roots become very thick and parsnip-like.
**Species cultivated** *D. longimamma*, thick tap root, stout tubercles, stem bright green with areole on top with several spines, central Mexico. *D. melaleuca*, rather shorter tubercles, otherwise similar, flowers with reddish tips to the petals, Mexico. *D. uberiformis*, stout tubercles, free-flowering, Mexico.
**Cultivation** Pot in a fairly light potting mixture, with added sharp sand, grit and broken brick, at the rate of a sixth part; repot when the plant reaches the side of the pot or every two or three years. Place the pots on the greenhouse shelf in sunshine. Water from April to September, gradually reduce to none at all from October to March.

Temperature, any summer warmth and a minimum of 40°F (4°C), in winter when the plants are kept dry. Propagation is by seed sown in a light seed mixture, just covering the seed with its own depth of soil, in a temperature of 70°F (21°C). Keep the seedlings moist and shaded from sun.

---

**Dolphin fly**—see Aphids

---

## Dombeya (dom-bay-a)
In honour of Joseph Dombey, an eighteenth century French botanist *(Sterculiaceae)*. Ornamental evergreen trees and shrubs mostly from tropical Africa and Madagascar.
**Species cultivated** *D. burgessiae*, up to 10 feet, bearing convex clusters of large, rose tinted, white flowers from August to December, South Africa. *D. × cayeuxii*, 10–15 feet, with pendent umbels of finely veined pink flowers, hybrid. *D. viscosa*, 10–15 feet, heads of white flowers, deep crimson at the base, with

a honeyed fragrance, Madagascar.
**Cultivation** These attractive shrubs require a minimum winter temperature of 75°F (24°C) and a medium consisting of equal parts of loam and fibrous peat. Water freely during the growing season. Propagate by cuttings, taken in April, of nearly ripe wood, inserted in sandy soil in a propagating frame with a temperature of 80°F (27°C).

---

## Don, George
George Don (1798–1856) was a Scot who was brought up in the nursery trade to become foreman at the Horticultural Society's Chiswick gardens from 1816 to 1821.

In 1822 he was sent by the Society to search for plants along the coast of West Africa, particularly to Sierra Leone, and thence to the West Indies, Brazil and New York.

Although Don's tour along the coastal fringes was so brief, he was most successful. In fourteen months he searched for plants in six different countries on the West African coast, collected in six of the main islands of the Atlantic including Madeira, Jamaica and Trinidad, called at four places on the

---

**1 Dolichos lablab, the Hyacinth Bean, is an ornamental vigorous climbing annual. 2 Cassia conspicua was introduced by George Don, an active collector of plants.**

Brazilian coast and, finally, plant hunted on Manhattan Island.

Don had strict and precise instructions for his voyage and kept a full diary on the orders of the Horticultural Society.

Most of his introductions were tropical fruits and palms probably little known or grown today, but the Society were highly satisfied with his work and papers were read to the members on his discoveries which included *Anona senegalensis* (the custard apple), *Adansonia digitalis* (monkey apple), *Inga biglobosa* (locust tree), a fig *(Ficus brassii)* and other tropical hot-house fruits, many from Sierra Leone.

Among his flowers were *Clematis grandiflora, Gardenia coccinea, Arum compressum, Cassia conspicua, Gomphia reticulata, Clerodendrum splendens,* ipomoeas, pancratiums, crinums and passifloras.

Named for him was *Memecylon donianum,* a species of glabrous tree or shrub, 'unknown to cultivation in this country' says G. Nicholson, of *The Gardener's Dictionary.*

He edited Sweet's 3rd edition of *Hortus Britannicus,* prepared the first supplement to J. C. Loudon's *Encyclopaedia of Gardening* and wrote *'A General System of Gardening and Botany'* (1831–37).

**Donkey's Ears**—see Kalanchoe tomentosa

**1** Doronicum plantagineum excelsum, a hardy perennial reaching 5 to 6 feet, sometimes listed as 'Harpur Crewe's Variety'. **2** Doronicum 'Spring Beauty', a double yellow cultivar.

---

## Dormant

The dormant period is one of apparent inactivity. Some plants, such as bulbs, corms and tubers, may undergo quite long periods of rest, usually in winter, but few plants are completely dormant in the sense that no development is taking place within them. Some plants, for instance lily-of-the-valley crowns, trilliums and certain bulbs, can have the dormant period prolonged considerably by refrigeration at a constant low temperature. This is of great value to commercial growers who can bring plants out of cold storage and time the flowering when market prices will be advantageous.

Deciduous trees and shrubs are considered dormant when they have dropped their leaves in autumn, but many of these plants have some dormant buds on the stems throughout the year. Many seeds have a period of dormancy after ripening and nothing will induce them to germinate until they have had this natural period of rest. Other seeds may germinate almost as soon as they fall to the ground.

Buds on fruit trees may belong to one of two classes—either wood or growth buds, or blossom or fruit buds. During the winter these buds usually cease to develop but some wood buds may remain dormant for years (see Fruit and Wood bud).

---

## Doronicum (dor-on-ik-um)

From the Arabic name *doronigi (Compositae).* Leopard's bane. Hardy herbaceous perennials, natives of Europe and Asia, early-flowering, with long-stemmed, daisy-like yellow flowers. The sap from the root of *D. pardalianches* is said to be poisonous. Doronicums last well as cut-flowers.

**Species cultivated** *D. austriacum,* 18 inches, golden-yellow, spring. *D. carpetanum,* 2 feet, yellow, May and June. *D. caucasicum,* 1 foot, yellow, April and May; var. *magnificum,* flowers larger. *D. clusii,* 1 foot, yellow, May and June. *D. cordatum,* 6–9 inches, deep yellow, April and May. *D. orientale,* 1 foot, yellow, April, *D. plantagineum,* 2–3 feet, yellow, spring; var. *excelsum* (syn. 'Harpur Crewe') larger, bright yellow flowers, April to June. Other good named varieties will be found in nurserymen's catalogues. The new German hybrid 'Fruhlingspracht', or 'Spring Splendour', 1 foot, is an interesting introduction with double yellow flowers during April and May.

**Cultivation** Plant in the autumn or spring in ordinary garden soil in sun or partial shade. Propagation is by

division of the roots in October or March. Doronicums are adaptable plants which may be moved or divided without damage even when they are in bud, provided this is done in moist weather.

## Dorotheanthus (dor-o-the-an-thus)

Named in honour of Frau Dorothea Schwantes, wife of a German botanist (*Aizoaceae*). Greenhouse succulents from South Africa, often found under *Mesembryanthemum*. They may be used for bedding out or as pot plants.

**Species cultivated** *D. bellidiformis*, dwarf spreading plant, leaves fleshy, flowers open in sunshine, colours, white, pink, red and orange. *D. gramineus*, short-stemmed and spreading, flowers bright carmine. *D. tricolor*, spreading habit, leaves long and curved, flowers white below and purple above. All these are natives of Cape Province.

**Cultivation** An open mixture is needed; out of doors see that the soil is well drained and plant in sunny positions. These plants are annuals and three plants in a pot make a good display; they do not require high temperatures. Propagation is by seeds sown on a light seed mixture. Do not cover the seed. The temperature should be 70°F (21°C). Keep the seed pans moist and shaded while germination is taking place, prick out the seedlings and grow them on in a frame. The plants should be potted up or planted out in June.

**1 Dorotheanthus (Mesembryanthemum) in flower at the Karoo Garden, Worcester, South Africa. 2 Paphiopedilum 'Sunbeam' shows the prominent dorsal sepal attached to the back of the bloom.**

## Dorsal (bot.)

A term meaning attached to the back, used mainly when referring to the flowers of certain orchids. The erect, often large, sepal of a cypripedium (paphiopedilum) bloom is known as the dorsal sepal. This is a prominent feature at the back of the flower.

**Dorset Heath**—see Erica ciliaris

## Doryanthes (dor-e-an-thes)

From the Greek *dory*, a spear, *anthos*, a flower, the flower stem being like the shaft of a spear up to 15 feet long (*Amaryllidaceae*). A genus of three evergreen species from Australia, half-lily and half-palm-like in appearance, with fleshy roots.

**Species cultivated** *D. excelsa*, Australian giant lily, 8–15 feet, with brilliant scarlet heads of flowers in summer, New South Wales. *D. guilfoylei*, 12–15 feet, with clusters of crimson flowers in summer, Queensland. *D. palmeri*, spear lily, 10–15 feet, with red, funnel-shaped flowers in summer, Queensland.

**Cultivation** These tall, striking plants are suitable only for a spacious greenhouse where a minimum winter temperature of 55°F (13°C) can be maintained. Pot them in the spring, using a mixture consisting of equal parts of loam and leaf soil, with a little sharp sand. Water sparingly in winter, moderately from April onwards. They are propagated by means of suckers detached at any time and put in small pots in a temperature of 60°F (16°C).

## Dorycnium (dor-iss-nee-um)

From the Greek *dory*, a spear. The name is said to have been adapted by Pliny who applied it to 'a herb wherewith they poisoned arrowheads and darts' (*Leguminosae*). A small genus of hardy and half-hardy shrubby plants from the

Mediterranean region. The only species cultivated is *D. hirsutum* which grows 18 inches tall and has pink or white pea-like flowers in summer on erect, hairy stems. **Cultivation** This plant does best in a light sandy loam and a sunny position. Propagate by seed or by cuttings of half-ripened shoots taken after flowering and inserted in sandy soil in a cold frame.

### Dot plant
This is the name given to a plant of taller growth, often of standard form, used in formal bedding schemes to relieve the flat effect of a large bed of lower-growing plants. Plants often used for this purpose include fuchsias, heliotropes, pelargoniums, and roses, grown as standards. Other plants grown under glass and bedded out in the summer as dot plants are abutilons, daturas, the fast-growing *Eucalyptus globulus,* with attractive glaucous leaves, the rubber plant, *Ficus elastica,* whose large leathery, well-developed leaves have a bronze sheen, the graceful *Grevillea robusta* and the variegated form of the purple-flowered tree mallow, *Lavatera arborea.* Particularly popular on the Continent are the brilliant cannas with their luxuriant leaves. A striking centre-piece for a formal bedding scheme can be achieved by planting a specimen *Cordyline australis.* This may be seen at its best in Cornwall, England. In these days few private gardens have sufficient staff to maintain elaborate formal bedding, but in some parks colourful examples are still to be seen, notably at holiday resorts abroad.

### Double flowers
A double flower is one that has more

1 Standard Fuchsias used as dot plants in a summer bedding scheme. Dot plants break monotony and lend height to the display. Various plants may be used for this purpose. 2 Bellis perennis 'Alice', the small double form of the Common Daisy. 3 Picea sitchensis growing at Bedgebury. This was introduced by David Douglas.

than the characteristic number of petals. There are many examples, camellia, daffodil, paeony, tulip and helianthemum (sun rose). In members of the daisy family *(Compositae),* for example the common daisy, *Bellis perennis,* the doubling effect is produced by the replacement of disk florets with ray florets. Sometimes in the process of doubling stamens and carpels are transformed into petals and thus the plants cannot form seeds and are sterile. Botanically, double flowers are often described as *plena* or, more often, *flore pleno (Kerria japonica flore pleno),* or abbreviated thus, *fl. pl.*

### Douglas, David
David Douglas (1798–1834), a Scot from Scone, was one of the first, and probably the most successful, plant hunter that the Horticultural Society (later the Royal Horticultural Society) ever sent abroad. His contributions to arboriculture have never been surpassed and his discovery of hardy herbaceous plants, which now grace our borders, put him among the top class of botanical travellers.

Although he was first sent by the Horticultural Society in 1823 to collect fruit trees, oaks and plants in North America, travelling from New York to Philadelphia and the Great Lakes, his

main field of endeavour was the wild Indian country of the Pacific Coast of America, from British Columbia to California and as far inland as the Rockies.

He sailed to Fort Vancouver on the Columbia River, where he was under the aegis of the Hudson's Bay Company, in 1825, and made incredibly difficult journeys into the interior until 1827, when he returned to England. He was back at Fort Vancouver in 1829 and from there travelled through Oregon to California, where he collected until 1832 when he left for Hawaii for a brief respite. But in the same year he returned to the Fraser River country in British Columbia and made another excursion down into California. He left America for the last time in 1834 to sail to Honolulu where he fell into a pit in

1 Pinus ponderosa, the Western Yellow Pine. 2 Iris douglasiana, a native of California, flowers in May. These are but two of the many plants introduced by David Douglas. 3 Douglasia nivalis, one of a genus named in honour of Douglas.

which a young bullock had already fallen and was trampled to death in July 1834 at the age of 35.

According to one authority it was said: 'No other collector has reaped such a harvest in America or associated his name with so many plants'. It is estimated that he collected 800 species of which 217 were new. Among these are *Clarkia elegans, Gilia capitata, Mimulus cardinalis* and *M. moschatus,* lupins, godetias, berberis, coreopsis, *Garrya elliptica, Ribes sanguineum, Mahonia aquifolium* and mignonette.

His tree finds, which altered the

European landscape, included the Douglas fir, now named *Pseudotsuga menziesii, Picea sitchensis, Pinus lambertiana, P. ponderosa, P. radiata, P. contorta,* and the firs, *Abies grandis, A. nobilis, A. magnifica, A. menziesii, A. douglasii, A. amabilis* and *A. bracteata.* Commemorative plants are *Iris douglasii, Clematis douglasii* and *Limnanthes douglasii.* Dr John Lindley named for him the genus of alpines, *Douglasia.*

## Douglasia (dug-lay-se-a)

Commemorating David Douglas, the famous plant collector, who travelled mainly in north west America (*Primulaceae*). A small genus of alpine plants related to *Androsace*. They are all natives of North America with one exception. These tufted evergreen little

495

plants are charming but require skill to cultivate them successfully.

**Species cultivated** *D. laevigata,* 2 inches, rosy-pink with a yellow eye, April, requires a lime-free, moist scree soil. *D. montana,* 2 inches, rose-pink, spring. *D. nivalis,* 2 inches, flowers pink, April. *D. vitaliana* (syn. *Androsace vitaliana*), 2 inches, known as the golden primrose, this is the one species found in Spain and central Europe. It forms a grey-green mat covered with solitary yellow flowers in April and is a good plant for a sunny trough garden or scree. The form *praetutiana* is particularly attractive and reputed to be more free-flowering.

**Cultivation** Douglasias do best in a soil consisting of equal parts of peat and loam with some sharp sand. Good drainage is essential. Propagation is by seed sown in deep sandy peat in March or April and placed in a cold frame. Lightly cover the seed with a sifted soil. Cuttings may be taken in June, or plants may be carefully divided in the autumn.

---

**Dovedale Moss**—see Saxifraga hypnoides

---

**Dove Tree**—see Davidia

---

**Downingia** (dow-nin-je-a)
Named for A. J. Downing, American landscape gardener and patron of botany

*(Lobeliaceae).* A small genus of annuals from North America which may be treated as hardy annuals or grown as pot plants in a cool greenhouse.

**Species cultivated** *D. elegans* (syn. *Clintonia elegans*), 6 inches, blue with white lip, summer. *D. pulchella* (syn. *Clintonia pulchella*), 6 inches, trailing, bright blue, marked white and yellow, summer.

**Cultivation** These are useful little plants for filling gaps on the rock garden or for edging. In warm gardens the seed may be sown in May where the plants are to flower, or the seedlings may be transplanted if required. For growing as pot plants sow in March in a warm greenhouse, or in a cold frame in April. Sow thinly in large pots containing a mixture of equal parts of loam, leafmould and sharp sand, and later thin out the seedlings to about 4 inches apart. When they are making good growth give weak liquid manure until they flower.

---

**Doxantha**—see Bignonia

---

**Draba** (dra-ba)
From the Greek *drabe,* acrid, a reference to the taste of the leaves *(Cruciferae).* A genus of over 250 annual, biennial and

Draba rigida flourishes in a sunny position in the rock garden in well-drained soil. It flowers in spring.

perennial plants from the colder areas of the world. Those cultivated are perennials for the rock garden or alpine house.

**Species cultivated** *D. aiziodes,* 3 inches, yellow, March, the earliest to flower, Europe. *D. aizoon,* 3 inches, yellow, April, Europe. *D. alpina,* 3 inches, yellow, April, Europe and Asia. *D. brunifolia,* 3 inches, yellow, June, Caucasus. *D. bryoides,* 2 inches, hard green cushions, tiny golden flowers, April, Caucasus; var. *imbricata,* 1 inch, both scree plants or for alpine house. *D. carinthiaca* (syn. *D. johannis*), 3 inches, white, May, Carpathians and Pyrenees. *D. dedeana,* 3 inches, little cushions of grey-green with white flowers, May, Spain. *D. mollissima,* 2 inches, grey-green cushion with clusters of yellow, fragrant flowers on tiny stems, April, sensitive to damp, suitable for the alpine house, Caucasus. *D. olympica,* 3 inches, golden flowers, April, Asia Minor. *D. polytricha,* 2 inches, pale yellow, April, for the alpine house, Turkish Armenia. *D. rigida,* 2 inches, yellow flowers in clusters, Armenia.

**Cultivation** Plant in March or April between rocks in sandy soil and in a sunny position. Good drainage is essential for these cushion-forming plants. Any dead rosettes should be removed or the rot may spread. Propagation is by seed sown in pans of sandy soil

1 Dracaena (Cordyline) terminalis, a stove-house plant grown for its ornamental foliage. 2 Dracaena godseffiana, a handsome foliage plant from the Congo. 3 Many garden-raised forms have Latin names such as Dracaena victoriae.

in March; by careful division of the roots in March, or by rosettes taken in June and rooted in a propagating frame in sandy soil.

### Dracaena (dras-ee-na)

From the Greek *drakaina*, a female dragon; *D. draco*, the dragon tree, yields the colouring matter known as dragon's blood *(Liliaceae)*. Evergreen plants from the tropics grown in warm greenhouses for the handsome, often variegated, foliage. They are related to *Cordyline* and often confused with that genus. The flowers of dracaena are usually larger and the rootstock is not creeping as in *Cordyline*.

**Species cultivated** *D. concinna*, 6 feet, leaves green with red margin, Mauritius. *D. draco*, dragon tree, 40–60 feet, leaves glaucous, Canary Isles, where there is an aged, world-famous specimen over 70 feet high. Hardy in the Isles of Scilly and parts of Cornwall. Young plants are decorative under glass. *D. fragrans*, up to 20 feet, glossy green, recurved leaves, yellow flowers in clusters, fragrant, Guinea. *D. godseffiana*, 3 feet, leaves green with cream spots, flowers yellowish or red, Congo. *D. goldieana*, 4–6 feet, leaves glossy yellowish-green, marked silver-green, tropical West Africa. *D. sanderiana*, 5 feet, leaves green with a broad white margin, Congo.

**Cultivation** Pot in February or March in a mixture of 2 parts of loam, 1 part of peat and 1 part of leafmould and sharp sand. Stand in a light position. The minimum winter temperature should be about 60°F (16°C). Water moderately in winter, freely during the spring and summer. Propagation is by seed sown in March in sandy soil in a temperature of 85°F (29°C). Cuttings may be made in March or April from the main stem, cut into 2 inch lengths and partially buried horizontally in sandy peat. Or the plants may be propagated by pieces of the fleshy root placed in sandy peat in spring, or by the tops of stems placed in sand in March or April.

### Dracocephalum (drak-o-sef-a-lum)

From the Greek *drakon*, a dragon, *kephale*, a head, a reference to the gaping flower mouth *(Labiatae)*. Dragon's head. Annual and perennial plants of European and Asian origin.

**Species cultivated: Annual** *D. moldavica*, Moldavian balm, 1½ feet, blue or white flowers in whorls, July and August.

**Perennial** *D. austriacum*, 1–1½ feet, blue, July. *D. grandiflorum*, 6–9 inches, blue, summer. *D. hemsleyanum*, up to 1½ feet, light blue, grey foliage, summer. *D. isabeliae*, 1½ feet, violet-blue, stems covered with white hairs, summer. *D. purdomii*, 1 foot, purple, summer, rock plant. *D. ruyschianum*, 1½ feet, purple, June. *D. sibiricum* (syn. *D. stewartianum* and *Nepeta macrantha*), 1½–3 feet, lavender-violet in many-flowered whorls, foliage silvery-grey, summer.

1 Dracophyllums are shrubs for the cool greenhouse, preferring a peaty soil. 2 Dracunculus vulgaris, the Dragon Arum, growing at the foot of a brick wall. The spathes reach 1 foot or more.

**Cultivation** These plants thrive in a cool, partially shady border in a light loamy, well-drained, soil. Propagation of annual and perennial varieties is by seeds sown in the open in April, or cuttings of the perennials may be inserted in sandy soil in a cold frame in April or May. Perennials may also be divided in the autumn or preferably in March.

## Dracophyllum (drak-o-fill-um)
From the Greek *drakon*, a dragon, *phyllum*, a leaf, referring to the resemblance of the leaves to those of the Dragon Tree, *Dracaena draco (Epacridaceae)*. Grass trees. A genus of evergreen shrubs and trees, mainly from New Zealand, a few from Australia and New Caledonia, all with tiny heath-like or grass-like leaves. A few species may be found growing in the open where subtropicals thrive; elsewhere they need the protection of a cool greenhouse.
**Species cultivated** *D. capitatum*, 2–4 feet, 1 inch wide heads of white flowers, April to June, Australia. *D. gracile*, 3–4 feet, white flowers in a 1 inch long oval head, June, Australia. *D. paludosum*, 4–6 feet, white flowers in short spikes, summer, Chatham Islands. *D. secundum*, 1–2 feet, spikes of white flowers, April, New South Wales. *D. uniflorum*, 5–6 feet,

solitary white flowers, summer, New Zealand.
**Cultivation** In the greenhouse these shrubs should be potted in peat with enough sharp sand to ensure free drainage. Prune hard in March, when the plants should be repotted with as little root disturbance as possible. Maintain a minimum winter temperature of 40°F (4°C). Propagation is by short cuttings rooted in a propagating case with bottom heat.

## Dracunculus (drak-un-ku-lus)
The Ancient Greek name, a diminutive of *drakon*, a dragon *(Araceae)*. Dragon arum. Hardy tuberous-rooted perennials from the Mediterranean region, related to *Arum*. There are but two species and of these the only one likely to be found in cultivation is *D. vulgaris* (syn. *Arum dracunculus*), which grows to about 3 feet. The large spathe is deep purple with striped purple mouth, the tall spadix is equally dark in colour, the leaves are much divided into segments. Plants give

off an offensive odour when in flower in June and July, attracting flies for pollination purposes. Seedlings of this species were depicted in stone relief in the Great Temple of Thutmose III in Egypt, *circa* 1450 B.C.
**Cultivation** Plant the tubers 3 inches deep in sandy soil in October or November. They like a sunny position and a well-drained border. Propagation is by division of the tubers in October or March.

**Dragon Arum**—see Dracunculus

**Dragon's blood**—see Dracaena

**Dragon's Head**—see Dracocephalum

**Dragon Tree**—see Dracaena draco

## Drainage
The soil must have adequate drainage otherwise air may be excluded and the more beneficial micro-organisms may be destroyed. Soils which have poor drain-

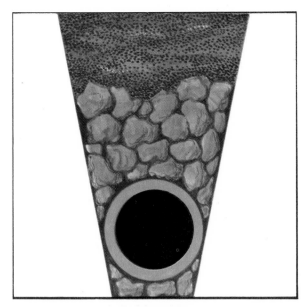

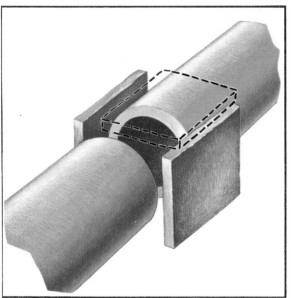

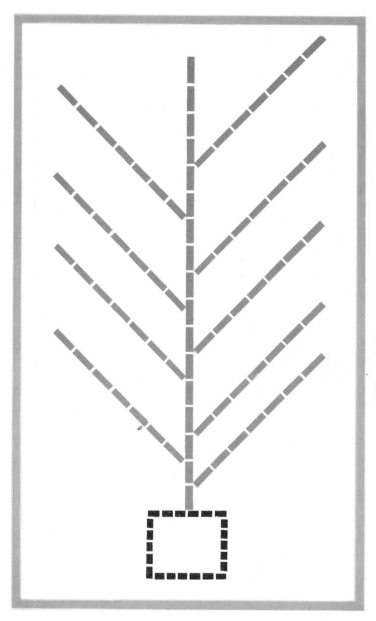

age are often sour and acid. It will be necessary to improve this acidity by applications of agricultural lime. Wet soils are cold. This means that plant growth is severely retarded. The situation is even more critical in the northern, colder parts of the country. Waterlogged soils cause roots to rot and a combination of all these problems can produce complete failures in some gardens.

Soils which are well-drained have sufficient natural coarse, gritty material or sand and many soils have a high proportion of small stones also. A high humus or organic content will also ensure good drainage. It is usually the clay soils which are the most difficult with regard to drainage, although a hard 'pan' or layer beneath the surface of some soils can also present a problem. Such a pan is usually produced by mechanical cultivation which, in some instances, can consolidate the lower soil layers. Setting the plough or cultivators to cultivate to the same depth season after season will also produce this hard, unbroken layer. Varying the cultivating

*Top left:* **A section through a tile drain.** *Bottom left:* **A junction protected with slates prevents the entry of silt.** *Right:* **The herring-bone system of drainage ensures the removal of excess water.**

depth occasionally usually overcomes this difficulty.

Clay soils are composed of finer particles and these tend to pack so tightly together that they soon form a solid mass through which excess water cannot pass easily. Improving the drainage here consists in opening up these fine particles. This can be done by liming the soil. The particles of soil cling together in large granules after this treatment. If sharp, gritty material such as coarse sand or well-weathered cinders is worked in, the clay particles will be separated and made more open. Bulky materials such as peat, composted vegetable waste and strawy manure are invaluable as soil conditioners. Gypsum is another preparation which has proved excellent for the breaking up of heavy, waterlogged clay soils.

Where cultural methods are not sufficient to provide a marked improvement in difficult conditions, it will be necessary to improve drainage by a system of drains or drainage trenches. The most efficient method is to use field or pipe drains. These are expensive, especially if drainage on a large scale is necessary. The pipes are sold in several sizes; those 2 inches or 3 inches in diameter are the best for the amateur.

Trenches are dug out to receive these pipes, at least 15 inches deep. All trenches should slope in one direction and this slope need not exceed 1 in 40. The trenches should be arranged in a herringbone fashion and should lead to one main trench which runs from the highest point in the garden to the lowest. The side or intermediate trenches should meet this main trench at an approximate angle of 45°.

The pipes should be laid, for preference, on a 2 inch layer of coarse gravel or cinders. Each pipe should be kept about ½ inch away from its neighbour and the junction covered with a piece of

slate, broken tile or a small piece of tough plastic sheeting. More gravel or cinders should be carefully placed around and on top of the pipes as work proceeds. The gaps between the pipes are essential to allow excess water to enter them and drain away inside the pipes. Frequent checks should be made with a little water from a watering can or hose pipe to see that water flows steadily along the pipes.

The main pipe line must be taken to a suitable outlet such as a ditch or dry well. The latter can be constructed by digging out a large hole as deeply as possible and filling it in with stones, clinker, gravel or ashes. This hole must be at least 2–3 feet square and deep. Under no circumstances must drainage water be allowed to flow on to neighbours' property. Where a stream or ditch is available for the emptying of drainage water, the local Public Works Department should be consulted to make quite sure whether it is permissible to discharge the water in this way.

An efficient drainage system can be provided if trenches are lined with rubble and coarse cinders. A similar system of trenches should be taken out and the bottom half filled with rubble. This layer of rubble should be then covered with about 6 inches of coarse

1 Drainage is of particular importance in such places as the scree garden and the lawn. Tile drains covered with clinker and stones assist the rapid percolation of water. 2 A dry well is easy to construct and helps to dispose of surplus water where there is no ditch available for this purpose.

cinders. The trench is then filled up with soil. Surplus water will run through the coarser base material and finally into the large drainage sump at the lowest part of the garden.

It is possible to use a third system, although this is not quite so satisfactory as the others. This method employs brushwood which is laid in bundles at the bottom of the trench systems. The brushwood is then covered with soil to the surface of the surrounding ground. The unsatisfactory part of this method is that the brushwood gradually rots away and loses its efficiency. It will be necessary to renew the system every few years, and unless the layout is small, this will involve a great deal of time and labour.

Where a new site is taken over, it is a very good idea to examine it thoroughly to see whether or not the soil requires attention to drainage. If it does it will provide an excellent opportunity to

gather all the usual kinds of rubble which can be found on a new or neglected site. Builders often leave behind them a surprising amount of broken bricks, old paint tins, and lumps of concrete.

All this type of waste should be placed in convenient piles in the garden and used in the bottom of drainage trenches. If insufficient is available from the garden, it is quite likely that the local builder will be only too glad to supply some from his building sites.

During the planning of a drainage system for a waterlogged or poorly drained garden, it is a good plan to look ahead and visualise the positions for structures such as sheds, greenhouses or home extensions. All these buildings shed water and it will certainly aggravate the situation if this water is allowed to flow into the garden.

The position of a convenient drainage trench should be marked with a stake so that, later on, excess water from a gutter or down-spout can be directed into this drainage trench. The emptying of a fish pond is also facilitated if the water is directed on to an area of ground which is drained in this way, of if an outlet pipe is built into one of these drainage trenches.

**Draw hoe**—see Hoes

## Drawn

A term used by gardeners to describe a plant of weak, elongated growth, usually due to over-crowding or poor light. Fast-growing bedding plants pricked out too thickly in boxes are liable to develop in this way, antirrhinums, stocks, nemesia, for instance. Unless seed is sown thinly in pots, boxes or in the open ground the same trouble may occur with many plants. To overcome this tendency with plants in a greenhouse, seedlings and young pot-grown plants are often placed on shelves near the glass where the light is good. Nevertheless it may be necessary to shade some such plants from the hottest midday sun in the early stages.

## Dried blood—see Blood

## Drill

This is a shallow furrow made in the soil usually in a straight line, in which seeds are sown. There are various ways in which this may be done. The usual way is to push into the soil a stick to which is attached a length of cord or string. This is drawn taut just above the soil to another stick pushed in the ground at the required distance. Then a hoe, or sometimes the edge of a rake, is drawn parallel to the length of line making a furrow of the required depth.

It is important that the depth of the drill is uniform throughout its length and that the depth is correct for the seeds which are being sown. Obviously such large seeds as those of peas and

1 An example of drawn Busy Lizzie.

beans will require a deeper drill than the small seeds of flowering annuals, such as mignonette, polyanthus or clarkia. Where seed is being sown in a frame or small flower bed a cane is often used to mark a straight line in the soil by pressing it lightly on the surface. A furrow may then be carefully drawn along the impression with a dibber.

When the seeds have been sown they are covered with the soil which was displaced by making the drill. This may be done by drawing a rake diagonally

2 Drills are depressions made for sowing seeds, using a line and draw hoe or dibber.
3 Drimys winteri, Winter's Bark, needs wall protection except in mild districts.

across the drill or by using the edge of a wooden label for small drills. For most seeds a depth of ½ inch is adequate for the drill, but when sowing large seeds, such as broad beans or peas, it may be necessary to make the drill up to 2 inches in depth, according to the type of soil.

## Drimys (drim-iss)

From the Greek *drimus,* acid, a reference to the taste of the bark and the leaves *(Magnoliaceae).* A small genus of evergreen decorative but tender shrubs.

**Species cultivated** *D. aromatica,* 10–15 feet, aromatic leaves, copper-tinted young growths, small white flowers, April and May, Tasmania. *D. colorata,* pepper tree, 10 feet, leathery, yellowish-green leaves, blotched red and purple, small white flowers followed by black berries, New Zealand. *D. winteri,* Winter's bark, 15–20 feet, ivory-white fragrant flowers, May. The long, pale green leaves have a peppery aroma, South America; var. *latifolia,* narrower leaves.

**Cultivation** These shrubs may be grown in the open in the mildest districts, in well-drained soils; elsewhere they need some protection and are not really suitable for outdoor cultivation in colder areas of the United States. Propagation is by cuttings of half ripe shoots inserted in sandy soil in a cold frame or by layers.

## Dropwort—see Filipendula

1 Drosanthemum hispidum grows to 2 feet and comes from Cape Province. 2 Droseras have the power to trap and digest insects. 3 Drosera rotundifolia, common Sundew, is an American native.

**Drosanthemum** (dros-an-the-mum)
From *Drosera* (the sundew) and the Greek *anthemon*, flower *(Aizoaceae)*. Greenhouse succulent shrubs, of the *Mesembryanthemum* group, with erect or prostrate stems, leaves three-angled to cylindrical, covered with sparkling papillae (tiny, pimple-like protuberances) reminiscent of the dew-like glands on the leaves of the sundew *(Drosera)*, hence the derivation of the name. The flowers open in the afternoon in sunshine.

**Species cultivated** *D. albiflorum*, dainty shrub, about 6 inches high, flowers white, Cape Province. *D. bicolor*, erect stiff stems, up to 1 foot high, flowers purple with a golden-yellow centre, Little Karroo. *D. hispidum*, shrub up to 2 feet high, leaves thick and fleshy, flowers deep purple, very free-flowering and handsome, South West Africa.

**Cultivation** Drosanthemums should be provided with a very porous soil, consisting of a fairly light potting mixture to which has been added a fifth part of coarse sand, grit, broken brick and granulated charcoal. They are easy to grow; plants should be out of doors during the summer and in a frost-free greenhouse in the winter. Propagation is by seeds or cuttings; seeds are small and should not be covered. Moisture and warmth soon brings seedlings along and they will flower the first year. Cuttings

soon strike in an equal mixture of peat and sharp sand; spray them occasionally.

**Drosera** (dros-er-a)
From the Greek *droseros*, dewy, a reference to the dew-like glands on the leaves *(Droseraceae)*. Hardy and greenhouse annual and perennial insectivorous plants, found widely, several in North America. Leaves bear sensitive gland-like hairs, reddish in colour, which discharge from their tips a sticky fluid on which small insects and other creatures are entrapped. These hairs also curve inwards when an insect comes into contact with them (see also Insectivorous Plants)..

**Species cultivated** *D. binata*, 4 inches, large white flowers, June to September, Australia. *D. capensis*, about 6 inches, purple, June and July, South Africa. *D. longifolia*, 3 inches, white, July, Europe, including Britain. *D. rotundifolia*, sundew, annual, 4 inches, white, July and August, Europe, North America.

**Cultivation** Use a mixture consisting of living sphagnum moss, peat, charcoal and sharp sand. Stand the pots in saucers of water in a sunny greenhouse. Water freely except in winter. Propagation is by seeds sown at any time on the surface of living sphagnum moss and peat in well-drained pots in a propagating frame, with a temperature of 55–65°F

1 The fruit of the Sloe is a drupe, in which the seed is protected by a hard wall or stone as well as by flesh. 2 Dryandra formosa, an Australian shrub growing to 10 feet in a cool greenhouse.

(13–18°C). Root cuttings are the best means of increasing *D. binata*. Pieces about 1 inch long are embedded in pans of moss and peat in a closed frame with a temperature of about 70°F (21°C) in the spring.

## Drought

A term loosely used to describe a period which is comparatively rainless. Often a drought is any period of fourteen days or more without measureable rainfall. During such weather many plants flag and make little growth unless some means of irrigation is available. As plants obtain nourishment from the soil in the form of solutions, it is evident that adequate water is of the utmost importance. A good gardener can help to conserve moisture in the soil by deep digging, which encourages plants to root deeply, and by incorporating plenty of garden compost, peat, or manure. An adequate water supply, particularly for commercial crops, is however the answer to the drought problem. It has been shown that in a normal summer in southern England, the application of 2 inches of water by overhead irrigation will double the carrot crop yield and the same can be said of many other crops. Inadequate amounts of water applied spasmodically can cause trouble in that plants may be encouraged to form surface roots which are liable to be damaged if the soil dries out. A fine spray of water applied over for an extended period is far more beneficial than a flood of water given during a short period. Watering is one of the most important operations, yet in some establishments it is left to the least experienced, sometimes with disastrous results (see also Irrigation and Watering).

## Drupe

A drupe is a fruit with a hard kernel (a 'stone') with a fleshy surround called the pericarp. The term is occasionally used by fruit growers when referring to 'stone fruits' such as the plum and cherry. The individual sections of blackberry, loganberry and raspberry fruits are also drupes.

## Dryandra (dri-and-ra)

Commemorating Jonas Dryander, eighteenth century Swedish botanist *(Proteaceae)*. About 50 species of evergreen shrubs of south western Australian origin, closely related to *Banksia,* with striking cone-like heads of flowers; at least one species is grown in the open in California *(D. formosa).*

**Species cultivated** *D. floribunda,* hollyleaf dryandra, 6–12 feet, blue-green,

attractive, holly-like leaves, creamy-white flowers up to 2 inches across, May. *D. formosa,* the species most commonly encountered, 8–10 feet, rich orange, fragrant flowers surrounded by light orange bracts, freely borne all along the branches, March–May. *D. nobilis,* 6–7 feet, large yellow flowers, May.

**Cultivation** In the cool greenhouse these handsome plants require a light, well-drained soil. The minimum winter temperature should be about 40°F (4°C). A mixture of equal parts rough fibrous loam, peat and coarse sand is suitable. Water freely during the summer months; sparingly during the winter. Propagate by seed or by cuttings, which are not easy to root, taken in August, made from firm side-shoots inserted in sandy soil in a shaded frame with a little bottom heat.

## Dryas (dri-as)

From the Greek *dryas,* a dryad or wood nymph or goddess, or from the Greek *drus,* an oak, since the leaves are somewhat reminiscent of oak leaves *(Rosaceae).* Three species of hardy, evergreen creeping plants from the mountainous regions of the Northern Hemisphere. They are admirable plants for a sunny rock garden or a gravelly bank, forming a mat of attractive foliage throughout the year, with pleasing flowers, like small single roses, in May and June.

**Species cultivated** *D. drummondii,* 3 inches, yellow, bell-shaped flowers, June, North America. *D. octopetala,* mountain avens, 3 inches, white, May and June, northern Europe, Britain, North America. *D.* × *suendermannii (D. drummondii × D. octopetala)* 3–4 inches, white, flowers, yellow in the bud stage, June, hybrid.

**Cultivation** These little plants thrive in a sunny position in a peaty mixture. *D. octopetala* is found mainly in limestone mountainous areas. Nurserymen supply pot-grown plants which may be planted at any time during favourable weather. Propagation is by seed sown in pans of sandy peat and placed in a cold frame in April or May. Cover the seed very lightly. Transplant the seedlings carefully as the roots are easily damaged. Seedlings may flower in the second year. Cuttings about 2 inches long may also be rooted in sandy soil in a cold frame in August or plants may be increased by division of self-rooted branchlets

## Drying Flowers—see Everlasting Flowers

1 Dryandra nobilis, a shrub up to 7 feet comes from west Australia. Grown in a cool greenhouse, it flowers in May. The Dryandras are closely related to the Banksias. 2 Dryas octopetala, the Mountain Avens, a trailing, mat-forming evergreen for the rock garden. It is frequently found in the wild, on limestone rocks in the Northern Hemisphere including Europe, Asia, North America.

1 Dryopteris abbreviata in a rock crevice. 2 Dryopteris cristata, native to North America, Asia, Europe. Requires boggy conditions and a peaty soil. 3 Dryopteris borrei crispa graces a path. There are many other species, some hardy, others suitable for the greenhouse.

## Dryopteris (dri-op-ter-is)

From the Greek *dryas*, a wood nymph, *pteris*, a fern, or the Greek *drus*, an oak, meaning oak fern *(Polypodiaceae).* A large genus of decorative, easily grown, hardy and greenhouse ferns, widely distributed over much of the world. They have handsome fronds, varying greatly in size from species to species, some a mere few inches long, others (not described here) 6 feet or more long.

**Species cultivated: Hardy** *D. aemula,* hayscented buckler fern, 1–1½ feet, Britain. *D. cristata,* 1–1½ feet, Europe, North America. *D. filix-mas,* male fern, 2–3 feet, Europe and North America. There are many different forms. *D. fragrans,* 6–9 inches, Arctic North America, Japan. *D. goldieana,* 1 foot, eastern U.S.A. *D. linnaeane,* oak fern, 9 inches, Britain and Northern Hemisphere. *D. marginalis,* 1½–2 feet, eastern U.S.A. *D. oreopteris,* mountain buckler fern, 1½–2 feet, North America, Europe. *D. phegopteris* (syn. *Thelypteris phegopteris),* beech fern, 6–9 inches, found in Northern Hemisphere. *D. thelypteris,* 1–2 feet, Britain, Europe, North America, Asia.

**Greenhouse** *D. decomposita,* 1–2 feet, Australia. *D. effusa,* 4 feet, tropical America. *D. otaria,* 1 foot, Ceylon, Phillippines. *D. sieboldii,* 9–12 inches, Japan.

**Cultivation** The hardy species need a shady position with a light, leafy, moist soil. Topdress annually with leafmould. Do not remove dead fronds until April and protect crowns with bracken in severe weather. Plant in April or early May. The greenhouse species should be potted or planted in March or April and given a shady position. The compost should consist of equal parts of loam, leafmould, peat and sharp sand. The winter temperature should be 40–50°F (4–10°C), rising in summer to 65°F (18°C).

Water freely during the growing season, moderately during winter. Propagation of hardy species is by division in April or by spores sown in pans on the surface of sandy soil and placed in a shady cold frame. Greenhouse species may be propagated by division in spring or by spores sown at any time in a similar manner but in a propagating frame with a temperature of about 80°F (27°C).

## Dry rot

In many cases of plant disease where crop products such as fruits, tubers, corms, rhizomes etc are attacked by a parasite the tissues are affected by a discoloration and a brown rot. This rot, however, can be of various kinds and is not always the wet or slimy type which many people associate with rotting tissue. Often the inner tissues develop a brown discoloration and begin to dry up and shrivel. A typical case is dry rot of potatoes due to infection by the fungus *Fusarium caeruleum* which affects the seed tubers. Large areas on the skin sink and shrivel and the inner flesh turns brown and dries up. Gladiolus corms can

1 A section of a dry wall showing the slope of the stones and plants in the crevices. 2 Dwarf Genistas. 3 Encrusted Saxifrages in a dry wall. These are among the many plants which do well in a dry wall in a sunny position.

develop a dry rot due to the fungus *Sclerotinia gladioli,* in which the corms develop black spots or even large black blotches which soon sink and the whole corm shrinks and becomes 'mummified'. Infected corms should be destroyed.

## Dry set

This term is rather specialised in that it applies to an affliction of tomato fruits which is one of the type called non-parasitic (see Disease). The effect is that after the flower petals fall the young fruit fails to swell and remains no larger than the head of a match. This is one of the non-parasitic disorders and is caused by the atmosphere being too hot and dry when pollination of the flowers is taking place. The best way of avoiding losses from dry set is to syringe the tops of plants daily while they have flowers.

## Dry walling

A wall built of pieces of stone without using mortar is known as a dry wall. Such a wall is both useful and decorative in a garden when suitable plants are established between the stones and along the top. Usually these walls are not very high; the very nature of their construction prevents them being stable if made more than 4 feet high. Because of this they are usually found as divisions or terrace walls in gardens. They also have an important part to play as edging or flanking walls along pathways and drives. One of the problems associated with undulating or steep gardens is the retention of soil. Where small banks have to be dealt with, a low dry wall is an ideal method to adopt. Larger bulks of soil require a more substantial wall construction. For walls of this kind the term retaining wall is more appropriate, for plants must have moisture which they get from the soil in a 'dry wall'.

Various types of stone may be used—sandstone, limestone or even granite—but do not make the mistake of using what is known as waterworn Westmor-

land limestone in a natural sandstone district. It will look completely out of character. If the stones are about the same thickness—not less than 3 inches—this will make the construction less complicated. However, one of the most popular materials is the broken type paving slabs, approximately 2 inches thick. This is particularly attractive if the rough or broken face is kept to the outside of the wall as it is built up. A ton of this material will cover approximately 9 square yards. Small coloured slabs may be purchased with a split or rough face. These make up into most attractive walls. They are about 9 inches wide and various lengths can be obtained, the usual sizes being, 9, 12, and 18 inches. Colours include grey, green, stone, brick red, grey-green and a mixture of any or all of these will produce a pleasant, restful effect. Prices will vary considerably according to the quantity ordered, carriage distance and quality and colour of the walling stone. Walls may also be constructed of peat blocks and these are particularly useful for growing plants requiring acid conditions.

1 A low retaining dry wall for a border on which Phlox subulata and Dianthus flourish. 2 The Sempervivums or House-leeks flourish in the crevices of dry walls, given a sunny position. They thrive in very little soil.

**Construction** A firm, solid base is essential for the construction of a successful dry wall. The site should be marked out and a trench taken out slightly wider than the stones to be used. The trench should be about 6 inches deep and filled with small rubble to within 1 inch of the surface. This rubble must be thoroughly consolidated by ramming. The final inch of trench should be filled either with ashes or soil to provide a level surface for the first course of stones.

The construction of the wall starts with the laying of the first course on the prepared site. Where random sizes of stones are used, the largest pieces should be picked out and used for this first layer or course, particularly at the ends. A wide base ensures a firm wall. Although a dry wall should look as natural as possible, it is essential to take some

care with levels. Use a spirit level frequently to check this, otherwise an unstable, irregular wall will be produced.

Subsequent courses should be built up so that the pieces are bonded together. This is accomplished by making sure that stones are placed over the joints between stones in the previous row. The same method is used during the construction of a brick wall. Although the pieces of stone can be laid on top of each other, it is far better to add a $\frac{1}{2}$ inch deep layer of soil between the courses. This will enable suitable plants to be established in the crevices or joints.

The soil should be prepared carefully and must contain a high proportion of humus material. This will prevent it from drying out too quickly, and at the same time it will encourage the development of a vigorous root system. A suitable mixture can be made up of 3 parts of fibrous medium heavy loam, 1 part of horticultural peat or composted vegetable waste, plus some coarse, gritty sand. Mix thoroughly together and make sure it is well moistened before it is used. Any gaps behind the

1 In this dry wall, Dianthus and Sedums provide colour and interest, both with their flowers and their foliage. 2 In sloping gardens, such as this one, dry walls retaining different levels can provide much interest.

wall, between it and the bank should be filled with soil, which should be well consolidated to avoid air pockets. Although low walls may be built vertically, to provide extra strength and particularly stability, it is a good plan to construct those walls which are several feet high with a slight inward slope or 'batter' to the soil behind. The slope should be about 15–20° where a bank of soil is retained. Make sure that free access is allowed to this soil for the plants' roots.

One of the problems in building a dry wall is to keep the whole length of wall sloping at the same desired angle. This can be achieved by driving in a stake at each end—or with a long wall other intermediate stakes may be used—at the required angle. Attach a line or cord between the stakes which can be moved upwards as the building progresses. With a vertical wall upright stakes will help to keep the wall face in a straight line. For the top layer of stones choose large flat pieces which will adequately cover the layer beneath. This will conduct rain water into the soil rather than immediately behind the lower stones, when there would be a tendency to wash the soil away from behind the wall. It is, in

any case, a wise precaution to leave small 'weep holes' at the foot of the wall to allow surplus water to escape easily. If this is not done water may build up behind the wall in very wet weather and seriously weaken it, possibly bringing it down. It is important to make sure that there are no roots of perennial weeds in the soil behind the walling, or endless trouble may ensue. When laying, place the stones sloping slightly inwards and downwards. This will help to keep the soil between them moist.

**Planting** A dry wall is greatly enhanced by the naturalising or planting of suitable plants. Although these can be inserted carefully after the wall has been constructed, it is much better to plant as each course is built up. As the next course is added, the weight of the stones will keep the plants in position. This method of planting will also ensure that the roots are carefully spread out and in contact with the soil all around. Plants must be thoroughly soaked before they are planted.

If planting cannot be done while the wall is being built it is possible to do it afterwards. Soil between the stones should be scraped out to make a planting hole, and when planting pot-grown rock plants they should be well watered and

the ball of soil should be gently squeezed into an oblong shape before planting, to enable it to be inserted between the courses. If a plant dies in the wall, as is bound to happen from time to time, scrape out the remains and the old soil around the roots, before filling the cavity with fresh loamy soil in which the new plant is made firm.

**Dry-wall plants** A great variety of rock plants may be grown in or on top of a dry wall, the trailing or drooping kinds being particularly effective when growing down the face of the wall. Plants that enjoy a sunny position include aethionemas, *Alchemilla alpina*, alyssums, androsaces, *Anthemis cupaniana*, *Arabis albida flore pleno*, *Arenaria ledebouriana*, armerias, *Artemisia stelleriana*, aubrietas, *Calamintha alpina*, *Campanula kemmulariae*, C. *portenschlagiana*, cheiranthus (wallflowers), *Corydalis lutea*, *Cotyledon oppositifolia*, *Cymbalaria muralis*, *Dianthus caesius*, and others, *Dryas octopetala*, erinus, erodiums (stork's bills), *Euphorbia myrsinites*, *Genista lydia*, *Gypsophila dubia*, haberleas, *Hypericum polyphyllum*, *Iberis sempervirens* 'Snowflake', lewisias, linums, *Phlox subulata*, *Polygonum vaccinifolium*, *Primula marginata* 'Prichards' Variety' *Saponaria ocymoides, Saxi-*

*fraga aizoon,* sedums, sempervivums, *Zauschneria californica* (the Californian fuschia). This last-named plant is not suitable for severe regions and requires a hot, dry place.

On the top of the dry wall plant helianthemums (sun roses), cistus (rock roses), some of the more compact hardy geranium species (cranesbills), *Gypsophila repens, Lithospermum* 'Grace Ward', sempervivums (houseleeks), thymus in variety, sedums, and *Zauschneria californica.* Where the wall is shady, plant *Arenaria balearica* which will make a mossy green carpet studded with tiny white flowers during the summer, *Ramonda myconi* with large lilac-coloured flowers and, among other ferns, the neat little hardy *Polypodium vulgare,* or common polypod.

---

**Ducksfoot**—see Podophyllum peltatum

---

**Dumb Cane**—see Dieffenbachia

---

**Duranta** (du-ran-ta)
Commemorating Castor Durantes, sixteenth century Italian botanist and physician *(Verbenaceae).* A small genus of evergreen trees and shrubs from tropical America, with small flowers in long spikes.
**Species cultivated** *D. lorentzii,* shrub to 10 feet, flowers white, Argentine. *D. plumieri,* up to 15 feet, lilac-blue, August, West Indies. *D. repens,* 15 feet, lavender flowers and golden, waxy berries borne, at the same time, Mexico.
**Cultivation** Durantas require warm greenhouse conditions and should be grown in a mixture consisting of equal parts of peat and loam. Propagation is by cuttings taken in early spring and rooted with bottom heat.

---

### Dusting
This is the process of applying as dry dust, the substances known as fungicides and insecticides to plants so as to cover them with a protective film as a guard against attack by parasitic fungi or insects. The chemicals used for dusting are in a very fine state of division so as to give a good cover to the plants. In this country spraying is more favoured than dusting despite the added trouble of mixing with water because dusting can only be done when there is no wind and the foliage ought to be slightly damp to get a good adhesion to the leaves. Despite this a good deal depends on local conditions as to whether dusting will be more suitable for a crop. Dusting appliances vary from small handworked pump or bellows types up to larger knapsack dusters and on to power driven large rotary fan machines. For very large areas even small aeroplanes are employed in dusting operations on field crops and trees.

---

**Dusty Miller**—see Primula auricula, Centaurea gymnocarpa and Senecio cineraria

---

**Dutch hoe**—see Hoes

---

**Dutch Honeysuckle**—see Lonicera periclymenum

---

**Dutch Iris**—see Iris

---

### Dutch light
A type of frame widely used in some horticultural areas. Each 'light' consists of a wooden frame of deal or cedar containing one sheet of glass measuring 56 inches by 28¾ inches. The glass used for this purpose is usually 21 oz horticultural glass. The great advantage of these lights is that they are easily moved by one person. A frame can be quickly erected by using straw bales for walls with the lights placed across the top. Care must be taken in windy weather that lights on frames are made secure in some way. Such lights are also used to construct the Dutch type of greenhouse, which can be erected on rails so that the whole structure can be pushed along to cover successive crops. This operation must be done with care for if the ground is uneven the glass is easily broken. When not in use Dutch lights can be neatly stacked. In a private garden these

1 Duranta plumieri, is a shrub for the warm house. It comes from Mexico and the West Indies and flowers in August. 2 Dutch light cold frames being prepared for planting. The 'lights' comprise a single pane of glass.

lights are most useful for frames or they can be made into a small greenhouse.

**Dutchman's Breeches**—see Dicentra cucullaria

**Dutchman's Pipe**—see Aristolochia macrophylla

## Dwarf

Many plants in cultivation are naturally smaller than the original species. The dwarf character is hereditary and such plants have been propagated because they are particularly attractive or have some economic value. Some fruit tree stocks, selected over the years at the East Malling Research Station, in Kent, and appropriately known as Malling stocks, have the quality of restricting the size of varieties worked on them. When a variety is budded or grafted on to a dwarf or semi-dwarf stock, a normally vigorous apple such as 'Golden Delicious', will be restricted in growth to a height of 10 feet or so. This is most useful in gardens where space is limited. These stocks are also used for grafting cordon and espalier training trees. Other plants are dwarfed artificially by having their roots restricted and pruned from time to time, as with Japanese specimen pines, wisteria, and the like, which may be only a foot or two in height, but many years of age (see Bonsai). Plant breeders also play their part in raising by careful selection dwarf varieties, for instance, dwarf delphiniums and dwarf sweet peas, which are popular because they require the minimum of support.

**Dwarf Chestnut**—see Castanea pumila

**Dwarf Conifers**—see Conifers

**Dwarf Huckleberry**—see Gaylussacia dumosa

**Dwarfed trees**—see Bonsai

## Dyckia (dyke-e-a)

Named in honour of Prince Salm-Reifferscheidt-Dyck, who had a fine collection of succulent plants and produced an illustrated work on the subject (Bromeliaceae).

A large genus of South American stemless perennials which form an ornamental rosette of thick, spiny leaves and spikes of flowers, usually yellow in colour.

**Species cultivated** *D. altissima*, 2–3 feet, with branching panicles of bright yellow flowers in August, Brazil. *D. frigida*, 1–2 feet, orange-yellow flowers in branching spikes in early spring, Brazil.

**Cultivation** Dyckias require a minimum winter temperature of 55°F (13°C) and little water during the winter months. They may be stood in the open from June to September. Pot in a mixture consisting of 2 parts of loam, 1 part of

Dwarf plants are increasing in popularity. 1 A dwarf hybrid broom, Cytisus. 2 Dwarf hybrid Echiums. 3 Thuja orientalis minima aurea, a dwarf conifer.

leaf soil and a little sharp sand. Propagate by offsets or suckers taken at any time and placed in small pots in a warm greenhouse.

**Dyer's Greenweed**—see Genista tinctoria

## Earthing up

This is an old gardening term referring to the process of banking up soil around plants as potatoes and sometimes celery. Potato plants are usually earthed up as they develop, but with celery this should not be done until the heads are fully developed, as the plants make little or no growth after earthing up. The work is usually done with the aid of a hoe, although in large vegetable gardens a mechanical cultivator fitted with the necessary attachment will make a neat and quick job with long rows of potatoes and the like. A garden fork with its tines bent at right-angles, is useful for earthing up and for other forms of cultivation. In windy gardens it is sometimes necessary to earth up around the stems of broccoli, the taller varieties of kale and cauliflowers, to keep them firm in the ground.

**1** Earthing up potatoes is an operation carried out to ensure that the tubers are not made green by exposure to light. **2** When earthing up, you should make the sides as upright as possible so that the spores of Potato Blight will not contaminate the tubers. **3** The Earthworm, Lumbricus terrestris. **4** Earthworm casts on the surface of a lawn in autumn.

With celery and leeks the earthing up is done to blanch the stems and a spade is often used to pile up the soil to the required height and to firm the wall of soil, thus made, using the back of the spade to smooth the soil. Care must be taken not to get soil between the stems and into the heart of the celery. When growing for show purposes gardeners often wrap brown paper around the celery stems before earthing up. Where leeks are grown for exhibition planks

of wood are placed on each side of the row, about 5 inches away from the plants, and the trough made by the planks is gradually filled with sifted soil as the leeks develop (see also Celery, Leeks and Potatoes).

**Earthnut**—see Arachis hypogaea

## Earthworms

These are generally considered to be beneficial since their activities are claimed to improve the soil in various ways. Aeration is said to be improved by their burrowing and water penetration into the soil made easier. They bring up subsoil and mix it with surface layers and break down decaying material so that it becomes available more quickly to growing plants.

Of the four common species that are distributed widely, *Eisenia, Allolobo-*

Earwigs can damage many plants. 1 Hay or straw put into an inverted flower pot will trap these insects. The traps should be emptied daily. 2 The female Common Earwig greatly enlarged.

*phora, Octolasium* and *Lumbricus,* the two most likely to annoy the gardener are *Allolobophora nocturna* and *Allolobophora longa.* These are the species which make wormcasts, which are a nuisance on sports grounds and unsightly on the lawn.

Possible control measures include the use of mowrah meal, at the rate of 6–8 oz per square yard and well watered in; derris applied according to makers' instructions; potassium permanganate at ½ oz per gallon of water per square yard, or copper sulphate, 1 lb dissolved in 10 gallons of water per 50 square yards. Only potassium permanganate is safe where there is a chance of seepage into fishponds or streams and all worms

which come to the surface must be swept up at once, in all cases, because of possible danger to domestic pets and wild life. Proprietary worm-killers are available, which should be used according to the manufacturer's instructions.

## Earwigs

These interesting little creatures, *Forficula auricularia,* are among the few insects which tend their young. Eggs are laid in an underground nest and the mother earwig stands over them until they hatch. She then keeps her family around her until they are well able to fend for themselves.

There has been much speculation

about the name 'earwig'. Some people consider it is a corruption of 'earwing', referring to the shape of the delicately folded flight wings; others point out that the forceps on the end of the body, particularly the curved ones of the males, resemble ear-piercing instruments. As for the theory that they crawl into the human ear, this may well have happened occasionally in more primitive times to people sleeping rough in straw, etc., on the ground. Even now, there are occasional plagues when earwigs enter houses in vast numbers and cause alarm and annoyance by dropping out of folds in the curtains, from the lids of food containers, from door jambs and other unlikely places.

They feed at night and are scavengers, feeding on almost anything, but best known for the damage they do—mostly clean-cut holes—to the leaves and flower-petals of plants such as chrysanthemum, dahlia and clematis etc. By day, they like to find a cosy shelter that fits them like a glove, such as a tubular petal or the 'tail' of a nasturtium flower. This makes it easy to trap them in rolls of corrugated cardboard, or flower pots filled with hay and placed upside down on bamboo canes in the vicinity of such plants as dahlias.

They are susceptible to a fairly wide range of insecticides. Check with your state experiment station.

**Easter Cactus**—see Schlumbergera

**Easter Lily**—see Lilium longiflorum

**Ebony Wood**—see Bauhinia variegata

## Ecballium (ek-bal-e-um)

From the Greek *ekballein,* to cast out, referring to the violent discharge of the seeds from the ripe fruits *(Cucurbitaceae).* Squirting cucumber. There is but one species of this genus, the Mediterranean *E. elaterium,* an interesting and curious plant for the front of a border. It is a trailing plant with greenish-white flowers, insignificant but freely borne in June. The fruits are small, oblong, green and prickly. They become swollen when ripe and eject their small black seeds at the slightest touch, to a distance of many feet, hence both the generic and common names.

**Cultivation** Sow the seeds in April in gentle heat and after hardening off the seedlings plant them out towards the end of May.

## Eccremocarpus (ek-re-mo-kar-pus)

From the Greek *ekkremes,* pendant, and *karpos,* fruit, describing the pendulous seed vessels *(Bignoniaceae).* An attractive evergreen half-hardy annual climbing plant. There are very few species and of these one only is in cultivation. This is *E. scaber,* the Chilean glory flower. It grows up to 15–20 feet, clinging to suitable supports by means of tendrils at the ends of the leaves. The flowers, borne in clusters from late spring to autumn, are tubular in shape, scarlet or orange-red and yellow in colour. There is a golden-flowered variety, *aureus,* and an orange-red variety, *ruber.*

**Cultivation** *E. scaber* is very easily raised from seed sown in pots of sandy soil in March to May and germinated in a temperature of about 60°F (16°C). Seed will even germinate out of doors in milder gardens if sown in April or May. Plant out in June in a light, rich soil against any appropriate style walls, with trellis, wires, etc., for support. The growths are weak, so that they will do no harm if the plant is allowed to scramble over shrubs. In mild winters the roots are hardy, but in exposed gardens should be covered with old ashes or matting in severe weather. In favoured gardens in the mild areas and extreme south, the plant appears to be quite hardy except, perhaps, in very severe winters. In most places, however, it is readily grown treated as an annual. Seed is set very freely in long capsules which turn dark brown as they ripen. Self-sown seedlings occasionally appear in the spring, particularly where they have germinated between paving stones and thus the seed has had some protection during the winter.

1 **Ecballium elaterium**, the Squirting Cucumber, is an annual and a native of the Mediterranean. 2 **Eccremocarpus scaber**, the Chilean Glory Flower, is a climbing plant which will grow outside, treated as an annual in the North.

## Echeveria (ek-ev-eer-e-a)

Commemorating Atanasio Echeverria, Mexican botanical artist (*Crassulaceae*). Greenhouse and half-hardy, low-growing succulent plants, formerly included in *Cotyledon*; mostly of upright growth with large fleshy leaves in rosettes, many well coloured and waxy in appearance.

**Species cultivated** *E. agavoides*, very thick fleshy leaves, long and pointed, flowers red and carmine, central Mexico. *E. bella*, forms clumps, flowers orange-yellow, Mexico. *E. gibbiflora*, stems strong, erect, leaves broad and shiny, flowers light red with yellow centre, Mexico; vars. *caruncula*, with raised rough parts to the centre of leaf; *metallica*, leaves bronze edged with red. *E. harmsii* (syns. *E. elegans, Oliveranthus elegans*), much branched shrubby plant, 1–1½ feet tall, each branch ending in a rosette of leaves, large flowers, 1 inch long, red, tipped yellow, a most handsome species, Mexico.

**Cultivation** The medium should be made from a fairly light potting mixture, with a sixth part added of grit, sand and broken brick. Pot the plants in March and place them in a sunny position. Old plants get very leggy and lose their lower leaves. The tops can then be cut off and rooted and the old stem will send out fresh shoots. Water from April to September, but give none in winter unless the plants are in a warm room when they should be watered once a month. They may be planted out of doors in early June and removed to the greenhouse in September. Some, particularly *E. gibbiflora metallica*, are used in summer bedding schemes as edging plants. Propagation is by seed sown in rather light seed mixture at a temperature of 70°F (21°C), in early spring. Shade the seedlings from strong sunshine, prick them out when large enough. Plants are also readily increased from cuttings, including leaves. It is also possible to flower young shoots. Flower scapes cut off and dried can make roots.

## Echinacea (ek-in-ay-se-a)

From the Greek *echinos*, hedgehog, referring to the whorl of prickly, pointed bracts close beneath the flower head (*Compositae*). A genus of two North American species of hardy herbaceous perennial plants.

**Species cultivated** *E. angustifolia* (syn. *Rudbeckia angustifolia*), 2–3 feet, purplish-red, summer. *E. purpurea* (syn. *Rudbeckia purpurea*), purple coneflower, 3–4 feet, purplish-red, August. The crimson cultivar 'The King', 6 feet tall, is outstanding, with flowers 5 inches across

1 Echeveria elegans makes an attractive pot plant for the home. 2 Echeveria gibbiflora, an attractive succulent plant. 3 Echinacea purpurea, the Purple Coneflower, a fine border plant.

2 Three Mexican cacti: 1 Echinocactus grusonii rarely flowers in the cold. 2 Echinocereus reichenbachii, a Hedgehog Cactus from Texas and Mexico. 3 Echinocereus blanckii, will withstand cold if kept dry.

from August to October. 'Robert Bloom', is a newer cultivar, 3 feet tall, with large, carmine-purple flowers in July and August. Other named cultivars appear from time to time in nurserymen's lists.
**Cultivation** Plant in autumn or spring in a deep, rich, light loamy soil and in a sunny position. Propagation is by division in spring; by root cuttings in February, or by seed sown in boxes of light soil in March in a temperature of about 55°F (13°C), or sown out of doors in a sunny position in April.

## Echinocactus (ek-i-no-kak-tus)
From the Greek *echinos,* a hedgehog, and *Cactus,* referring to the numerous spines *(Cactaceae).* Greenhouse cactus plants. Many new genera have been formed from this genus, including: *Astrophytum, Epithelantha, Ferocactus, Gymnocalycium, Hamatacactus, Malacocarpus, Notocactus,* and *Parodia,* all of which are described in separate articles within this Encyclopedia. Most species are large growing and are not easy to flower in Britain owing to the lack of strong sunshine.
**Species cultivated** *E. ingens,* stem globular becoming columnar when old, greenish-grey, woolly at the top, ribs increasing in number with age, flowers reddish-yellow. *E. grusonii,* golden barrel cactus, mother-in-law's chair, a great favourite, a football-shaped plant with many strong, golden-yellow spines. It is not likely to flower in Britain. *E. visnaga,* large-growing species, flowers glossy yellow. All are from Mexico.
**Cultivation** The medium should consist of a fairly light potting mixture, with a sixth part extra of sharp sand, grit and broken brick in well-drained pots. The plants should be given a position in a sunny greenhouse. Repot every three or four years or when the plant reaches the side of its pot. Water sparingly from March to September; keep quite dry in winter. Temperatures: 65–75°F (18–24°C) in summer and 40°F (4°C) in winter. Give plenty of ventilation in hot weather. As these plants rarely make offsets propagation is from seed sown in a light seed mixture. Just cover the seed lightly, keep moist and shaded in a temperature of 70°F (21°C).

## Echinocereus (ek-i-no-seer-e-us)
From the Greek *echinos,* a hedgehog, and *Cereus,* referring to the very prickly nature of the plants *(Cactaceae).* Greenhouse cacti, first introduced in the late seventeenth century; a large genus with erect and spreading stems and mostly

515

with large and spectacular flowers.

**Species cultivated** *E. berlandieri,* thick sprawling stems with strong spines, flowers large, pink, Mexico. *E. blanckii,* stems sprawling, flowers purple, Mexico and Texas. *E. dubius,* stems yellowish-green, fleshy, flowers pink, south-east Texas. *E. reichenbachii* (syn. *E. caespitosus*), stems stiff, erect, with numerous yellowish spines, flowers pinkish-purple, Mexico, Texas. *E. rigidissimus,* the popular rainbow cactus, stem erect, stout with many ribs closely covered with short spines, which are coloured reddish near the top of plant, flowers pink, Mexico and Arizona. Almost all shades of colour are to be found in this genus.

**Cultivation** A suitable medium is a fairly light potting mixture with a sixth part extra of grit, coarse sand and broken brick. Grow the plants on a sunny shelf in the greenhouse. Pot every two years for adult plants, every year for young seedling plants. Water the plants when the soil dries out from March to September, but give no water in winter. Temperatures should be 65–75°F (18–24°C) in the growing period, 40°F (4°C) in winter. Propagation is by seeds sown in rather light seed mixture in early spring; keep moist and at 70°F (21°C), shaded from direct sunshine. Several species with branching habit can be increased by taking sideshoots as cuttings. Dry them well and stand them on sharp sand to root.

---

### Echinocystis (eki-no-sis-tis)

From the Greek *echinos,* hedgehog, and *kystis,* a bladder, descriptive of the spiny fruits *(Cucurbitaceae).* An American genus of half hardy or tender, annual or perennial, prostrate or climbing herbaceous plants. Some of the climbers are suitable for covering arbours or trellis.

**Species cultivated** *E. fabacea,* wild cucumber, 10 to 30 feet, leaves palmate, flowers whitish, male in racemes, female solitary, followed by rounded, spiny fruits, 2 inches long, half hardy, with a large tuberous root. *E. macrocarpa,* similar to above, with more deeply lobed leaves and larger handsome fruits to 4 inches long, splitting open like a flower to reveal a white interior and large, beautifully mottled seeds. Both are tendril climbers from America.

**Cultivation** These plants will do well in ordinary garden soil in a warm sheltered site. Propagation is by seeds sown under glass in February or March or outdoors.

---

### Echinofossulocactus

(ek-i-no-foss-u-lo-kak-tus)

From the Greek *echinos,* a hedgehog, the Latin *fossula,* a groove, and *Cactus,* referring to the grooved, prickly plants *(Cactaceae).* Greenhouse cacti, sometimes found under the genus *Stenocactus.* An easily recognised genus as the plants are globular and later columnar, with many ribs, up to 35 in some species.

Echinofossulocactus lamellosus, a many-ribbed Mexican cactus, produces red flowers on a short tube.

These ribs are very thin and wavy, thus presenting plenty of skin to the atmosphere but not to the direct rays of the sun. The flowers are all produced at the growing tip of plant.

**Species cultivated** *E. crispatus,* about 25 ribs, with strong spines, purple flowers. *E. hastatus,* 35 wavy ribs, stiff spines, flowers yellowish-white. *E. xiphacanthus,* very strong flattened, sword-like spines, flowers pale mauve. All are from Mexico.

**Cultivation** The medium should be very porous, made from fairly light potting mixture, plus a sixth part of sharp sand, grit and broken brick added. Use a pot just larger than the base of the plant. Repot in March or April, water sparingly at all times and give none in winter. Temperatures should range from 65–80°F (18–27°C) in summer, down to 40°F (4°C) in winter. Plants like plenty of sunshine. Propagation is by seed sown in rather light seed mixture in pans in early spring in a temperature of 70°F (21°C). Shade the seedlings from sun while young. Few plants make offsets.

---

### Echinops (ek-in-ops)

From the Greek *echinos,* a hedgehog, *opsis,* like, referring to the spiky appearance of the flower heads which resemble a rolled-up hedgehog *(Compositae).* Globe thistle. Hardy herbaceous perennial and biennial plants for the border.

**Species cultivated** (All perennial) *E.*

*bannaticus*, 2–3 feet, violet-blue globular heads of flowers, summer, Hungary. *E. humilis*, 3–5 feet, large blue heads, September, Asia; var. *nivalis*, white. The cultivar 'Taplow Blue' has bright blue heads in summer. *E. ritro*, 3–4 feet, steel-blue, summer, southern Europe. *E. sphaerocephalus*, 6 feet, flowers silvery-grey, summer, Europe and western Asia. **Cultivation** Plant in autumn or spring in ordinary soil, in sun or partial shade. Echinops are trouble-free plants for a large border or for a wild garden. The metallic lustre of the flower heads keeps them decorative for a long time when dried. The species *E. ritro* is probably the best for this purpose. Propagation is by root cuttings or division in October or March, or by seed sown in the open in a sunny position in April.

**1 Echinops, a good border plant. 2 The Echinops, or Globe Thistles, natives of Spain, eastwards to Abyssinia. 3 Echinopsis obrepanda, a Bolivian cactus.**

### Echinopsis (ek-in-op-sis)

From the Greek *echinos*, a hedgehog, *opsis*, like; the spiny plants resemble a rolled-up hedgehog *(Cactaceae)*. Hedgehog cactus. Greenhouse cacti, first introduced in the early nineteenth century, among the commonest cactus plants in cultivation. They are globular when young, columnar with age. They have several deep ridges or ribs with areoles and stiff spines; their large, often fragrant flowers open for about 36 hours. **Species cultivated** *E. eyriesii*, to 6 inches tall, 11–18 ribs, flowers white, fragrant, Mexico. *E. leucantha*, 14 ribs, strong

spines, flowers brownish-green outside, inside white, Chile, western Argentina. *E. multiplex*, makes many offsets, pale green body, ribs 13–15, flowers pink, fragrant, southern Brazil. *E. tubiflora*, globular when young, columnar with age up to 18 inches in height, flower a long tube, white to pink, brown on the outside, southern Brazil.

**Cultivation** The medium should be made up from a fairly light potting mixture with a sixth part of coarse sand, grit and broken brick added, in well-drained pots. Give the plants a sunny place in a window or greenhouse. Repot every two or three years. Some species flower better if their offsets are removed. Temperatures: March to September, 65–75°F (18–24°C), September to March, 40–45°F (4–7°C). Propagation is by rooting offsets

1 Echium vulgare, a biennial growing to 3 feet in ordinary soil. 2 Echium x scilloniensis was raised at the gardens of Tresco Abbey. 3 Edgeworthia gardneri, a deciduous shrub from Nepal requiring cold greenhouse protection.

which are usually freely produced; some form roots while still attached to the parent plant. New kinds are raised from seed when offsets are not available; sow in rather light seed mixture, in a temperature of 70°F (21°C); keep the seedlings moist and shaded and prick them off when large enough to handle and the cotyledon has been absorbed.

### Echium (ek-e-um)

From the Greek *echis*, a viper, referring either to the supposed resemblance of the seed to a viper's head or the belief that the plant was efficacious against the adder's bite *(Boraginaceae)*. Viper's bugloss. Hardy and half-hardy annual, biennial and perennial plants mainly from the Mediterranean region and the Canary Islands.

**Species cultivated: Annual and biennial** *E. creticum*, 1–1½ feet, violet, July, annual. *E. plantagineum*, 2–3 feet, rich bluish-purple, summer, annual or biennial. *E. vulgare,* 3–4 feet, purple or blue, summer, biennial, Europe. *E. wildpretii*, 2–3 feet, rose-pink, summer, biennial.

**Perennial** *E. albicans*, 6–18 inches, rose, becoming violet, summer. *E. fastuosum*, 2–4 feet, deep blue, April to August, greenhouse, but hardy in the mild areas. *E.* × *scilloniensis*, 4–6 feet, blue,

May onwards, hybrid originating in the gardens of Tresco Abbey, Isles of Scilly, where other half-hardy species are also grown out of doors.

**Cultivation** Plant out the perennial kinds in ordinary well-drained soil and in a sunny position in May. Seed of the annual kinds is sown in a sunny position in the open in April or August. The perennials are propagated by seed sown out of doors in spring.

### Edelweiss—see Leontopodium alpinum

### Edgeworthia (ej-wer-the-a)

Commemorating E. P. Edgeworth, a botanist, in the service of the East India Company in the nineteenth century *(Thymelaeaceae)*. A small genus of tender, early-flowering shrubs, allied to *Daphne*.

**Species cultivated** *E. gardneri* (E), 4–6 feet, rich yellow flowers, early spring, Sikkim. *E. papyrifera* (syn. *E. chrysantha*) (D), paper bush, Mitsumata, 4–6 feet, rich yellow fragrant flowers with silky hairs, borne in large terminal clusters, early spring, China, grown in Japan for paper making, less tender than *E. gardneri*, hardy in the milder counties.

**Cultivation** Edgeworthias can only be

grown out of doors in the mild and maritime districts. When grown as a cool greenhouse pot plant use a compost consisting of 2 parts of sandy loam and 1 part of turfy peat. Good drainage and ample water during the growing season are all that is required. Propagation is by cuttings taken in the spring, placed in sandy soil in a propagating frame, or under a bell-glass.

## Edging plants

These are low-growing plants used for the front of flower beds, either annuals raised under glass and bedded out in the spring, or sown in the open where they are to flower, or perennials. Although they are seen more often in public parks these days, rather than in private gardens, they can, nevertheless be most colourful. The contrast of colours is a matter of individual taste. Yellow, red and blue are contrasts in all their shades, and the variations formed by the union of any two of these produces a harmonious effect.

A great variety of plants can be used for this purpose. Edging plants raised from seed include candytuft (iberis), convolvulus, such as 'Royal Marine', which carpets the ground, *Dimorphotheca*, 'Glistening White', the cheerful yellow edged white, free-flowering *Limnanthes douglasii, Linaria maroccana*, mignonette, the sky-blue *Nemophila insignis*, 'Tom Thumb' nasturtiums, midget Sweet Williams and Virginian stock. Plants used for bedding out in May include dwarf antirrhinums and dahlias, ageratum, dwarf asters, lobelia, mesembryanthemum, nemesia, dwarf petunias, portulaca, *Phlox drummondii*, tagetes, and verbena. In early spring polyanthus and small primulas, such as the purple 'Wanda' and the cherry-pink 'E. R. Janes' are most attractive and good use should be made of crocuses, scillas, muscari and other miniature bulbous plants. Pansies and violas may be bedded out to give colour throughout the summer months.

For a more permanent edging use can be made of box (buxus), dwarf lavender, and the trailing evergreen *Euonymus radicans*, particularly in its silver and golden variegated forms. A neat form of edging between a lawn and a border is made with paving stones interplanted with various dianthus, thymes, campanulas, aubrietias and saxifrages.

For the formal bedding schemes the following are among the many plants used for edging: alternantheras with various-coloured foliage which can be clipped to keep them dwarf, echeverias with their beautifully coloured rosettes,

1 Violas, used as edging plants, flower over a long period if they are picked regularly. 2 Edging plants, as Alyssum, Lobelia, Candytuft, Dwarf Nasturtiums and French Marigolds play a useful role in summer bedding schemes.

the mat-forming *Cerastium tomentosum,* or snow-in-summer; mesembryanthemums in many brilliant colours, sedums, sempervivums, the creeping *Herniaria glabra,* and *Stellaria graminea aurea.* These and many other bedding plants are still used extensively in formal planting schemes in parks, particularly at British resorts (see Bedding).

## Edging tools

A lawn is only as neat as its edges so the purchase of an efficient edging tool is an important investment. The choice of tool must depend on the amount of lawn which has to be dealt with. For the more extensive ones, a mechanically propelled type will be necessary to reduce time and labour. This does not mean to say that the hand-operated types do not save time—they do, for there are several ingenious designs available.

One interesting tool has a long arm, at one end of which is a trigger-like handle that operates the cutting blades at the other end. These can be rotated so that the vertical and horizontal edges of the lawn can be dealt with. The complete unit is mounted on wheels so that it is pushed along as work proceeds. In operation this design is comfortable to use, but can be a little hard on the hand

muscles if used continuously.

Another rapid edge cutter has star-like blades which are rotated by rubber wheels as it is pushed along. A similar tool has cutters operated by a ribbed metal roller. Both designs are very easy to operate. The simplest edger consists of a pair of long handled shears. Several designs are available with such refinements as moulded rubber grips, aluminium shafts or stainless steel, hollow ground blades. Models are available which can turn vertically or horizontally.

For complete ease of edge trimming there are some motorised tools available which are astoundingly rapid in their work. One is powered by a 2-cycle engine and the complete machine weighs only about 25 lb. It is claimed that about eight miles of edges can be cut on one quart of fuel.

Battery power is playing an important part in mechanised garden tools. The battery-operated lawn edger is specially designed for the smaller areas. The capacity of the small battery is quite

surprising as it is capable of allowing the trimmer to cut about two miles of lawn edge. The method of cutting is similar to that of the motor-powered model. The weight is a little over 20 lb. and the plug-in battery charger makes the recharging of the battery a very simple matter. One distinct advantage of this particular tool is that it is very quiet in operation. The edging iron or verge-cutter is a useful tool with a straight handle about 3 feet in length, to which is fitted a half-moon-shaped steel blade. It is used for trimming the edges of lawns and also sometimes for making the vertical cuts when lifting turf with a turfing iron.

## Edraianthus (ed-ri-an-thus)

From the Greek *edraios,* stemless, *anthos,* flower *(Campanulaceae).* Low-growing tufted perennial plants from the Mediterranean region, closely related to *Wahlenbergia,* suitable for the rock garden.
**Species cultivated** *E. caudatus* (syn. *E. dalmaticus*), 3 inches, semi-prostrate, purple, funnel-shaped flowers, July. *E. dinaricus* (syn. *Wahlenbergia dinarica*), 3 inches, violet, June. *E. graminifolius,* 3 inches, purple, variable, bell-shaped, summer. *E. pumilio* (syn. *Wahlenbergia pumilio*), 2 inches, violet, large, funnel-

1 An edging-iron is used once a year with a line to straighten the edges of lawns. 2 Edging shears in use. 3 Edraianthus Serpyllifolius Major, a hardy prostrate plant for the rock garden.

shaped, spring, a good plant for the scree. *E. serpyllifolius* (syn. *Wahlenbergia serpyllifolia*), prostrate, purple-violet, May and June. *E. tenuifolius*, 4 inches, violet-blue, summer.

**Cultivation** These dwarf plants need a gritty, well-drained soil and a sunny position. They require ample water in the spring and early summer, but dislike winter wet. Propagation is by seed sown in March, or by cuttings made of the soft tufts in late May and rooted in a sandy compost in a propagating frame.

**Edwardsia**—see Sophora

**Eelgrass** —see Vallisneria spiralis

### Eelworms or Nematodes

These are minute, transparent, worm-like creatures which require a specialist to identify them and advise on control. This is necessary because it is hardly possible to see them with the naked eye and only microscopic examination reveals whether they are plant-parasitic or harmless species.

Those of horticultural importance include the leaf and bud eelworms, *Aphelenchoides sp.* They live mostly in the leaf tissues but can move over the plant when there is a film of moisture present to aid their progress. Adult eelworms can survive in dried leaves for about eighteen months and normally they also survive in the stools and in the soil nearby when the plant dies down. *Aphelenchoides ritzema-bosi* attacks plants such as chrysanthemum, causing the leaves to turn black, hang down and eventually fall. *A. fragariae* includes strawberry and violet among its hosts.

The stem and bulb eelworm, *Ditylenchus dipsaci*, has a number of different strains which attack a certain range of plants, e.g. the narcissus strain may be found in narcissus, onions, parsnips, scillas etc., while the phlox strain attacks phlox, oenothera, gypsophila etc.

The eelworms live in the plant tissues e.g. in narcissus bulbs, where they increase rapidly and move through the soil to infest other bulbs in the vicinity. They can continue to thrive after the bulbs are lifted and even after they have decayed and dried up the eelworms can survive in a desiccated condition for years.

Symptoms of attack vary with the host plant. Narcissus bulbs may show concentric brown rings when cut across and the leaves and flowers may be stunted and distorted. Phlox stems split and the leaves may become filled and bloated or narrowed to a whiplike effect.

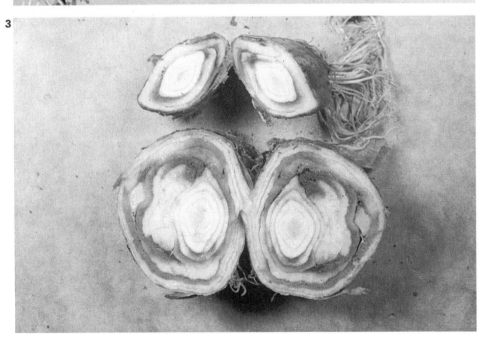

**1** Tomato roots showing the presence of the Root Knot Eelworm, Meloidogyne. **2** The influence of the Root Lesion Eelworm on the bulbs of Narcissus. Attacked bulbs become progressively weaker. **3** Narcissus bulbs cut in half to show the concentric brown rings caused by the Stem and Bulb Eelworm.

Warm water treatment is used to control Chrysanthemum Eelworm in dormant stools: 1 After lifting remove basal shoots. 2 Wash stools free of infected soil. 3 Immerse them in water heated to 110°F (43–44°C) for 20 to 30 minutes; wash and place in sterilised soil.

Rootknot eelworms, *Meloidogyne sp.*, cause swellings on the roots of plants such as tomato, lettuce, begonia etc. The female eelworms are minute, white, radish-shaped creatures, very difficult to see, embedded in the tissues. They produce vast numbers of eggs and from these young eelworms hatch, some remaining in the root and others spreading into the surrounding soil.

Root eelworms, *Heterodera sp.*, attack plants such as potatoes, tomatoes, beet, peas etc. The female cysts, globular and white at first, becoming golden and later dark brown, can just be seen attached to roots and tubers, although they are smaller than pinheads. They contain great numbers of young coiled inside eggs, and these can survive for a long time in the absence of suitable food-plants. However, if these become available once more, within about ten years, a chemical exudation from the plant roots causes many of the eelworms to hatch and infest the plants.

Eelworm control varies according to the plants concerned. For the amateur, it usually consists in destroying affected plants and keeping susceptible plants off the ground for a number of years. Control by injection of chemicals into the soil tends to be very expensive and home-made hot water baths for the treatment of chrysanthemum stools and bulbs need careful construction. Recent reports also indicate marigolds may eliminate soil forms up to 3 years.

Details of above apparatus and of some of the more important eelworms and their recommended methods of control are given in the bulletins issued by the US Department of Agriculture and many state experiment stations.

As far as phloxes are concerned it is possible to raise stocks free from infestation by taking root cuttings and growing them on in clean soil.

**Egeria**—see Elodea

**Eggplant**—see Aubergine

**Eglantine**—see Rosa eglanteria

**Egyptian Lotus**—see Nymphaea lotus

**Ehretia** (eret-ia)
Commemorating the eighteenth century German botanical artist G. D. Ehret. *(Ehretiaceae,* formerly *Boraginaceae).* A genus of 50 species of tender to hardy shrubs and trees, deciduous and evergreen, characterised by a globose, single-seeded fruit or drupe. Some of the hardy species make interesting specimen trees.

**Species cultivated** *E. dicksonii,* (D), tree to 30 feet, leaves oval, to 7 inches long, flowers small white, fragrant, in terminal 4 inch long panicles; fruit ½ inch wide, yellow when ripe, China and Formosa. *E. thyrsiflora,* similar to the preceding but up to 40 feet, flowers smaller, ¼ inch wide, in larger panicles, fruit ⅛ inch diameter, orange turning to black, China and Japan.

**Cultivation** The ehretias should be planted in fertile, well-drained soil in a site preferably sheltered from the north and east. Propagation is by half-ripe cuttings in a propagating frame or under mist in late summer or by seeds sown in gentle warmth in early spring.

## Eichhornia (i-kor-ne-a)

Commemorating J. A. F. Eichhorn, a nineteenth century Prussian statesman *(Pontederiaceae)*. A genus of five tender aquatic plants from South America and one from tropical Africa. The water hyacinth, *E. crassipes,* is a floating aquatic which increases so rapidly that it endangers navigation on some rivers in various parts of the Tropics and sub-Tropics like Florida. Vast sums are spent on trying to eradicate it.

**Species cultivated** *E. azurea* (syn. *Pontederia azurea*), submerged aquatic for a tropical tank, rampant, lavender-blue and yellow, summer. *E. crassipes,* (syn. *E. speciosa*), water hyacinth, pale violet, with pale green inflated leaf petioles which float the plant, summer. *E. martiana* (syns. *E. paniculata E. tricolor*), purple, summer. *E. nutans,* small blue flowers, foliage both floating and submerged, tropical Africa.

**Cultivation** Pot the plants in September in bowls of sifted soil and charcoal, putting several plants in each bowl, and fill with water. Reduce water gradually so that the plants remain in wet soil for winter in a frost free place. Restart in March in a temperature of about 65°F (18°C). Propagation is by division in early summer or by severing the stolons from the runners.

## Elaeagnus (el-e-ag-nus)

From the Greek *elaia,* an olive tree, *agnos,* a willow-like plant *(Elaeagnaceae)*. Hardy deciduous and evergreen decorative shrubs with insignificant, but fragrant, silver-coloured flowers, resembling small fuchsias.

**Species cultivated** *E. angustifolia* (D), oleaster, 15–20 feet, branches spiny, silvery, willow-like leaves, fruits large, oval, silvery-amber, southern Europe and western Asia; var. *orientalis,* larger leaves. *E. commutata* (syn. *E. argentea*) (D), silvery berry up to 10 feet, silvery leaves, silvery-yellow, fragrant flowers, May, northern North America. *E.* × *ebbingei* (E), up to 10 feet, handsome hybrid *(E. glabra* × *E. pungens)*, silvery-green foliage, flowers small pendent, silvery-white, fragrant. *E. glabra* (E), up to 15 feet, narrow silvery leaves, Japan. *E. macrophylla* (E), 10 feet, strong

1 **Eichhornia crassipes speciosa, Water Hyacinth, a plant for indoor lily pools. In South America, Africa and Florida it can impede navigation. 2 Elaeagnus grow well on a dry bank.**

1 Elaeagnus pungens, the type, will grow to 15 feet. It is a useful shrub though not as handsome as its variegated leaf varieties. 2 Elaeagnus pungens aureo-variegata has gold-splashed leaves. 3 Elaeocarpus dentatus.

grower, round silvery leaves, yellow, fragrant flowers, October and November, Japan. *E. multiflora* (D), up to 10 feet, flowers creamy, April and May, leaves silvery beneath, deep orange edible fruit, Japan. *E. pungens* (E), up to 15 feet, silvery white fragrant flowers, October and November; best known in its vars. *aureo-variegata (maculata)*, 6 feet, handsome, slow-growing shrub with large glossy leaves heavily splashed with gold; *simonii*, larger leaves, silvery-white below. Other varieties of this plant include *dicksonii*, slow growing, bright yellow variegation; *reflexa*, taller, more vigorous, undersides of leaves covered with brown scales; *variegata*, creamy-yellow marginal variegation. *E. umbellata* (D), 15 feet, strong growing and spreading, flowers creamy-white, May, fruit silvery, becoming deep red, Himalaya.

**Cultivation** Plant the deciduous species from October to December, and the evergreen species in April or September. All thrive in dryish, ordinary soil either in an open, exposed situation, if hardy, and in a warm climate or indoors, if tender. Propagation is by cuttings placed in sandy soil in a cold frame in September, by layers in spring, or by seed sown in March in boxes of light soil in a temperature of 55°F (13°C).

**Elaeocarpus** (el-ay-ee-o-kar-pus)
From the Greek *elaia*, an olive and *carpos*, a fruit; some species have olive-like fruits (*Elaeocarpaceae*). A genus of

200 species of tender evergreen trees and shrubs, few of which are in cultivation. Some of them make handsome plants for the larger greenhouse or conservatory.

**Species cultivated** *E. dentatus,* 15–20 feet, leaves leathery, oblong, flowers white or straw coloured, petals lobed at tips, New Zealand. *E. reticulatus* (syn. *E. cyaneus*), a large shrub or small tree to 15 feet or more tall, leaves prominently net-veined, oblong-lanceolate, toothed, flowers small, white, fragrant, with five fringed petals; fruits ovoid, blue, Australia.

**Cultivation** These plants require the protection of a cool greenhouse, with a minimum winter temperature of 40°F (4°C). They should be grown in large pots or tubs of well-drained medium; an enriched, drained mixture is suitable. In a large greenhouse they may be planted out into a bed or border. Propagation is by seeds sown in spring or by half-ripe cuttings taken with a heel in summer.

---

**Elaeodendron** (el-a-o-den-dron) From the Greek *elaia,* an olive and *dendron,* a tree *(Celastraceae).* A small genus of tender trees and shrubs, mostly natives of southern Africa and India. A few species are sometimes grown for their graceful habit and attractive fruits.

**Species cultivated** *E. capense,* large shrub to 18 feet, with pendulous branches clothed in lanceolate, somewhat unequal sided spine-toothed leaves. Flowers greenish, inconspicuous, followed by ovoid yellow fruits ½ inch long. *E. orientale,* juvenile leaves slender, the adult leaves broader, about 2½ inches long, flowers greenish-yellow, followed by olive-like fruits, Madagascar and Mauritius. This species makes a graceful pot plant while young.

**Cultivation** These plants need the protection of a warm greenhouse with a minimum temperature of 50–55°F (10–13°C). They should be grown in pots or tubs of a lime-free, well-drained, peat and loam mixture. Propagation is by seeds or by cuttings rooted in late spring.

---

**Elder and Elderberry**—see Sambucus

---

**Elecampane**—see Inula helenium

---

### Electricity in the garden

Electricity is a most versatile power when applied to gardening and it provides a means of doing many tasks more quickly, more efficiently and with less labour. These are tremendous advantages which are being appreciated by more and more gardeners every year.

Electricity is the only system which

**1** One type of greenhouse in which electricity is used for heating, ventilation, soil warming, lighting and shading. The aim is for complete automation. **2** Electrically driven hedge-shears are a boon in gardens with long hedges.

provides complete, trustworthy automation for several applications. It is clean, relatively easy to install and the installations are neat in appearance. Electrical apparatus is safe only if it is installed by an experienced electrician and only if the correct or approved types of fittings are used. There is a high level of dampness in the garden and in most horticultural structures and equipment and it is vital, therefore, that waterproof fittings and cable are used. Local electricians will often be pleased to offer sound, practical advice on proposed installations and will also undertake the work.

As a time saver, electricity will enable you to perform more jobs around the garden. It will also open up many more exciting possibilities for you. One of the most important uses of electricity is for heating which can be installed in the greenhouse, in a frame or the garden shed. There are several ways in which this can be done. One of the cheapest is in the form of soil warming. Bottom heat is provided for propagation benches, the staging and greenhouse borders and frames. It can be put to good use in the cloche runs too. It is a much cleaner and more reliable system than the old-fashioned use of rotted manure or hot beds.

**Soil warming** This is provided by specially manufactured heating wires or cables which can be either low voltage or regular voltage. The former uses a transformer which reduces the line voltage to a low, safe level of about 12 volts. The heating element is usually galvanised wire, covered with plastic, of a given length and gauge which will provide a calculated electrical resistance. Elements of different lengths can be purchased so that any given area can be warmed to a certain temperature. Usually a loading of 6 watts per square foot is sufficient.

Larger voltage warming uses special wire covered by insulation and, in the more expensive types, a protective sheath. Unlike the low voltage outfits, the wires are connected direct to the main power supply.

The approximate running costs of soil warming are modest for each square foot of bed which is warmed. For a frame of 32 square feet the cost per week would then be very reasonable if 10–12 hours each night is allowed. Costs will rise, of course, if higher temperatures are required.

Hot beds are formed quite simply. The heating wire must be laid over the base of the bed in even patterns, usually in parallel rows about 4–6 inches apart. The wires can be retained in position by special wire pegs. The required loading for a given area is ascertained by multiplying the area by 6. For example, a hot bed 8×4 feet has an area of 32 square feet. Multiplied by 6 the loading required is 192 watts. A 200 watt cable or

Tomato plants being grown in a specially constructed, raised bed. The soil temperature can be accurately controlled by electrical soil warming cables. Tomato plants respond well to soil warming.

transformer would be correct.

Heating for a hot bed is usually given by the dosage method during the night. A certain number of hours of warming is applied, at least 12 hours in the colder northern gardens and 10 hours in the more favoured southern areas. Automatic control can be used in the form of a special switch which will switch the electricity on and off at pre-set times.

Once in position, the warming wires are covered with soil to a depth of 6 inches. For complete safety, the hot-bed system is recommended as little damage will occur if the wire is accidentally cut by a spade, fork or trowel. The cost of units will vary according to the type. A non-automatic type for an area of 32 square feet costs comparatively little and an automatic system is surprisingly

cheap, too, compared with even a modest greenhouse heater.

**Propagation** In the greenhouse or frame propagation is made much easier by the use of electricity and a greater degree of temperature control is possible so that growing conditions are as near perfect as possible. A home-made propagator can be constructed from deep boards about 1 inch thick and 6–8 inches in depth. The top of the 'box' is covered by sheets of glass or clear plastic sheeting. The box need not have a bottom if placed on the greenhouse bench.

A higher soil temperature is required for this type of work and temperatures of 55–60°F (13–16°C) are necessary. This means that the loading per square foot of propagator area must be increased, but only slightly, by 1½ watts to 7½ watts per square foot. A propagating case of 6×2 feet is more than sufficient for average purposes. The cables should be laid over 2 inches of washed sand and covered with 3 inches of sand. The pots, boxes or seed pans are placed on the sand and warmth is retained by packing

granulated peat around the receptacle afterwards.

A further refinement is the use of cables which will warm the air inside the propagator. These are clipped neatly in place around the sides of the frame by means of special stainless steel spring clips. These cables need not produce a very high temperature when used in conjunction with soil or sand warming and a temperature of 50°F (10°C) is adequate for normal purposes. Automatic control can be achieved if twin thermostats are used, one in conjunction with the cables in the sand, and one above for air temperature control.

Commercially-made propagators of various designs and sizes can be obtained. The size is determined by the amount of use there is for them. Some models are supplied with a special plastic dome as an extra to give more headroom. Most modern propagators have plastic or glass fibre bodies which ensure trouble-free service. Many are equipped with accurate thermostats which regulate the temperature of the sand bed and ensure low running costs. Heating is supplied by warming cables which are laid on a sand bed and covered by another layer of the same material. Seeds are sown in pots, pans or boxes which are placed on the warmed sand and surrounded by granulated peat to retain the warmth. Cuttings can be treated in the same way. The top of the propagator is covered by glass or plastic. In this way soil tem-

1 England's Humex Mist Propagators use a patented detector to apply a fine mist at frequent intervals. 2 The Humex Big Top Propagator has thermostatically controlled bottom heat and air warming. 3 In the Humex Mist Propagator, bottom heat is supplied to the rooting cuttings by soil warming cables.

peratures of 60–65°F (16–18°C) can be maintained and concentrated in the small area of a propagator instead of heating the vaster area of the greenhouse. This is a great advantage when one realizes the running costs of a propagator, especially in the Northeast.

Very simple and much smaller propagators can also be purchased which are really 'heating plates'. These provide bottom heat and on them the boxes or pots are stood. Some of the latest models have their heating elements and thermostats bonded in completely by a special plastic process. This ensures a very neat, compact unit which is completely safe and rugged. One model propagator is supplied with an aluminium glazed top. It has air warming and bottom heating cables both independently controlled by accurate thermostats. The running costs when both are in use amount to only a moderate amount.

**Heating** In some parts of the country, electricity plays a vital part in heating the greenhouse by warming the air inside the whole structure. Its chief assets are that it can be controlled automatically and that it is reliable. Unfortunately the cost per unit (1000 watts) is not low everywhere although temperatures of 40–45°F (4–10°C) are fairly economical to maintain. On the other hand, for a lean-to green-

house, 10×8 feet on a brick base and heated to 45°F (7°C), another 5–10° can result in expensive quarterly accounts, especially if the winter is a long, hard one. This is taking into consideration the fact that the system is automatically controlled by a reliable, sensitive thermostat.

It is important, therefore, if you have a greenhouse to plan the fullest possible use of all the space where you intend to use electricity as a form of heating. If you cannot attend to the greenhouse frequently, there is no doubt that automatic electric heating is the answer.

There are several ways in which the greenhouse can be heated. These are by tubular heaters, convector types and fan heaters. Each has its own particular advantages and the final choice must depend on individual requirements and situations. The selection must also be guided by the amount of heat or power which is required. This is calculated on the temperatures which are desired and also on the heat loss through the greenhouse. Heating should always be based on the average minimum outside winter temperature. If, for example, an

inside temperature of 50°F (10°C) is required, the heating apparatus must be capable of raising the temperature by more than the difference.

The calculation for heat loss is quite a complicated one but it is not necessary for you to make this calculation; the specialist heating firms make a particular point of helping their customers to purchase just the right capacity of heater or heating equipment if certain essential details are supplied. These are, usually, the size of the greenhouse—length, breadth, height ,of eaves and height to ridge. Also the type of construction, whether of wood, metal, all glass sides or brick or wooden sides. The required minimum temperature (winter) is also essential. From your address, the specialist heating firm will also be able to make due calculation for district conditions. Obviously a greenhouse in the northernmost parts will take much more heating than one in the warmer southern parts of the country.

The firms will also suggest the best type of heater to use, but it is useful to have some idea of the various types available. The tubular heaters are very popular in England. They use a minimum of space in the house. They are fastened to the sides, and sometimes to the end of the greenhouse, low down near the borders. They are made from special grade metal and are completely waterproof. Their electrical loading is usually 60 watts per foot length. Installation is quite simple and no complicated wiring is necessary. The requisite loading to produce the desired temperature is easily achieved by multiples or banks of these tubes. Unfortunately, they are not easy to find in the US.

Convector heaters heat the greenhouse by drawing air in at the base, warming it over an element and finally passing it out through a slit or grill at the top. There are not many large types of heater available, and they are more suited to the smaller house.

A popular heater is the fan heater which heats the air by a special element and blows the hot air out into the greenhouse. The fan which distributes the air revolves at high speed and ensures that all parts of the greenhouse are heated. The 'moving' air thus created greatly reduces dampness and produces a buoyant atmosphere for plants. Placing the heater requires a little care so that plants nearby are not scorched by direct blast. Usually this type of heater is placed on the floor of the greenhouse near the door and pointing down the centre of the path towards the opposite gable end.

Usually these heaters have their own built-in thermostat which provides quite accurate control. Most models are supplied with a switch so that the heating element can be isolated and air circulation only allowed. This is useful in the warm summer months to keep air moving and to prevent 'hot spots'. It does not cool the air in any way, unless the temperature outside is a little lower, when this air is drawn into the house.

Another version of fan heating uses plastic tubing which is perforated at intervals. This tubing is fastened along the sides of the greenhouse, low down and one end is sealed. The other end is attached to a special fan heater or blower which pushes warm air along the tubing and out of the holes in it. As most of these heaters are rated above 3 kilowatts, they are more suited to the larger greenhouse.

Immersion heaters also exist which will quickly transform an existing hot water, solid fuel system to automated electric heating. These heaters can also be used for the installation of a new system using 3–4 inch diameter pipes.

An outdoor frame can be heated by air and soil warming cables and this is a very economical system to adopt. For a frame of 24 square feet it will not cost much to provide frost protection.

1 English water-filled heaters automatically supply heat with humidity, as required by plants. 2 Humex tubular heaters are for greenhouses in relatively mild areas. They are easily fixed in position. The electrical loading is 60 watts per foot of single tube.

**Soil sterilisation** Clean soil is important for healthy growth at all stages and sterilisation by electricity is a quick, clean and time-saving system. Specially designed, compact units can be purchased that will deal with various amounts of loam. The soil is brought to a temperature of 180°F (82°C) which kills weed seeds, pests and diseases.

**Pest control** Another method of dealing with greenhouse pests by electricity is with a special 'lamp' which volatilises insecticides. Tablets are inserted through a hole in the lamp and the heating element volatilises them.

**Automatic ventilation** One of the most serious problems is that of keeping the greenhouse cool. Electrically operated fan extractors are useful here, particularly for the gardener who is away for most of the day. These are attached to the gable end of the greenhouse opposite to the door and as high up as possible. Connected to a thermostat, the extractor fan comes into operation as soon as the temperature exceeds that which has been set on the thermostat. It is essential to select a fan of sufficient power and diameter to suit the cubic capacity of the greenhouse. For 500 cubic feet a 9 inch diameter fan is usually adequate. For a capacity of up to 1000 cubic feet a 12 inch diameter fan will be necessary.

There are still other ventilating systems, however. One type used in the

1 English Humex Soil Sterilizer has ½ cubic foot, 1,500 watt, immersion element, which produces steam for partial sterilisation. 2 A thermostatically controlled fan can change the air 30 times per hour.

larger home greenhouses consists of a horizontal pipe or rod bearing rocker arms. As the rod is rotated by a motor the arms open hinged vents. In smaller houses one or more small motors activate built-in vertical rods which lift the vents (ridge type only).

**Automatic watering** Electricity can even play its part where watering is concerned. A completely automatic system can be installed, which controls the amount and frequency of the watering. The 'brain' of the outfit is a control unit which contains a solenoid valve which switches the piped water supply on and off. When used as a watering device, a detector probe is inserted into a special compartment in the unit which can be flooded with water through a porcelain block. As soon as the porcelain block absorbs all the water from its own basin and the probe's compartment, an electrical circuit is made and the solenoid valve turns on the water. As soon as the block and the compartment are flooded, the solenoid is switched off and the water ceases to flow. Another system, run by a timer, opens or shuts valves which, in turn, supply water through a system of pipes or tubes which are

fastened to the benches. Usually the water to the plants is delivered through a perforated plastic pipe or individual pot waterers.

Where the apparatus is required for water application for propagation purposes, it is essential to provide a very small amount and this is done by the use of special mist spray heads. These are usually fixed at intervals to a length of pipe, the heads themselves being about 2 feet above the staging. The detector probe is removed from its special compartment in the control unit and placed on a stick just above the cuttings where it will be wetted by the mist heads. The detector, in such a position, will dry out quite quickly and will provide more frequent watering. The detector is often referred to as a 'leaf' when used in this way, as it will dry out in the same way as a leaf does.

**Lighting** Lastly there is the use of electricity for illuminating the greenhouse, not only to enable you to attend to your plants in the long winter evenings, but to encourage out of season growth for certain plants.

Good gardening depends not only on skill but also on patience, but sometimes there is an opportunity to hurry things along. The growth of some plants and their flowering and fruiting times can be influenced by adjusting or varying the number of hours of light and darkness

per day. All that is required is low intensity light. Plants can be divided into two types—long-day plants and short-day ones. Increasing the length of day by lighting will induce the flowering of long-day types during short daylight hours. Short-day plants such as mid season and early-flowering chrysanthemums can have their flowering times delayed if a day length of over $14\frac{1}{2}$ hours is provided from mid August to about mid October.

There are available specially designed growth lamps of various wattages. For the treatment of chrysanthemums, 100 watt lamps are suitably suspended about 6 feet above the rows and spaced 5–6 feet apart. More intense lighting of 400 watts is suitable for raising seedlings such as tomatoes early in the season. Much experimental work is being done on this subject in Alaska at present.

For average amateur requirements 100 watt lamps or multiples of these are quite satisfactory. For bulb forcing, one such lamp suspended over daffodils and tulips supplied with an air temperature of 60°F (16°C) will encourage much more rapid growth. Twelve hours dosage per 24 hours will be sufficient and this can be more conveniently regulated if a time switch is employed. About 9 square feet of area can be dealt with efficiently by one of these bulbs which should be placed 3 feet above the bowls or boxes.

Artificial light is ideal for the cultivation of saint paulias and specially designed growing-cabinets can be purchased for this purpose. Growth lamps noted above in the roof of an electric propagator will encourage more rapid and vigorous growth of seedlings, especially during the duller early spring months. In all instances, it is *vital* that only specially manufactured apparatus and fittings are installed and the installation should always be carried out by a competent individual.

**Installation kit** The exception to the rule of not attempting to install electrical equipment oneself is provided by the 'do-it-yourself' kit which enables you to fit out your greenhouse with a comprehensive array of socket outlets, wires switches and lights. The manufacturer supplies dummy (stiff card) matrices for plug points. These are pinned in the desired position in the greenhouse. The distance between each is then carefully measured so that the necessary amount of cable can be supplied. The distance between greenhouse and dwelling house is also measured, either for underground plastic cable or above-ground installation. In Britain, details are entered on a special order form. Eventually the kit arrives completely wired pro-

Elsholtzia stauntonii, a semi-woody plant from China, that partially dies back each winter. The leaves, when crushed, have a minty smell.

fessionally, including the proper fixture, protected wire cable, ready connected to suitable connectors.

So complete is the kit that even the special cable clips are supplied so that an extremely neat installation can be fitted. The cost is surprisingly reasonable. A kit comprising a lighting unit, six socket outlets, a wire unit, switch fuse and the necessary cable is relatively cheap (see also Frames and Frame gardening, Greenhouse gardening, Heating, Lawnmowers, Lighting in the garden, Machinery in the garden and Sterilisation).

**Elephant Grass**—see Pennisetum purpureum

**Elephant Wood**—see Bolusanthus speciosus

**Elettaria** (el-et-ta-re-a)
The native Malabar name *(Zingiberaceae)*. A genus of two perennial herbaceous plants from India. The species cultivated is *E. cardamomum,* a plant with a creeping rhizome and bamboo-like shoots bearing slender, pointed leaves, about 6 inches long, with an aroma of cinnamon. The flowers, borne in loose spikes, are white with a yellow and blue lip. In its native country it grows up to 10 feet. In northern areas it rarely exceeds 1 foot when grown as a house plant. It produces the cardamom seed used for Oriental curries.
**Cultivation** This plant requires a very warm, shaded, greenhouse with high humidity from spring to autumn, but should be kept on the dry side during the winter. It should be potted in mixture consisting of 4 parts of turfy loam, 1 part of leafmould, and 1 part of sharp sand. Propagation is by division of rhizomes in February or March. It may be grown as a house plant in a warm, draught-free room, away from direct sunlight.

**Eleusine** (el-u-sin-see)
From Eleusis, a city in Greece, noted for its Temple of Ceres, the Roman Goddess of agriculture *(Gramineae).* A small genus of tropical annual grasses, some of which are grown as grain crops. *E. indica* and the allied *E. coracana* are the so-called finger millets. They are sometimes seen in botanical gardens and grown by tropical bird fanciers. In appearance they are rather like a large-growing annual meadow grass, up to a foot or more tall, with a distinctively fingered inflorescence.
**Cultivation** These grasses may be grown in pots of any ordinary medium under glass or out of doors in a warm sheltered spot. Propagation is by seeds sown in late spring.

**Elisha's Tears**—see Leycesteria formosa

**Elm**—see Ulmus

**Elodea** (el-o-dee-a)
From the Greek *elodes,* a marsh. A genus of a few species of aquatic plants from South America, related to *Anacharis (Hydrocharidaceae).* The only species likely to be cultivated is *E. densa* (syn. *Egeria densa),* an oxygenating plant for the aquarium or pond, with small dark green leaves and clusters of tiny white flowers enclosed by a broad spathe.
**Cultivation** Plant in spring or summer by attaching a clump of the plant to a stone and sinking it in the pool or aquarium. Propagation is by pieces detached at any time during late spring or summer.

**Elsholtzia** (el-shol-se-a)
Commemorating Johann Sigismund Elsholtz, seventeenth century German physician and naturalist *(Labiatae).* A small genus of semi-woody, aromatic shrubs, one only of which is generally cultivated. This is the Chinese *E. stauntonii,* which grows 4–5 feet tall and bears purplish-pink flowers freely in panicles from August to October. The leaves have a mint-like smell when crushed.
**Cultivation** This shrub likes a sunny position and a loamy soil. The top growth usually dies back considerably in winter and dead wood should be pruned away in April, when new flowering stems will soon appear. Propagation is by cuttings of green shoots taken in August and rooted in sandy soil in a frame.

## Elymus (el-e-mus)

Said to be derived from the Greek *elus*, meaning rolled-up, or named after a kind of millet, the seeds of some species being ground into flour *(Gramineae)*. Lyme grass, wild rye. Perennial grasses widely distributed over the temperate regions. **Species cultivated** *E. arenarius*, sea lymegrass, 2–4 feet, rigid stems of blue-green, broad leaves, rolled inwards and ending in a sharp point, 5 inch spikes of seagreen flowers in June and July, creeping rootstock, much used on exposed sandhills to bind the sand; the grass is not eaten by cattle. *E. canadensis*, 5 feet, dark green, smooth stems, flower heads July and August, North America. *E. glaucus*, 3 feet, blue-green, erect, hairy, Turkestan. *E. virginicus*, 3 feet, flower spikes 6–7 inches long, summer.
**Cultivation** These grasses are hardy and may be grown in ordinary soil, but *E. arenarius* and *E. virginicus* are particularly suited to sandy soils. Propagation is by seed sown in spring.

## Emasculation

A term used by plant breeders to describe the act of removing the anthers from a flower to prevent it becoming fertilised by its own pollen. This may be necessary when pollen from one selected flower is to be artificially transferred to the selected seed-bearing parent flower. Such flowers are usually protected with muslin or plastic bags to prevent fertilisation by bees or other insects.

1 Elymus, a genus of erect perennial grasses that prefer sandy soils.
2 Embothrium coccineum lanceolatum, an evergreen shrub from South America.
3 Embothrium coccineum longifolium and lanceolatum are not fully hardy.

## Embothrium (em-both-re-um)

From the Greek *en*, in, *bothrion*, a little pit, a reference to the pollen cases *(Proteaceae)*. A small genus of evergreen, slightly tender flowering shrubs from Chile, which must have a lime-free soil. One species only is cultivated, *E. coccineum*, the firebush which grows 10–30 feet tall and has recurving racemes of brilliant scarlet flowers in May and June. It is a striking spectacle when in full flower. The variety *lanceolatum* makes a graceful, slender tree and is hardier, while *longifolium* has longer, narrower leaves than the type.
**Cultivation** These shrubs are seen in coastal districts and sheltered inland gardens in the British Isles and California where *E. coccineum* has been introduced. Plant in March or April in sandy peat with protection in somewhat cooler areas, if possible, or among taller evergreens which make a splendid background for the scarlet-clad branches. When grown in pots in a greenhouse, plants will flower when they are quite small. Pot in March in 2 parts of peat, 1 part of lime-free loam and 1 part of sharp sand. Prune in March when necessary. Stand plants in the open during the summer and water them freely. When under glass from October to April water them moderately only. Propagation is by cuttings inserted in spring in sandy peat in a propagating frame with a temperature of 75°F (24°C), or by sowing seed in spring in sandy peat in the same temperature.

## Embryo (bot.)

A term used to describe the rudimentary plant within a seed. It is the earliest stage in the development of living organisms and in plant life the embryo may occupy the whole seed or sometimes be embedded in part of the seed.

**Emilia** (em-il-e-a)
Derivation unknown, probably a commemorative name *(Compositae)*. A small genus of perennials or annuals of which one species only is in cultivation. This is *E. saggitata* (syns. *E. flammea, Cacalia coccinea*), the tassel flower, a half-hardy annual growing 1–2 feet tall. It has small, bright scarlet flowers clustered closely together in heads, in summer. There is a yellow form *aurea,* and seed is also obtainable of mixed colours.

**Cultivation** Sow seeds in pans or boxes of a regular seed mixture in February or March and place in a warm greenhouse. Prick out the seedlings when they are large enough to handle, and after hardening them off, plant them out about 1 foot apart in May in a sunny bed. Alternatively, seed may be sown in the open in April where the plants are to flower. Plants do well in a dry and sandy position.

---

**Empetrum** (em-pet-rum)
From the Greek *en*, in or upon, *petros*, a rock; the plant is found in rocky places *(Empetraceae)*. There is probably one species only in this genus, *E. nigrum*, an evergreen, hardy, procumbent shrub of heath-like appearance, known as the crowberry, a native to parts of North America. It grows to 6–10 inches tall and bears small pink flowers in May, followed by edible brownish-black berries. The form *purpureum* has reddish-purple berries.

**Cultivation** This little plant requires a lime-free soil and is suitable for a peaty, moist soil on shady parts of the rock garden, where it should be planted in the spring. Propagation is by cuttings inserted in sandy peat during the summer in a cold, shaded frame.

---

**Encephalartos** (en-sef-a-lar-tos)
From the Greek *en*, in, *kephale*, head, *artos*, bread, referring to the farinaceous interior of the trunk *(Cycadaceae)*. Caffer or Kaffir bread. A genus of African evergreen plants, mostly tree-like in appearance, the feathery leaves clustered at the top of a stout stem, the fruit borne in cones. A few species are grown in stovehouses in this country as decorative foliage plants.

**Species cultivated** *E. altensteinii*, 8 feet or more, leaves up to 5 feet long, with very many leaflets, cones large, 1 foot or more in length. *E. caffra*, 8–10 feet, leaves to 2 feet long, leaflets numerous, cones to 1 foot long. *E. horridus*, 8–10 feet, leaves to 2 feet long, leaflets fewer than in above species, cones to 1 foot long. *E. villosus*, very short stem, leaves 6–8 feet, leaflets numerous, cones to 2 feet.

**Cultivation** These plants are grown in large pots containing a mixture of 2 parts of loam and 1 part of sand. They need ample room as their leaves are large, and should be given a light

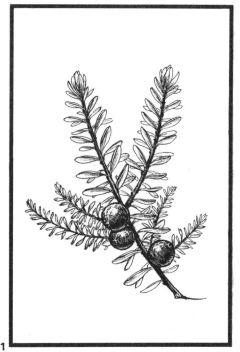

1 Empetrum nigrum, the Crowberry, an evergreen, hardy, procumbent shrub, flowering in May.
2 Encephalartos villosus produces leaves 8 feet long and cones up to 2 feet.
3 Emilia flammea, the Tassel Flower, an erect annual reaching 1 or 2 feet.

position. Ample water is needed from April to August, but after that little should be required until the following spring. The winter temperature should be 55–60°F (13–16°C), rising to 75°F (24°C) in the summer. Propagation is by seed sown in a light, sandy compost in srping in a propagating case in which a temperature of 85–95°F (29–35°C) can be maintained

## Encephalocarpus
(en-sef-al-o-kar-pus)

From the Greek *en*, in, upon, *kephale*, head, *karpos*, fruit; the flowers and seeds are carried on top of the stem *(Cactaceae)*. A genus of a single species, *E. strobiliformis* (placed originally in the genus *Ariocarpus*). This is a greenhouse cactus from Mexico, with a globular stem, about 3 inches across, the greyish-green tubercles or scales very compressed and packed tightly round the stem. Small bunches of hair or wool are borne in the areoles. The outer petals of the flowers are greenish, fringed at the top, the inner a bright violet.

**Cultivation** Provide a porous soil such as a fairly light potting mixture, with a fifth part extra of sharp sand or other roughage. Do not repot more often than every four years, as this is a slow-growing plant. Give it a very sunny position, water sparingly in summer and keep quite dry in winter. Maintain a minimum winter temperature of 45°F (7°C), rising to 65–85°F (18–29°C) in summer. Propagation is by seed sown in rather light seed mixture as for *Ariocarpus*.

## Enchytraeid Worms

Small, transparent or whitish worms, sometimes called 'Pot Worms', found in plant pots and out of doors where the soil is rich in humus. They are often mistaken for eelworms but plant parasitic eelworms are too small to be detected with the naked eye except when in cyst form (see Eelworms). Enchytraeid worms are not usually primary pests of plants but feed on tissue already decaying from other causes. If present in great numbers, they may be reduced by watering with potassium permanganate at the rate of ½ oz per gallon of water, or with derris at normal dilutions.

## Encyclia—see Epidendrum

## Endive

Although the leaves of endive *(Cichorium endivia)* look similar to those of lettuce, they are very bitter and few people enjoy eating them green. However, after blanching there is no trace of bitterness and endive replaces lettuce in late autumn and winter salads.

**Cultivation** Seeds may be sown as early as April but to produce plants for blanching in the autumn, a sowing is made in June. Allow 1 foot between the rows and the seed drills should not be deeper

1 Encephalocarpus strobiliformis, a greenhouse cactus from Mexico.
2 Endive, Cichorium endiva, a hardy annual, the leaves are used in salads.
3 Endymion hispanicus, the Spanish Bluebell, flowers in May. (Scilla in US.)

than 1 inch. If the soil is on the dry side, flood the seed drills with water. Sow reasonably thinly when the water has drained away. Provided the soil is in good heart and able to produce fine lettuces, no fertilisers need be used. Thin the seedlings to 9 inches apart when they are large enough to handle. Some of the seedlings may be transplanted to a cold frame or unheated greenhouse for plants to be blanched in November or early December. Keep down weeds by hoeing or by mulching with sedge peat and water well if July or August are dry months. Cover the row with cloches in October.

The first batch of plants may be blanched in October. Complete darkness

is essential. Partial darkness results in yellow endive which has traces of bitterness. The plants must be quite dry when blanching is started. Damp plants are liable to rot. The process takes from four to six weeks and although some success may be obtained by covering the cloches or the frame with black polythene sheeting, far better results are forthcoming where the plants are dug up with a ball of soil around the roots. The plants are then replanted beneath large clay pots, from which all light is excluded by covering the drainage hole with a piece of slate or tile (see Blanching).

## Endymion (en-dim-e-on)

Named for *Endymion*, a beautiful youth in Greek mythology, who slept perpetually on Mount Latimus, kissed by *Silene*, the moon *(Liliaceae)*. Bulbous plants usually included in *Scilla*, sometimes described as *Hyacinthus*, commonly known as bluebells, but botani-

1 Endymion non-scriptus (Scilla n.), Bluebell, or Wild Hyacinth that is found in large colonies in woods.
2 Enkianthus campanulatus, a shrub growing to 8 feet that requires lime-free soil. Light shade is tolerated.

cally sometimes a small separate genus.
**Species cultivated** *E. hispanicus*, Spanish bluebell, 12–18 inches, variable, deep blue, pale blue, pinkish and white, scentless. Individual bells are larger than those of English bluebell and the stems are stouter, May, Spain and Portugal. There are various named hybrids, including the pure white *alba maxima*, the porcelain blue 'Blue Queen', the deep blue 'Excelsior' and the rosy-lilac 'Rose Queen'. *E. non-scriptus*, bluebell (but not the bluebell of Scotland, which is *Campanula rotundifolia*, the English harebell), 12–18 inches, misty blue, occasionally pink or white, nodding, slightly fragrant, bell-shaped flowers, May, Britain and western Europe.
**Cultivation** These plants are ideal for naturalising in dappled woodland or partially shaded areas where the large bulbs should be planted about 3–4 inches deep in the autumn. Once planted they should be left undisturbed until they have formed thick clumps, when they may be divided. Lifting is quite a task. They thrive best in a heavyish loamy soil, and are not averse to clay, provided it is not waterlogged.

### Engleheart, The Rev. George Herbert

All but a handful of the daffodils that we grow in our gardens and see at shows today are relative newcomers. Not until the middle of the last century was any great interest taken in this now immensely popular florist's and garden flower; the first book about it and its culture was not published until 1875. Shortly after, in 1885, Engleheart

became vicar of Chute Forest near Andover. The vicarage had a large garden, and for the first time he began to work seriously at gardening, and made experimental crossings of daffodils. This work eventually led to Engleheart being acclaimed as 'the father of the modern daffodil'.

He was born on Guernsey and obtained a scholarship at Oxford, becoming first a curate at Leicester. He was a man of high scholarship, publishing translations of Greek, Latin and French poems into English and vice-versa, a superb calligrapher in Greek and English, and a talented artist. But it was as a breeder of daffodils that he excelled, transforming that flower after about 18 years work when, in 1898, he exhibited his 'Will Scarlett' at the Birmingham Daffodil Show. He had six bulbs, three of which he sold to a nurseryman for £100—a hitherto undreamed of price—retaining the others for further breeding. Many other successes followed such as the white 'Beersheba' still widely grown.

### English Bluebell—see Endymion non-scriptus

### English Iris—see Iris xiphioides

### English Ivy—see Hedera helix

### Enkianthus (en-ke-an-thus)
From the Greek *enkuos*, enlarged, *anthos*, a flower, possibly a reference to the rounded, bell-shaped flowers (*Ericaceae*). A small genus of deciduous shrubs for a lime-free soil. The drooping urn-shaped flowers are interestingly veined, and during the autumn months the whorls of the leaves are beautifully coloured.
**Species cultivated** *E. campanulatus*, 6–8 feet, erect habit, flowers sulphur-yellow, veined bronze-crimson, May, leaves richly coloured in the autumn, Japan. *E. cernuus*, 6–8 feet, cream, May, Japan; var. *rubens*, deep red flowers, fine autumn colour. *E. chinensis* (syn. *E. sinohimalaicus*), up to 20 feet, salmon-red flowers, May and June, western China. *E. perulatus* (syn. *E. japonicus*), 4–6 feet, white flowers, May, autumn leaves bright scarlet, Japan.
**Cultivation** Plant in dappled shade in early autumn or in April. The soil must be lime-free and some leafmould or peat should be dug in to retain moisture. Propagation is by cuttings of firm shoots taken in the spring and inserted in sandy soil in gentle heat, or by seed sown in peaty soil in the spring.

## Entelea (en-tel-ee-a)

From the Greek *enteles*, perfect, the numerous stamens are all fertile *(Tiliaceae)*. A genus of but a single species, *E. arborescens*, from New Zealand, a large evergreen shrub, which has the distinction of producing the lightest wood known, with a specific gravity less than that of cork. The whole shrub is covered with soft scurfy hairs. The oval heart-shaped leaves are toothed, often somewhat three-lobed, 4 to 9 inches or more long. The flowers are 1 inch across, white, with a bold central boss of yellow stamens, borne in erect clusters. The seed capsule, 1 inch across, is covered with long sharp bristles.

**Cultivation** This is a shrub for the cool greenhouse with a winter minimum temperature of 40°F (4°C). It may be grown out of doors in parts of southern California. Under glass it should be grown in large pots or tubs, or planted out in a greenhouse border. A fairly fertile potting mixture is suitable. Propagation is by seeds sown in spring or by cuttings taken in summer and rooted in a propagating frame with bottom heat.

## Entomology

The study of insects, from the Greek word *entomos*, cut-into, and restricted to the Class *Insecta*. Insects are recognised by the following characters in the adult stage: the body divided into three segments—head, thorax and abdomen; one pair of antennae (feelers) on the head; three pairs of legs on the thorax

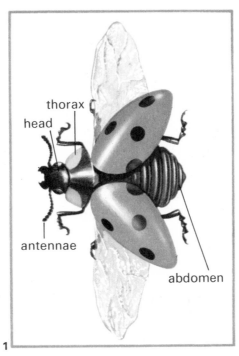

and none on the abdomen. There may also be wings on the thorax and, in common with some other Classes, insects have a hard covering or 'exoskeleton' protecting the body. The number of different kinds of insects found in most areas exceeds twenty thousand.

## Eomecon (ee-o-mee-kon)

From the Greek *eioe*, the dawn, and *mekon*, a poppy *(Papaveraceae)*. Dawn poppy. A genus of but one species, a herbaceous perennial from China, *E. chionanthum*, which grows 12–18 inches tall and bears white flowers on branching stems in May and June. The leaves are grey-green, heart-shaped, rather fleshy and slightly waved.

**Cultivation** This plant is almost hardy and the creeping rhizomes should be planted in October or March in sandy peat or leafmould in a sunny bed, but in the south the position is best shaded from the midday sun. In exposed districts protect with an airy mulch in severe weather. Propagation is by division of the rhizomes in March or early April.

## Epacris (ee-pak-ris)

From the Greek *epi*, upon, *akros*, the summit; the plants grow on high ground in their native countries *(Epacridaceae)*. Australian heaths. Evergreen flowering heath-like shrubs from Australia, Tasmania and New Zealand. They make useful and decorative winter-flowering plants when grown in a cool

**Entomology is the study of insects. These are recognised in the adult stage by a body divided into three segments—head, thorax and abdomen. Wings may also be present on the thorax.**
**1 A Ladybird showing these characteristics.**
**2 Eomecon chionanthum, the Dawn Poppy, an herbaceous perennial from China. The cultivar 'Snow Poppy' grows 1 to 2 feet.**
**3 Epacris longiflora, an evergreen shrub that requires a cool greenhouse. It will grow to 4 feet and flowers in May.**

1 Ephedra distachya, a hardy, evergreen shrub reaching 3–4 feet. It is grown for its red fruits.
2 Epidendrums are orchids found from the West Indies to south Brazil.

greenhouse or conservatory.

**Species cultivated** *E. impressa*, common Australian heath, 2 feet, white, pink or red tube-like flowers borne on loose branches, March. *E. longiflora*, fuchsia heath, 2–4 feet, tubular red flowers tipped with ivory on arching stems, May. *E. obtusifolia*, 1–3 feet, fragrant, white, short, open bell-shaped flowers, September to November. *E. purpurascens*, 2–3 feet, white and red, winter.

**Cultivation** Pot in the spring in a mixture of 3 parts of fibrous peat, and 1 part of sharp sand. Stand the pots in a sunny position in the open from July to September, the rest of the year in a light, airy greenhouse with a winter minimum temperature of 45°F (7°C). Water moderately at all times. Good drainage is essential. Syringe overhead frequently from March to July. Erect varieties should be pruned after flowering to within 1 inch of the main stem, and pendulous varieties about half-way along the branches. Propagation is by seeds sown immediately they ripen on the surface of sandy peat in a propagation frame with a temperature of 55°F (13°C), or by cuttings taken in August or April and inserted in sandy peat in a propagating frame in a cool greenhouse.

**Ephedra** (ef-ed-ra)
The ancient Greek name for the horse-

tail, another plant which these plants resemble *(Gnetaceae)*. Shrubby horsetail. Low-growing, hardy or tender, evergreen shrubs, their tiny flowers of little ornamental value, but some with attractive, berry-like fruits.

**Species cultivated** *E. andina*, low shrub, spreading in habit, wiry stems, almost leafless, orange fruits. *E. distachya*, 3–4 feet, upright branches from a procumbent base, red fruits, southern Europe. *E. gerardiana*, 2 feet, branchlets slender and spreading, fruits red, Himalaya. *E. major* (syn. *E. nebrodensis*), 3–4 feet, densely branched, fruits red, North Africa, northern India. All the above are hardy.

**Cultivation** Plant in the autumn in ordinary well-drained soil on a sunny bank where the branches can sprawl around. Propagation is by layering the branches during the summer.

---

**Epidendrum** (ep-e-den-drum)
From the Greek *epi*, upon, *dendron*, a tree, growing on trees *(Orchidaceae)*. A large genus of about 1000 species of mainly epiphytic orchids. Immense variation exists, from minute, leafy plants to tall-stemmed species reaching 10 feet and more, some plants with stout pseudobulbs and others with long thin stems known as reed-stemmed species. Most are interesting while many are very decorative and well worth growing. The genera *Barkeria*, *Encyclia* and *Nanodes* are here treated as belonging to *Epidendrum*.

**Species cultivated** (A selection only) *E. aromatica*, very fragrant, yellowish-white and red, summer, Mexico. *E. atropurpureum*, reddish-brown, lip white and crimson-purple, a very fine species, summer, Central America. *E. brassavolae*, yellow, white and purple, summer, Guatemala. *E. ciliare*, narrow segments, white with fringed lip, various, tropical America. *E. dichromum*, rose flushed white and purple, summer, Brazil. *E. endresii*, a small-growing species, pinkish-white with violet spots on lip, various, Costa Rica. *E. fragrans*, very fragrant yellowish-white with reddish-brown on lip, various times, Central America. *E. frederici-guilielmii*, crimson-purple, summer, a very fine species, Peru. *E. ibaguense*, a reed-stem type, orange-yellow to red, various times, Colombia. *E. lindleyanum (Barkeria)*, rose-purple, summer, Mexico. *E. mathewsii (Nanodes)*, dwarf species, purplish, Central America. *E. medusae (Nanodes)*, yellowish-green and purplish-brown, Costa Rica. *E. melanocaulon (Barkeria)*, rose-red, summer, Mexico. *E. nemorale*, rose-mauve, lip white and purple, sum-

1

2

**1 Epidendrum hanburii, a spring flowering orchid introduced from Mexico in 1843.**
**2 Epidendrum parkinsonianum is pendulous, requiring a shelf in the intermediate orchid house.**

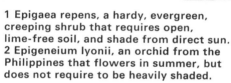

1 Epigaea repens, a hardy, evergreen, creeping shrub that requires open, lime-free soil, and shade from direct sun.
2 Epigeneium lyonii, an orchid from the Philippines that flowers in summer, but does not require to be heavily shaded.

mer, Mexico. *E. pentotis*, very fragrant, flowers in pairs, yellowish-white, lip marked with reddish-brown, autumn, Brazil. *E. prismatocarpum*, yellowish-white, spotted purple, summer, Central America. *E. radicans*, a reed-stem species, orange-scarlet, various times, Mexico. *E. skinneri (Barkeria)*, deep rose, autumn, Guatemala. *E. stamfordianum*, sprays of yellow, red-spotted flowers, fragrant, summer, Central America. *E. wallisii*, bright yellow with maroon spots, various times, Colombia. *E. xanthinum*, orange-yellow, various times, Brazil.

**Cultivation** A general mixture is 3 parts of osmunda fibre and 1 part of sphagnum moss in pots or baskets. Species with firm pseudobulbs and hard leaves require abundant light with shade to prevent scorching and a minimum temperature of about 55–60°F (13–16°C) in winter, when they also require a decided rest. The summer temperature can be up to 80°F (27°C) and over. The reed-stem types like a generally higher temperaature at all seasons, with greater humidity. The delightful species of the *Barkeria* section with their delicate, quill-like stems are best grown in pans

hung near the glass and should have a decided rest in winter. The *Nanodes* section appreciate generally moister conditions. Propagation by division at potting time and by cuttings taken below the stem roots in the reed-stem section.

### Epidermis

The outer skin or layer of cells covering a plant. In woody plants bark later replaces the epidermis on the trunk and branches.

### Epigaea (ep-e-jee-a)

From the Greek *epi,* upon, *ge,* the earth; the plants are prostrate *(Ericaceae)*. Two species of hardy, evergreen, creeping shrubs, requiring a lime-free soil.

**Species cultivated** *E. asiatica*, prostrate, mat-forming shrublet, flowers, white, flushed pink, March and April, Japan. *E. repens,* May flower, trailing arbutus, prostrate with bristly branches, white flowers, pink in the bud stage, fragrant, April and May, north-east America.

**Cultivation** Plant in September, October or April in sandy, moist peat on a shady rock garden or border. Topdress each spring with a peaty compost. In dry

weather spray the plants overhead with water. Cool, shady conditions are essential for these little plants which are not the easiest to cultivate. There is a hybrid between the two species, *E. × intertexta* ('Aurora'), with rose-pink flowers in April, which is reputed to be less difficult to please. Propagation is by seed sown in March, or by division in September or April.

### Epigeneium (ep-ee-jen-ee-um)

A genus of interesting epiphytic orchids *(Orchidaceae)*. Pseudobulbs are produced at intervals on creeping rhizomes. Several have very pretty flowers, others have large, dramatic flowers of very striking appearance. All were at one time included in the genus *Dendrobium*.

**Species cultivated** *E. amplum*, a lesser version of the next species, summer, Java. *E. coelogyne*, solitary, magnificent blooms of bizarre colouring, brownish green, purple striped, lip black brown, up to 7 inches long, summer, Burma. *E. elongatum,* up to 10 flowers on a stem, white with yellow lip, winter, Java. *E. lyonii,* long spikes of up to 25 closely set flowers, rich red purple, summer, Philippines, a very fine species. *E. triflorum,* white with yellow lip, arching spikes of about a dozen blooms, very free flowering, autumn, Java.

**Cultivation** These orchids require a medium of 3 parts of osmunda fibre and 1 part of sphagnum moss. Maintain a minimum temperature of 55°F (13°C). They do well in a variety of conditions. They should not be overpotted; repotting should be done when new growths appear. Some shading is needed, though it should not be too heavy. Propagation is by division.

---

## Epilobium (ep-e-lo-be-um)

From the Greek *epi,* upon, *lobos,* a pod; the flowers appear to grow on the seed pod *(Onagraceae).* Willow herb. Hardy perennial plants for the wild garden. The willow herbs comprise some pretty plants, but the majority are far too rampant and some seed themselves with abandon. The rosebay willow herb or fireweed, *Epilobium angustifolium (Chamaenerion angustifolium),* can become a menace and is the plant which became a dominant feature on bombed sites during and after the war years. The seeds are readily carried by the wind and once the plant is established it quickly spreads by means of its long, underground stolons.

**Species cultivated** *E. dodonaei* (syns. *E. rosmarinifolium, Chamaenerion palustre),* 1 foot, rose-purple, June to August, Europe. *E. hirsutum,* great willow herb, or codlins and cream, 3–5 feet, rose-purple, July and August, clammy to touch. Britain, central and southern Europe. *E. obcordatum,* 3–6 inches, creeping, large rosy-purple flowers, summer, California.

**Cultivation** Plant from October to March

1 Epilobium angustifolium (Chamaenerion angustifolium) commonly called the Rosebay Willow Herb or Fireweed.
2 Epimedium versicolor, a hardy perennial grown for its ornamental foliage.
3 Epimedium niveum in flower.

in ordinary soil, in sun or shade, or by the waterside, dwarf species on a sunny rock garden. Propagation is by seed sown out of doors in a shady position in the spring or in August or by division of the roots in October or March.

---

## Epimedium (ep-im-ee-de-um)

From *epimedion* the ancient Greek name used by Pliny *(Berberidaceae).* Decorative hardy perennials for the rock garden or wild garden. In the spring the small shield-shaped leaves are pale green with pink, rose and pale lemon tints. They become deeper green in the summer and are attractively veined; by the autumn they take on rich tints of deeper colouring. The light, arching sprays of flowers are borne in spring and early summer.

**Species cultivated** *E. alpinum,* bishop's hat, 9 inches, rose-purple and yellow on branching stems, June, southern Europe. *E. diphyllum* (syn. *Aceranthus diphyllus),* 6 inches, white, drooping, April and May, Japan. *E. grandiflorum,* 9–15 inches, a most attractive species with variable flowers, white, pale yellow, deep rose to violet, June, Japan. The hybrid 'Rose Queen' has crimson-carmine flowers. *E. perralderianum,* 1 foot, bright yellow, June, young leaves rich bronze, Algeria. *E. pinnatum,* barrenwort, 1 foot, arching stems of bright yellow flowers, May to July; var. *colchicum (elegans),* larger flowers more numerous, Persia. *E. pubigerum,* 1½ feet, pale yellow or white, May, Balkans, Asia Minor. *E. × rubrum* (syn. *E. alpinum rubrum),* 9 inches, crimson and yellow, April, a hybrid. *E. × versicolor,* 1 foot, red when young, becoming pale yellow, a hybrid; var. *sulphureum,*

flowers pale yellow. *E. × youngianum*, 6–12 inches, white, tinged with green, April, a hybrid; vars. *niveum*, white flowers; *rubrum*, rose-red. *E. × warleyense*, 9 inches, coppery-red, April and May, a hybrid.

**Cultivation** Plant in the autumn or spring in sandy loam enriched with leafmould or peat. Choose a cool shady border or rock garden. They do well under trees, provided the situation is not too dry, where they retain their leaves throughout the winter. They are useful for suppressing weeds. Propagation is by division of the roots in the autumn.

---

### Epipactis (ep-e-pak-tis)
From the Greek *epipegnus*, to coagulate; said to be the effect on milk *(Orchidaceae)*. A genus of about 20 terrestrial,

**1** Epipactis palustris, the Marsh Helleborine is a hardy orchid that grows about 12 inches high. It is found wild in Britain and across Europe to Serbia. The flowers appear in July.
**2** Epiphyllums, a type of cactus, produce their flowers on leaf-like branches.
**3** Epiphyllum 'Niobe', a hybrid easily grown and propagated by cuttings.

---

hardy orchids, mostly with small greenish flowers in long spikes. A few have more attractive flowers and are occasionally found in cultivation.

**Species cultivated** *E. gigantea*, green and rose with red lines, summer, North America. *E. helleborine*, green and purple, summer, Europe. *E. palustris*, white, yellowish and purple, summer, Europe.

**Cultivation** Plant in early autumn in

moist shaded borders, or in marshy places by rock garden pools. Propagation is by division of the plants in spring.

---

### Epiphyllum (ep-if-il-lum)
From the Greek *epi*, upon, *phyllon*, a leaf; the flowers are produced on the leaf-like branches *(Cactaceae)*. Succulent greenhouse plants, epiphytic cacti, previously known as *Phyllocactus*, introduced in the early nineteenth century when they became very popular in warm houses. Many now in cultivation are not true species but hybrids between a *Selenicereus* and a *Nopalxochia*.

**Species cultivated** *E. anguliger*, bushy growth with erect stems, well notched, very few spines at areoles, flowers tubular, scented, greenish-yellow outside and white inside, southern Mexico. *E.*

*crenatum,* branches thick and notched, to 3 feet high, flowers greenish-yellow to white, Guatemala. *E. oxypetalum,* branches thin and long, flowers reddish on outer petals, white inside, Brazil and Mexico. These species are epiphytic, growing in the forks of trees in bird manure and rotted leaves. The hybrid type usually found under the name of *E. × ackermannii* is the one often grown as a house plant and flowers every year, if grown under good conditions, especially in a sunny window. There are hundreds of named varieties of this hybrid, with very large flowers in a wide range of colours.

The following is a selection of named cultivars: *albus superbissimus,* white; *cooperi,* lemon-white, scented; 'Ensemble', flesh-pink; 'Gloria', orange-salmon; 'Hecla', small red; 'Innocence', white; 'Alice Roosevelt', white, rich yellow sepals; 'Silver Beau', large white; 'Springtime', pink, lavender flecked; 'September Morn', shrimp pink; 'Desert Song', pink; 'Bold Venture', bold orange; 'Buckeye', Bengal rose; 'London Prince', vermilion; 'London Youth', vermilion; 'Noblesse', red; *peacockii,* cerise-violet; 'Sarah Courant', light pink; 'Universe', carmine.

**Cultivation** These plants are easily grown and will thrive in almost any type of mixture. The best results, however, are obtained in a rich soil composed of 6 parts of loam, 2 parts of peat and 2 parts of sharp sand; some well-decayed cow manure may be incorporated in the lower part of the pot. Prune all old stems away after flowering, as once a flower has appeared at an areole no more will ever come from that spot. Encourage new growth each year as this will flower more freely. Repot plants when they become potbound, water them freely from April to September. Keep them in the greenhouse in winter and spring, but place them out of doors for summer. Plants do not like too strong sunshine in an unshaded greenhouse. Propagation is by seeds sown as for cacti, or by cuttings. These are easily obtained from young shoots, even a section of a shoot will make roots if dried at the cut part first. Root in sharp sand.

## Epiphyte
A plant which grows upon another plant without actually being parasitic. Many orchids and bromeliads are epiphytic, growing on the branches of trees but obtain their nourishment from the air and from decaying matter in crevices of the bark.

**1** Epiphyllum x ackermannii, is often grown as a house plant. It prefers a sunny window and fertile soil.
**2** Epiphytic ferns established on a tree for support only. Epiphytes do not obtain nourishment from their host plants. Many lichens and mosses are epiphytes.

### Episcia (ep-is-ke-a)
From the Greek *episkios,* shaded, a reference to the natural habitat of the plants *(Gesneriaceae).* Natives of tropical America, these herbaceous perennials are grown as decorative foliage and flowering plants in a warm greenhouse.
**Species cultivated** *E. chontalensis,* 6 inches, trailing, flowers white or pale lilac with yellow centre, autumn and winter. *E. cupreata,* 6 inches, trailing, flowers scarlet, leaves with red and silver bands. *E. fulgida,* 6 inches, trailing, scarlet, July.
**Cultivation** The episcias are admirable plants for hanging baskets or in large pans on raised staging. Pot or plant in March or April in a compost of equal parts of fibrous peat, peat and leafmould, with some sharp sand added. They require a shady position and a winter temperature of about 60°F (16°C), rising to 65–80°F (18–27°C) from March to September. Propagation is by cuttings inserted in sandy peat in March or April with a temperature of about 80°F (27°C).

---

### Epithelantha (ep-e-thel-an-tha)
From the Greek *epi,* upon, *thele,* a nipple, *anthos,* a flower; the flowers are borne on the tubercles (nipple-like protuberances) *(Cactaceae).* A genus of a single species, *E. micromeris,* a greenhouse cactus formerly known as *Mammillaria micromeris,* but as the flowers are not borne in the axils of the tubercles as in *Mammillaria,* but on the tips of the young tubercles, it was moved to a new genus. Plants are so densely covered with small white spines that the body cannot be seen. Plants are small, some-

times forming clusters. The flowers are small, ranging in colour from white to pink; var. *greggii* is larger. There are other varieties with slight differences only.
**Cultivation** A fairly light potting mixture, with a fifth part added of sharp sand, grit and broken brick is suitable. Some limestone chippings may be incorporated as the plants grow naturally on calcareous hills. Pot in March every three or four years as plants are very slow-growing. Water sparingly at all times; from April to September water only when the soil is quite dry. Do not water at all during the winter. The temperature should be 65–85°F (18–29°C) during the growing period, but can be allowed to fall to 40°F (4°C) in winter when the soil is very dry. Place the pots in a sunny spot in the greenhouse. Propagation is by seed sown in rather light seed mixture in March at a temperature of 75–80°F (24–27°C). Keep the pans moist and shaded, germination is slow and seedlings take a few years to become sizeable. Offsets which are developed on mature plants may be rooted but are rather slow to root, and should be placed on sharp sand only and sprayed overhead occasionally.

### Eragrostis (er-ag-ros-tis)
From the Greek *eros,* love, *agrostis,* grass, a reference to the beauty of these grasses *(Graminae).* Love grass. Hardy annual grasses with feathery, graceful inflorescences, decorative in the border or for use with floral arrangements, particularly attractive when used with sweet peas. The stems may also be cut

1 Episcias cupreata and lilacina, natives of tropical America, require a warm greenhouse when grown for ornamental foliage and flowers.
2 Epithelantha micromeris, a greenhouse cactus that produces small, pale pink flowers. The fruit is red, club-shaped and takes a year to ripen.
3 Eragrostis, Love Grass, a hardy annual.

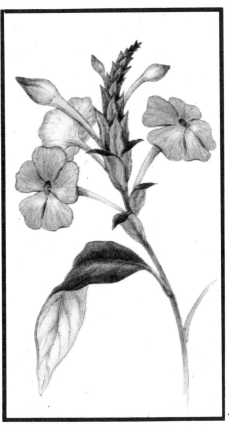

for winter use. This should be done as soon as the inflorescence is fully developed and the stems stood in an empty vase to dry, or hung heads downward in small bunches in an airy place.

**Species cultivated** *E. abessinica* (syn. *E. abyssinica*), 2–3 feet, Abyssinia. *E. interrupta* (syn. *E. elegans*), 1–2 feet, Brazil. *E. maxima*, 2–3 feet, Madagascar. *E. pilosa*, 6–12 inches, Europe. *E. sauveolens*, 1–2 feet, western Asia.

**Cultivation** Sow the seeds in April in ordinary soil in an open sunny place where they are. to grow.

---

### Eranthemum (e-ran-the-mum)

From the Greek *eras,* to love, *anthos,* a flower, a reference to the beauty of the flower *(Acanthaceae)*. Flowering and ornamental foliage perennials from south-east Asia, grown as warm greenhouse plants. The nomenclature has been much confused and many plants are referred to under this name, although botanically they are of different genera

---

**1 Eranthemum pulchellum, a winter flowering plant from India that is grown in the warm house. Pinch out the growing points to induce branching.**
**2 Eranthis x tubergenii produces larger flowers than the common Winter Aconite.**

(see also Pseuderanthemum, Stenandrium).

**Species cultivated** *E. pulchellum*, 1 foot, flowers blue, winter, India. *E. wattii* 12 inches, flowers purple, autumn, India.

**Cultivation** Pot in March and April in a mixture of equal parts of peat, leafmould, loam and sharp sand. Stand in a light position in the greenhouse from September to June with a minimum winter temperature of 55°F (13°C). Water moderately in winter, freely at other times. Stand in a sunny frame from June to September. Prune shoots to within 1 inch of the base after flowering. Propagation is by cuttings of young growths inserted in sandy peat in a propagating frame with a temperature of 75°F (24°C) from March to July.

---

### Eranthis (er-an-this)

From the Greek *er,* Spring, *anthos,* flower *(Ranunculaceae)*. Winter aconite. Hardy tuberous-rooted dwarf perennials. The cup-shaped yellow flowers with their conspicuous ruffs of green leaves are among the earliest to appear in the garden, where once planted, they should be left undisturbed.

**Species cultivated** *E. cilicica*, 4–5 inches, bright yellow, February and March, Greece and Asia Minor. *E. hyemalis*, 3–4 inches, lemon-yellow, February and March, western Europe. *E.* × *tubergenii*, 3–5 inches, golden-yellow, a hybrid raised in Holland, with larger, long-lasting flowers. 'Guinea Gold' is another hybrid with 2 inch wide, fragrant flowers, deep yellow, flushed with bronze.

**Cultivation** Plant from October to December about 2 inches deep and 2 inches apart in ordinary soil, in partially shaded borders or under trees. They may also be grown in pans containing a mixture of loam, leafmould and sharp sand in equal parts, and flowered in a cool greenhouse or not too sunny window. For this purpose plant the tubers close together and cover them with ½ inch of compost in October or November. After flowering plant the tubers in the garden. Propagation is by division of the tubers in October or November, or by seed which will germinate freely when sown in the open, where the plants are to grow, as soon as the seed is ripe.

---

### Ercilla (er-sill-a)

Commemorating Don Alonso de Ercilla, a sixteenth century Spanish nobleman. *(Phytolaccaceae)*. A genus of two self-clinging, evergreen climbing shrubs from South America, of which one only is generally seen in cultivation. This is the hardy *E. volubilis* (syn. *Bridgesia spicata*) from Chile, a tall growing species, climbing by sucker roots. The leaves are rounded oval in shape and in their axils are borne dense spikes of tiny off-white flowers, followed by attractive orange berries in autumn, though the fruits are not reliable.

**Cultivation** *E. volubilis* will grow in ordinary fertile garden soil against a sheltered wall or at the base of a tree. Propagation is by cuttings made from short lengths of stem, rooted in a cold frame in September.

---

## Eremurus (er-e-mur-us)

From the Greek *eremos,* solitary, *oura,* a tail, a reference to the single flower spike *(Liliaceae).* Imposing hardy herbaceous perennials with a curious, thick brittle rootstock, like a giant starfish. These natives of western Asia and the Himalaya region are best planted when quite young, although this may mean waiting three years or so before they flower, and once planted they should remain undisturbed for several years. They vary in height from 3–10 feet. There is a delightful range of colour.

**Species cultivated** *E. bungei* (syn. *E. stenophyllus bungei*), 3–4 feet, yellow, early July, Persia. *E. elwesii,* 6–9 feet, pink, May; var. *albus,* white. *E. himalaicus,* 6–8 feet, white, May and June, Himalaya. *E. × himrob (E. himalaicus × E. robustus),* 6–8 feet, pale pink, May and June, hybrid. *E. kaufmanniana,* 3–4 feet, yellow, June, Turkestan. *E. olgae,* 2–4 feet, white flushed with lilac, fragrant, July, Turkestan. *E. robustus,* fox-tail lily, 8–10 feet, peach-pink, June, Turkestan. *E. spectabilis,* 2–4 feet, pale yellow tinted orange, June, Siberia. *E. × tubergenii,* 5–7 feet, light yellow, May and June, hybrid. Named cultivars include 'Dawn', 6–8 feet, rose pink, June and July; 'Flair', 8 feet, golden yellow, flushed pink, June and July; 'Highdown Hybrids', 6–7 feet, various shades, summer; 'Shelford Hybrids', 6–7 feet, pink, coppery-yellow, etc., June and July; 'Sir Arthur Hazlerigg', 5 feet, coppery-orange, June and July.

**Cultivation** Plant in August, September or October in well-drained, rich, sandy loam in a warm, sunny bed, sheltered as much as possible from wind; a background of evergreens is admirable. Mulch each autumn with well-decayed manure. The lush green leaves appear in early spring and may be liable to damage by frost unless protected with some form of mulch or sand. If sand is placed over the crown in December or January the leaves will grow through it; the sand can easily be brushed away, and slug damage is not so likely as when other material is used. Propagation is by seed sown thinly in a cold frame in the early autumn. The seedlings should remain undisturbed for two years before transplanting. Germination of old seed is unpredictable. Division of the roots may be done carefully in October or March. The roots are easily broken when lifting and any damaged roots should be cut clean and dusted with lime.

---

## Erepsia (er-eps-ee-a)

From the Greek *erepsis,* meaning a roof or cover, in allusion to the roof-like

**The Shelford Hybrid Eremurus are imposing hardy, herbaceous perennials, growing to 7 feet and flowering in June.**

---

mass of staminodes *(Aizoaceae).* A genus of shrubby succulents from South Africa, a few only of which are in general cultivation, related to *Lampranthus* and formerly classified as *Mesembryanthemum.*

**Species cultivated** *E. haworthii,* a well branched sub-shrub to 2 feet tall, with crowded, grey-green tapered leaves 1 inch or more long; flowers up to 3 inches across, magenta purple. *E. inclaudens,* the best known species, with two angled stems and sabre-shaped fleshy, 1 inch long leaves; flowers 1½ inches across, bright violet purple. Other species likely to be occasionally met with in the trade or in botanic gardens and elsewhere are *E. anceps, E. aspera, E. compressa, E. gracilis* and *E. mutabilis,* all resembling the above in general appearance, but with variations in flower colour.

**Cultivation** These succulents may be grown in pots or pans in a cool greenhouse where a minimum winter temperature of 40–45°F (4–7°C) can be maintained. A well-drained medium is essential, a well-drained type being suitable with the addition of an extra part of limestone grit or extra sharp sand. Watering should be much reduced during the winter months but never entirely withheld. Propagation is by cuttings rooted in pots of sand during the summer.

## Eria (er-e-a)

From the Greek *erion*, wool; the flowers and flower stalks are often woolly *(Orchidaceae)*. A large genus of 350 species of epiphytic orchids, closely related to *Dendrobium*, usually with small flowers, often in long spikes. Many are insignificant in flower, while a few are very attractive with brightly coloured spikes of flowers, freely produced. Considerable variation of plant habit is found in the genus.

**Species cultivated** (A selection only). *E. bicolor*, white and yellowish, spring, Ceylon. *E. bractescens*, white, red and yellowish, summer, Burma. *E. globifera*, a very attractive miniature with single inverted flowers, creamy-white and reddish, winter, Annam. *E. floribunda*, many 5 inch spikes from tall cane-like stems, white and pink, spring. *E. ornata*, reddish-brown with orange bracts, summer, Malaya. *E. pannea*, white and orange-red, various times, Burma. *P. rhyncostyloides*, very handsome, many thick spikes of white, rose flushed flowers, summer, Java. *E. vestita*, white and yellow, pendent, summer, Malaya.

**Cultivation** Provide these orchids with a mixture of 3 parts of osmunda fibre and

1 part of sphagnum moss, in pots or baskets. They should have a general temperature of 60–65°F (16–18°C) in summer and a moist atmosphere, light shading and abundant watering. In winter rest the plants but do not let them dry out for long periods. Propagation is by division of the plants at potting time in spring.

## Erica (er-e-ka)

From the Greek *ereike*, the name for heath or heather *(Ericaceae)*. A large genus of evergreen, hardy and greenhouse flowering shrubs from Africa and Europe. The majority are compact, dwarf-growing, but some species attain the height of small trees. Most species require a lime-free soil, although *E. carnea* and its varieties, *E.* × *darleyensis*, *E. mediterranea*, *E. terminalis* and the tree heath, *E. arborea*, are to a varying degree tolerant of chalky soil. Hardy heaths are most effective and thrive better when grouped together than when dotted about singly. They are excellent plants for suppressing weeds. By making a careful selection it is possible to have heathers in flower in the garden almost throughout the year, provided there is sufficient space for a comprehensive collection.

**Species cultivated**: Hardy *E. arborea*,

1 Eria globifera, a miniature epiphytic orchid from Annam, flowering in winter.
2 Erica tetralix, the Cross-leaved Heath, flowers freely from June to October.
3 Erica cinerea coccinea, a form of the native Grey Heath, Scotch or Bell Heather, that flowers in June and July.

1 Erica carnea alba flowers profusely
from December to April on 12 inch stems.
2 Erica hyemalis from South Africa.

tree heath, 10–20 feet, panicles of
fragrant white flowers, April and May,
grey foliage, hardy only in the more mild
areas, Mediterranean; var. *alpina*, 6–8
feet, similar, but hardier, Spain. *E.
australis*, Spanish heath, 6–8 feet, rosy-
red, April and May, rather tender; 'Mr
Robert' is a fine white variety. *E.
canaliculata*, 12–18 feet, flowers white,
March to May, South Africa, hardy only
in mild regions, where it may be
damaged in severe winters. *E. carnea*,
dwarf to 18 inches, winter-flowering,
central Europe; vars. *gracilis*, rose-pink,
compact; *praecox rubra*, rose-red, early;
*vivellii*, carmine, dwarf, later-flowering,
winter foliage bronze. *E. ciliaris*, Dorset
heath, 9–18 inches, rosy-red, branching
spikes, June to October, south-west
Europe and south-west England; var.
*maweana*, larger flowers. *E. cinerea*, bell
or Scotch heather, also known as
fineleaved or twisted heather, 9–24
inches, branching, rosy-purple, June to
August, western Europe and British
moorlands; vars. *alba*, white; *alba major*,
white, taller; *atropurpurea*, bright purple; *coccinea*, dwarf, scarlet; *fulgida*,
dwarf, scarlet; *rosea*, rose-pink. *E. ×
darleyensis* (syn. *E. mediterranea hybrida*), 1½–2 feet, rosy-lilac, November to

May, an easily grown hybrid (*E. carnea* × *E. mediterranea*). *E. lusitanica* (syn. *E. codonodes*), Portuguese heath, up to 10 feet, white, tinged pink, slightly fragrant, March and April, rather tender, southwest Europe. *E. mackaiana* (syn. *E. mackayi*), 1–1½ feet, rosy crimson, July to September, western Ireland, northwestern Spain; var. *plena*, double flowers. *E. mediterranea*, 6–10 feet, hardiest of the tree heaths, rosy-lilac, honey-scented flowers, March to May, western Europe; vars. *alba*, white; *hibernica*, dwarfer, more compact; *superba*, pink, more compact. *E. pageana*, 1 foot, rich yellow, March and April. South Africa. *E.* × *praegeri* (syn. *E, tetralix praegeri*), 1–1½ feet, pale pink, June to October, hybrid. *E. scoparia*, 10 feet, flowers tiny, greenish, May and June, western Mediterranean, Madeira; var. *minima* (syns. *pumila*, *nana*), 1½–2 feet, dwarf form. *E.* × *stuartii*, 9–12 inches, deep rose, June to September, natural hybrid, Galway. *E. terminalis* (syn. *E. stricta*), Corsican heath, 5–8 feet, rose-pink, urn-shaped, June to September, western Mediterranean. *E. tetralix*, cross-leaved heath, 12–18 inches, rose-pink, June to October, Europe, including Britain; vars. *alba*, white; *lawsoniana*, dwarf, pink; *mollis*, grey leaves, white flowers; *rosea*, rose-pink. *E. umbellata*, 1 foot, cerise-pink, summer, hardy in the milder areas only, Spain,

Portugal, North Africa. *E. vagans*, Cornish heath, 2–3 feet, wide spreading habit, rosy-lilac, July to October, southwest Europe, including Cornwall; vars. *grandiflora*, rose-red; *kevernensis*, rose-pink; *kevernensis alba*, white; *rubra*, rosy-red. *E.* × *veitchii*, 3–6 feet, white, fragrant, February to April, hybrid tree heath. *E.* × *watsonii*, 12–18 inches, rosy-red, July to September, natural hybrid, Cornwall. *E.* × *williamsii*, 12–18 inches, leaves tipped gold, rosy-pink flowers, late summer to autumn, natural hybrid, Cornwall.

**Cultivars** include: *E. carnea* 'Cecilia M. Beale', white; 'James Backhouse', early, taller; 'King George', deep pink, dwarf; 'Prince of Wales', rose pink: 'Queen Mary', deep rose-red; 'Ruby Glow', dark red, dark foliage; 'Springwood', white, tall, early; 'Springwood Pink', rose-pink; 'Winter Beauty', rose-pink, very early. *E. ciliaris* 'Stoborough', white. *E. cinerea* 'C. D. Eason', deep pink. *E. darleyensis* 'George Rendall', deeper coloured flowers; 'Silberschmelze', white flowers. *E. mediterranea* 'Brightness', dwarf, rose-pink; 'W. T. Ratcliff', white.

*E. tetralix* 'Mary Grace', bright pink flowers, silvery foliage; 'Pink Glow', pink flowers, grey foliage. *E. vagans* 'Lyonesse', pure white; 'Mrs D. F. Maxwell', deep cerise. *E.* × *watsonii* 'Dawn', spreading habit, later flowering; 'H. Maxwell', taller, flowers clear pink. Many more are offered in specialist's catalogues.

**Greenhouse** *E.* × *cavendishiana* (*E. abietina* × *E. depressa*), 4 feet, yellow, May. *E. elegans*, 2 feet, red, May, South Africa. *E. gracilis*, 1–1½ feet, rose-purple in terminal clusters, September to December, South Africa. *E. hyemalis*, winter heath, 1½ feet, rose-tinted white, December to March, South Africa. *E. persoluta*, 1–3 feet, rosy-red, March to May, South Africa.

**Cultivation** For the hardy species a well-drained soil containing plenty of peat or leafmould is required and it should be lime free for all except *E. carnea*, *E.* × *darleyensis* and *E. mediterranea*, although *E. arborea* and *E. terminalis* may tolerate a little lime in the soil, but do better where it is absent. Plant deeply in April and May or in October and November. Heathers like an open sunny position and the best results are obtained by starting with small, really young plants, which will quickly get established. Old woody layers will not prove satisfactory. A topdressing of granulated peat or leafmould in the spring may be advisable where the soil is poor and light, but it is not essential on reasonably fertile soil. Plants should be clipped over lightly after they have flowered; this will keep them compact and they will live longer. Propagation is by small cuttings inserted in sandy peat in pots in July or August with gentle bottom heat; in hot weather they will need frequent overhead spraying. Plants may also be propagated by division in October, or by layering young growths in the spring, scooping out the soil round the plants, pressing the growths back into the dish-like depression so formed and filling up the centre with light, sandy soil. The shoots will root into this and may later be detached.

With the greenhouse species treatment is as follows: Repot autumn and winter-flowering plants in March, summer flowering plants in September. The mixture should consist of 2 parts of fibrous peat and 1 part of lime-free silver sand. Pot firmly. Water carefully at all times keeping the soil moist, but not wet. Maintain a minimum winter temperature of 40°F (4°C). Propagation of greenhouse species is by cuttings about 1 inch long inserted in sandy peat in a propagating frame in the spring with a temperature of about 65°F (18°C).

## Erigeron (er-ij-er-on)
From the Greek *eri,* early or *ear,* spring, *geron,* old, possibly referring to the hoary leaves of some species *(Compositae).* Fleabane. Hardy herbaceous, daisy-flowered perennials some of which continue to flower intermittently throughout the summer.

**Species cultivated** *E. alpinus,* 9 inches, purple and yellow, August, northern Alps. *E. aurantiacus,* orange daisy, 12–18 inches, orange, summer, Turkestan. *E. aureus,* 4 inches, bright gold, spring onwards, North America. *E. compositus,* 8 inches, purple, summer, North America. *E. glaucus,* 6–12 inches, purple to pink, summer, North America. *E. coulteri,* 20 inches, white or pale mauve, summer, North America. *E. leiomerus,* 4 inches, small, lavender-blue, North America. *E. macranthus* (syn. *E. mesa-grande*), 2 feet, violet, yellow centres, summer, North Africa. *E. mucronatus,* 15 inches, white, deep and pale pink, summer and autumn, Mexico, a useful wall plant. *E. philadelphus,* 3 feet, lilac-pink, summer, North America. *E. speciosus,* 18 inches, violet-blue, summer, North America. *E. trifidus,* 4 inches, pale lavender, summer, North America. *E. uniflorus,* 4 inches, white or purplish, summer, North America.

**Cultivars** include: 'B. Ladhams', 1½ feet, bright rose; 'Bressingham Strain', *(E.*

1 Erigeron 'Foerster's Liebling' is a semi-double form growing to 18 inches.
2 Erigeron mucronatus, a Mexican plant for the rock or wall garden. It spreads rapidly and can be damaged in severe winters, but is rarely killed.

*aurantiacus)*, 1–1½ feet, orange to yellow shades, May to July; 'Charity', 2 feet, pale pink; 'Darkest of All', 2 feet, deep violet; 'Dignity', 2 feet, mauve-blue; 'Felicity', 1½–2 feet, deep pink, large; 'Foerster's Liebling', 1½ feet, deep pink, semi-double; 'Gartenmeister Walther', 2 feet, soft pink; 'Merstham Glory', 2 feet, deep lavender-blue, semi-double; 'Prosperity', 2 feet, deep blue; 'Quakeress', 2 feet, pale blue overlaid silvery pink; 'Quakeress White', 2 feet, white; 'Unity', 2 feet, bright pink; 'Vanity', 3 feet, clear pink, late flowering; 'Wupperthal', 2 feet, pale blue.

**Cultivation** Plant in the autumn or early spring in a sunny position in ordinary soil on a rock garden, or towards the front of the border for the taller varieties. *E. mucronatus* is a good plant for paved areas or steps, where it can seed itself between the cracks. Cut down stems after flowering. Named varieties are propagated by division of the clumps in the autumn or spring, the species by seed sown in the open in light soil in a shady position from April to June.

---

**Erinacea** (er-in-ay-se-a)
From the Latin *erinaceus*, a hedgehog, a reference to the spiny branches *(Leguminosae)*. Hedgehog broom. There is but one species in this genus, *E. pungens* (syn. *Anthyllis erinacea*), a foot tall, spring-flowering shrub, deciduous and hardy, from Spain and North Africa. The hedgehog broom is slow-growing and likes a sunny position with well-drained soil on the rock garden.
**Cultivation** Plant in May or September in loam and peat at foot of south-facing wall or on rock garden in cool areas. Propagation is by cuttings inserted in sandy loam and peat in a cold frame in the autumn, or by seed.

---

**Erinus** (er-i-nus)
From the Greek *eri*, early; the plants flower in spring *(Scrophulariaceae)*. A small genus of tufted hardy plants for the rock garden, sink garden or sunny wall. The only species cultivated is *E. alpinus*, 3–4 inches, with rounded racemes of rosy-purple flowers in May, surmounting rosettes of hairy leaves; vars. *albus*, white; *carmineus*, carmine; 'Abbotswood Pink', 3 inches; 'Dr Haenaele', 6 inches, carmine and 'Mrs C. Boyle', 3–4 inches, pink, are excellent cultivars.
**Cultivation** These little plants thrive in gritty loam and peat. Once established they will sow themselves and the seedlings will overwinter in the open. Propagation is by seed sown in March or by division after flowering.

---

**1 Erinacea pungens, a spiny shrub sometimes called the Hedgehog Broom. Growing to about 1 foot in height, it is ideal for the rock garden.
2 Erinus alpinus, a tufted, hardy plant for the rock garden.**

## Eriobotrya (er-e-o-bot-re-a)

From the Greek *erion*, wool, *botrys*, a bunch or cluster, referring to the downy clusters of flowers *(Rosaceae)*. A small genus of east Asian shrubs and small trees of which one is cultivated. This is *E. japonica* (syn. *Photinia japonica*), the loquat, a somewhat tender evergreen flowering shrub from China. This reaches between 10–30 feet in height and, particularly after a hot summer, produces intermittently from autumn to spring, white or yellowish-white fragrant flowers, reminiscent of those of hawthorns. The edible fruits, about the size of a green walnut, are borne in bunches and are downy, pale orange-red in colour. The fruits rarely ripen in the open in England, but the leaves, dark glossy green, up to 1 foot long, woolly beneath, make it a striking shrub. It is grown in the open as far north as Norfolk, Va. and beyond but elsewhere requires some protection.

**Cultivation** Plant in the early autumn or in the spring in a light, loamy soil. It may also be grown on the back wall of a cold or slightly heated, sunny, lean-to greenhouse, where it should be watered moderately during the winter and freely from April onwards. Syringe with water during hot weather. Prune straggling shoots in April. Propagation is by seed sown in spring or autumn in pots of light soil, or by cuttings of firm shoots in August inserted in pots of sandy soil, both placed in a cold greenhouse or frame.

## Eriocephalus (err-ee-o-seff-al-us)

From the Greek *erion*, wool, *cephalus*, a head, referring to the woolly appearance of the heads after flowering *(Compositae)*. A genus of evergreen shrubs from South Africa, with silvery leaves. The only species likely to be found in cultivation is *E. africanus*, 2–3 feet tall, with silky hairy leaves and creamy-white flower heads at the ends of the stems, from January to March, followed by woolly fruits.

**Cultivation** This shrub needs the protection of a cool greenhouse with a minimum winter temperature of 40°F (4°C). A suitable potting mixture consists of 3 parts of sandy loam and 1 part of peat. Propagation is by cuttings of young shoots rooted in sandy medium in a propagating frame with bottom heat.

## Eriogonum (er-e-o-go-num)

From the Greek *erion*, wool, *gonu*, a joint; the nodes are downy *(Polygonaceae)*. Hardy herbaceous perennials suitable for the alpine house or frame. Mostly natives of California and Western America, they have woolly foliage

**1** Eriobotrya japonica, the Loquat, a somewhat tender evergreen shrub from China. The fruit is edible but rarely ripens in the upper part of its range.
**2** Eriogonum crocatum, a hardy sub-shrub.

1 Eriophorum angustifolium, Cotton
Grass, a native growing to 15 inches.
2 Eritrichium nanum, a connoisseur's
alpine plant that flowers in summer.

and, like other plants with similar
leaves, they dislike winter wet.

**Species cultivated** *E. arborescens,* 1–2
feet, bright rose in the bud stage,
becoming white, July. *E. jamesii,* 9
inches, white or pale yellow, June and
July. *E. ovalifolium,* 5 inches, cream,
turning purplish, summer. *E. racemosum,*
2–2½ feet, spreading, white to pink, July.
*E. torreyanum,* 9 inches, shrubby, cream,
summer. *E. umbellatum,* 12 inches,
spreading, yellow, September.

**Cultivation** Pot in early April in a well-
drained, sandy loam. Plants require
plenty of water during the growing
season, but they should be kept on the
dry side in winter. Propagation is by
seed sown in light soil in April, or by
cuttings taken with a heel in July.
Division of the roots is possible in March.

## Eriophorum (er-e-off-or-um)

From the Greek *erion,* wool, *phoreo,* to
bear; the heads are cottony or woolly in
appearance *(Cyperaceae).* Cotton grass.
A small genus of perennial herbaceous
plants, for moist, boggy places, related
to *Scirpus,* widely distributed throughout the Northern Hemisphere. The tufts
of elongated bristles surrounding the
spikelets in summer give the plants a
cottony appearance.

**Species cultivated** *E. alpinum,* 1 foot. *E.
angustifolium,* 15 inches, native plant. *E.
latifolium,* 1–1½ feet. *E. vaginatum,* 1 foot,
from Europe, northern Asia.

**Cultivation** These are plants for shallow
water by the edges of pools, or for the
bog garden. Plant in spring. Propagation
is by seed sown where the plants are to
grow or by division of the rootstocks.

## Eriophyllum (er-e-o-fil-um)

From the Greek *erion,* wool, *phyllon,*
leaf; the leaves are woolly *(Compositae).*
Hardy perennial plants for the rock
garden or border. The only species
cultivated is *E. caespitosum* (syn. *Bahia
lanata),* from North America, which
grows 1½ feet tall. It is yellow and has
daisy-like flowers freely produced in
summer.

**Cultivation** This little plant will grow in
ordinary soil in a sunny border or rock
garden. Plant from October to April.
Propagation is by seed which should be
sown ⅛th inch deep during April in
ordinary soil where the plants are to
flower or the roots may be divided in
early spring.

## Eritrichium (er-e-trik-e-um)

From the Greek *erion,* wool, *trichos,* hair,
referring to the silky hairs on the leaves
*(Boraginaceae).* Dwarf perennial alpine
plants for the connoisseur's alpine
house. They are beautiful in flower and
leaf but difficult to keep alive.

**Species cultivated** *E. nanum*, fairy borage, fairy forget-me-not, 3–6 inches, a dense cushion of silvery-grey, hairy leaves, bright blue flowers in May and June, from the highest European Alps. *E. rupestre pectinatum* (syn. *E. strictum*), 6–12 inches, tufted growth, silver-grey hairy leaves, blue flowers with yellow eye, May, Asian mountains.

**Cultivation** Although these are difficult plants they are so beautiful in flower that it is worth trying to grow them in a mixture of 3 parts of silver sand and 1 part of leafmould. The roots must be kept moist during the growing and flowering season, but the foliage must be kept damp-free at all times. Propagation is by seed sown in January. If the seed pan is placed in a refrigerator for about 48 hours after sowing this may encourage germination.

---

## Erodium (er-o-de-um)

From the Greek *erodios*, a heron; the style and ovaries resemble the head and beak of a heron *(Geraniaceae)*. Heron's bill. Hardy perennials, closely related to the hardy geraniums, or crane's bills. There are dwarf species suitable for the rock garden and taller border plants.

**Species cultivated** *E. absinthoides*, 1 foot or more, violet, pink or white, summer, south-east Europe, Asia Minor; var. *amanum*, 6 inches, white, leaves hairy white. *E. chamaedryoides* (syn. *E. reichardii*), 4 inches, white, veined pink, June, Majorca; var. *roseum*, deep pink.

*E. chrysanthum*, 6 inches, soft yellow flowers, summer, grey-green, ferny leaves, Greece. *E. corsicum*, mat-forming, rosy-pink with deeper veins, summer, Corsica; vars. *album*, white, *rubrum*, clear red. *E.* × *kolbianum* 3 inches, white to pink, summer, hybrid. *E. loderi*, 4–6 inches, white or pale pink, summer. *E. macradenum*, 6 inches, violet, blotched purple at base, summer, Pyrenees. *E. manescavii*, up to 2 feet, wine-red, summer, Pyrenees. *E. pelargoniflorum*, 1 foot, white, marked purple, summer, Anatolia. *E. supracanum*, 4 inches, white, veined pink, summer, Pyrenees.

**Cultivation** Plant out the taller varieties in March or April in ordinary soil and in a sunny position. These plants dislike acid soils. They very seldom need transplanting, although pot grown alpine species should be repotted in April every year, in a compost of equal parts of loam, leafmould, and sharp sand. Propagation is by seed sown in March or April for the taller species in a temperature of 55°F (13°C) and in July or August in a cold frame for the alpine species. Plants may be divided in April, and cuttings of dwarf species for the rock garden may be taken in May. The cuttings should then be rooted in a sandy soil, in a frame.

---

1 Erodium corsicum, a summer-flowering mat-forming perennial.
2 Eryngium maritimum, Sea Holly, a hardy perennial growing to 18 inches.

## Eryngium (er-in-je-um)

From the ancient Greek name *eryngeon*, the meaning of which is obscure *(Umbelliferae)*. A genus of over 200 species of hardy and nearly hardy perennial herbaceous plants, some with thistle-like leaves. Some species are seaside plants in the wild. All are more or less spiny and in some species a feature is the glistening, metallic bluish sheen that covers the stem, the inflorescence, and the floral bracts. If the stems are cut and allowed to dry slowly they retain their colour and sheen, thus providing useful winter decorations.

**Species cultivated** *E. agavifolium*, 5–6 feet, narrow spiny leaves up to 5 feet in length, flowers green, hardy in milder regions, Argentine. *E. alpinum*, 1–1½ feet, upper parts tinged blue, summer, Europe. *E. amethystinum*, up to 2½ feet, deep blue shiny flower-heads and upper stems, July to September, Europe. *E. bourgatii*, 1½–2 feet, leaves marked grey-white, flowers light blue on spreading branches, June to August, Pyrenees. *E. bromeliifolium*, 3–4 feet, long, slender leaves, flowers pale green to white, July hardy in the south and west, Mexico. *E. dichotomum*, 1–2 feet, blue, July and August, southern Europe. *E. giganteum*, up to 4 feet, rounded blue heads, July and August, Caucasus. *E. heldreichii*, 1–2 feet, bluish, summer, Syria. *E. leavenworthii*, 3 feet, purple, summer, North America. *E. maritimum*, sea holly, 1–1½ feet, pale blue, summer to autumn,

1 Eryngium giganteum, grows to 6 feet, and flowers in July and August. It was introduced from the Caucasus in 1820.
2 Eryngium grandiflorum, like most eryngiums prefers well-drained, sandy soil.
3 Eryngium oliverianum produces deep glowing amethyst flowers and stems in summer. The average height is 3 feet.

Europe, including Britain. *E.* × *oliverianum*, 3–4 feet, teazle-like, metallic blue flowers, July to September, a hybrid. *E. pandanifolium*, 6–10 feet, narrow, spiny leaves up to 6 feet in length, purple-brown flowers, late summer, Uruguay, hardy in warmer sections. *E. planum*, 2 feet, small, deep blue flowers, July and August, eastern Europe. *E. serra*, 6 feet, leaves up to 5 feet long, narrow, with spiny teeth, flowers white, to pale green, autumn, Brazil. *E. spinalba*, 1–2 feet, small bluish-white flowers, summer, Europe. *E. tripartitum*, 2–2½ feet, steel blue, with long bracts, summer, possibly a hybrid, origin unknown. *E. variifolium*, 1½–2 feet, leaves white veined, flowers whitish-green, summer, Europe. Cultivars include 'Blue Dwarf', 2 feet; 'Violetta', 2½ feet, violet-blue, both flowering in late summer.

**Cultivation** Plant in the autumn or in the spring, preferably in light sandy soil, although these plants are not particular, so long as the drainage is good. They like a sunny site and dislike cold, wet soil in winter. The thong-like roots require the soil to be deeply cultivated. Generally speaking, eryngiums from South America are half-hardy or hardy in the warmer regions only. They are, however, striking plants where they can be grown. Propagation is by seed sown in boxes and placed in a cold frame in April or May; by division of the plants in October or April, or by root cuttings.

## Erysimum (er-is-im-um)
From the Greek *erus,* to draw up; some species are said to produce blisters *(Cruciferae).* Alpine wallflower. Hardy annual, biennial and perennial plants, closely related to *Cheiranthus.* Some are rather weedy, but others make good edging plants for a perennial border, or on gravelly banks and retaining walls.

**Annual species cultivated** *E. perofskianum,* 1 foot, reddish-orange, summer, Afghanistan.

**Biennial** *E. allionii* see *Cheiranthus allionii, E. arkansanum,* 1½–2 feet, golden-yellow, July to October, Arkansas and Texas. *E. asperum,* 3 feet, vivid orange, early summer, North America. *E. linifolium* (syn. *Cheiranthus linifolius),* 1–1½ feet, rosy-lilac, early summer, Spain.

**Perennial** *E. dubium* (syn. *E. ochroleucum),* 1 foot, pale yellow, April to July, Europe. *E. rupestre,* 1 foot, sulphur-yellow, spring, Asia Minor.

**Cultivation** The alpine wallflowers like ordinary soil in dryish, sunny beds or on the rock garden. Propagation of annuals is by seed sown in April where the plants are to flower; biennials by seed sown out of doors in June in a sunny place, transplanting the seedlings to their flowering positions in August; perennials by seed sown in a similar manner, or by division in March or April, also by cuttings inserted in sandy soil in August in a cold propagating frame.

## Erythrina (er-ith-ri-na)
From the Greek *erythros,* red, the colour of the flowers *(Leguminosae).* A small genus of tender deciduous shrubs and half-hardy perennials.

**Species cultivated** *E. crista-galli,* coral tree, shrub to 6–8 feet, flowers bright scarlet in bold spikes on the ends of shoots, leaves leathery, somewhat glaucous, stems prickly, June to August, Brazil; var. *compacta,* less tall, more compact in habit. *E. herbacea,* 2–4 feet, herbaceous plant, flowers deep scarlet, borne in long spikes, June to September, West Indies.

**Cultivation** The coral tree can only be grown in the open in the warm climate gardens. Otherwise it should be grown in the warm greenhouse, in a large pot or tub containing equal parts of loam,

1 Erysimum rupestre, a spring flowering perennial for the rock garden.
2 Erythrina crista-galli compacta, a more compact form of the Coral Tree. The flowers appear from June to August.

peat, old manure and sharp sand. Repot when necessary in March. Water freely from April to September. Stand the container in the open during the summer. Cut the plant hard back in October, and keep it almost dry during the winter in a frost-free shed or greenhouse. This applies to both shrubby and herbaceous species. Propagation of shrubby species is by cuttings in the spring, removed with a piece of old wood attached and inserted singly in pots containing sandy peat in a propagating frame, with a temperature of 75°C (24°C). Herbaceous species may be divided in spring.

### Erythronium (er-e-thro-ne-um)

From the Greek *erythros,* red, the flower colour of the European species *(Liliaceae).* Small hardy bulbous plants grown there since the sixteenth century and coming mainly from the North American continent, although the species commonly grown, *E. dens-canis,* is a native of Europe. Some species have marbled leaves and others have plain green leaves, a general method of classification.

**Species cultivated** *E. americanum,* yellow adder's tongue, 6 inches, golden-yellow flowers speckled with red, May. *E. californicum,* 9–12 inches, creamy-white, petals spreading and reflexed at the tips, leaves heavily mottled. *E. citrinum,* 8 inches, creamy-white, lemon-yellow at the base, March and April. *E. dens-canis,* dog's tooth violet, 6 inches, the most popularly grown species, white to pale pink and reddish-mauve with a ring of orange-red marks at the base, March and April, leaves heavily marbled; vars. include *album,* white. *E. hendersonii,* 12 inches, pale lilac with dark purple markings at the base, early April, leaves heavily mottled, with pale green and pink lines. *E. revolutum,* trout lily, 9–12 ins., white to deep pink, April and May, mottled leaves. *E. tuolumnense,* 9–12 inches, golden-yellow flowers, April, light greenish-yellow leaves with pale mottling. Cultivars include: *E. dens-canis* 'Franz Hals', reddish-purple; 'Pink Perfection'; 'Purple King'; 'Rose Beauty'; 'Rose Queen'; 'Snowflake'. *E. revolutum* 'White Beauty'. *E. tuolumnense* 'Pagoda', 1–1½ feet, large golden-yellow flowers.

**Cultivation** Plant the bulbs in sheltered rock gardens, on banks or among shrubs which cast light shade, 3–5 inches deep and 4 inches apart, in August, in their permanent positions, because the plants do not like to be transplanted. Top dress annually with compost or rotted manure and loam and keep the

---

1 Erythronium tuolumnense, a hardy bulbous plant, 9 to 12 inches in height, that flowers in March and April.
2 Erythronium 'White Beauty', a bulbous plant that can be grown in pots, the rock garden and the front of mixed borders. Also used for naturalising.

1 Escallonia 'Apple Blossom', a compact growing evergreen shrub. It grows to 4 feet and flowers in June.
2 Escallonia 'Peach Blossom' grows to 6 feet and is suited to the finer gardens.

soil moist; never let the bulbs dry out or they will shrivel. Bulbs can be grown in pots in a mixture of equal parts of loam, peat and leafmould. Plant them in August, 1 inch deep only. Keep the pots free from frost through the winter, either in a cold frame or cold house and withhold water unless the soil dries out completely. In February put the pots into a greenhouse or living room and water regularly. The bulbs will then flower in March. Propagation is by offsets from the bulbs, separated at planting time, or by seed which is very slow to germinate and the resulting plants may take four or five years to flower.

## Escallonia (es-kal-o-ne-a)

Commemorating Senor Escallon, Spanish traveller in America (Saxifragaceae). Glossy-leaved shrubs, mostly natives of Chile, the majority of which are evergreen and many of which are hardy in the warm areas like the Deep South and California. A few are also hardy north to Virginia.

**Species cultivated** E. × edinensis (E or SE), 6 feet, rosy-pink, summer, hybrid. E. × exoniensis (E) 12–15 feet, white and rose, summer, hybrid. E. illinita (D), 10–12 feet, white, June to August. E. × ingramii (E), 12 feet, rose-pink, summer, hybrid. E. × iveyi (E), 10–12 feet, white, late summer to autumn, hybrid. E. × langleyensis (E or SE), 6–10 feet, rosy-carmine flowers, summer, does well against a north wall, hybrid. E. leucantha (E), 12–15 feet, flowers pure white in 1 foot long spikes, July. E. macrantha (E), 6–10 feet, fragrant crimson flowers, June,

used as a hedge in Britain's southern counties. E. montana (E), 5–6 feet, compact habit, flowers white, summer. E. montividensis (E), 10–12 feet, white, summer, wall protection helps. E. × newreyensis (E), 10 feet, white, pink flushed, summer, hybrid. E. organensis (E), 4–6 feet, rosy-red, summer. E. punctata (E), 6–10 feet, deep crimson, July and August. E. pterocladon (E), 8–10 feet, white, fragrant, June to August, Patagonia. E. revoluta (E), 15–20 feet, grey foliage, pink to white flowers, July to September. E. rubra (E), 12–15 feet, red, July and August; var. pygmaea, 1–2 feet, suitable for rock garden. E. virgata (syn. E. philsippiana) (D), 6–8 feet, white, June and July, the hardiest of all species, but not suitable for limey soil. E. viscosa (E), 8–10 feet, flowers white in drooping spikes, June to August.

Escallonias hybridise easily and several good named cultivars are even more vigorous and hardier than the parent plants. They include 'Apple Blossom' (E), 4 feet, soft pink flowers, June, compact growth; 'C. F. Ball' (E),

6 feet, bright carmine-red flowers, June to August, large leaves, especially attractive against a wall; 'Donard Beauty' (E), 4–5 feet, rosy-red, summer; 'Donard Radiance' (E), 4–5 feet, deep pink, July and August; 'Donard Seedling' (E), 5 feet, white and pale pink flowers, summer, a particularly hardy hybrid; 'E. G. Cheeseman' (E), 8–10 feet, large, bell-like cherry-red flowers, summer; 'Gwendolyn Anley' (E), 5–6 feet, blush pink, June and July; 'Peach Blossom' (E), 5–6 feet, summer; 'Pride of Donard' (E), 5–6 feet, rich red, May to July; 'Slieve Donard' (E), 5–6 feet, apple-blossom pink, summer; 'William Watson' (E), 4 feet, red, summer. Others, varying in height, flower colour, time of flowering and vigour, are listed in nurserymen's catalogues.

**Cultivation** Escallonias do best in rich, well-drained soil in sheltered positions, in cool areas or in the open where warm enough. Plant during October and November, but in uncertain districts, subject to cold winds, plant in March. Light pruning only is needed in spring

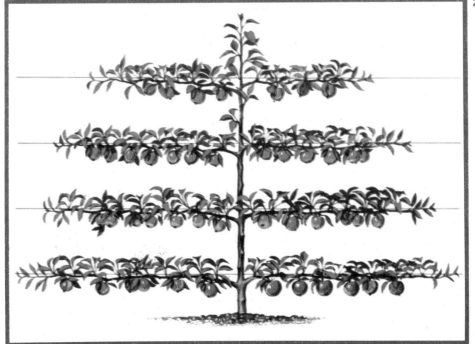

to maintain shape. Propagation is from cuttings made from short sideshoots in August and inserted round the edge of a pot of sandy medium. In general the hybrids are sturdier than the species.

## Eschscholzia (esh-olt-se-a)
Commemorating Johann Friedrich von Eschsholz, physician and naturalist, member of a Russian expedition to north west America in the early nineteenth century *(Papaveraceae)*. A small genus of hardy annuals from West Coast, America, bearing saucer-shaped flowers which open to the sun and close up during damp and cloudy weather.

**Species cultivated** *E. caespitosa*, 6 inches, flowers yellow, 1 inch across, summer; 'Sundew' with lemon-yellow flowers is a cultivar. *E. californica*, the California poppy. This grows to 1 foot tall and has 2 inch wide bright yellow or orange flowers in summer; var. *alba flore pleno* has double white flowers. There are numerous named varieties and strains to be found seedsmen's lists, in which the flowers vary from the palest lemon and apricot to a clear orange-red. Both single and double varieties are available, in heights from 9 inches–1 foot or so. The foliage is a consistent pale silvery-green, light, feathery and an exquisite foil for the flowers. They will be found under such names as 'Monarch Art Shades'; 'Carmine King'; 'Golden Glory'; 'Mandarin' and 'Toreador'. New strains are constantly being developed.

**Cultivation** A light, well-drained soil is most suitable, although these annuals will grow in any ordinary garden soil. Where they flourish they will seed themselves freely. Sow seed out of doors, in open, sunny positions in September or March to April where the plants are to flower and thin the seedlings to 6 inches apart, as soon as they are large enough to handle, to prevent them from becoming spindly. Once the flowers begin to fade cut them off to prevent the formation of seed and thus prolong the flowering season unless, of course, self-sown seedlings are required.

## Espalier
The literal meaning of this term is a fruit wall, a framework upon which fruit trees are supported. A well-constructed espalier has an upright post every 10 feet securely embedded in the ground and standing about 6 feet out of it. Horizontal wires are strung at intervals of about 15 inches along the posts, connecting one post to the next. The end posts are supported by diagonal stays to enable the wires to be pulled tight in order that the ultimate weight of fruit

Eschscholzia californica 'Monarch Art Shades', produces semi-double flowers in various shades. California poppies will flower over a long period.
2 A fruited apple tree trained espalier-fashion, with horizontal branches.

ESPOSTOA
HUANUCENSIS

shall not overload the erection.

Fruit trees are then planted at intervals along the fence so constructed, and trained in a horizontal fashion to the wires. Trees trained in this way have come to be called, quite erroneously, espaliers, though they may be referred to as espalier-trained trees.

There are two methods of training the young plants. In the first the stem is allowed to grow upright and as laterals develop they are tied in to the wires horizontally on each side of the main stem. On maturity the general effect along the fence is of horizontal ribbons of blossom and later fruit. The second form of training uses the side branches in exactly the same way but after they have been trained for a short distance in the horizontal position, they are turned upwards, thus forming a broad-based letter 'U'.

When fruit is grown on this system, more can be accommodated in a given space, light reaching all branches and air circulating freely, resulting in a

**1** Espostoa lanata, a cactus from Ecuador and Peru, covered with silky hairs. It produces white flowers that are nearly hidden in the wool. They are followed by red fruit with white, juicy flesh.
**2** Espostoa huanucensis.

heavier crop than would be possible were the dwarf trees grown as bushes.

Pears and apples are commonly trained in this way, either in the open or against walls. The method can also look effective for training apricots and soft fruits against walls and even foliage plants such as ivy are sometimes trained in this way on house walls.

## Espostoa (es-pos-to-a)

Commemorating Nicholas E. Esposto, Peruvian botanist *(Cactaceae)*. Greenhouse cacti, tall growing, stems usually clothed with whitish spines and wool.

**Species cultivated** *E. dautwitzii,* light green stem, 26–30 ribs, densely covered with yellowish hair or wool, small white funnel-shaped flowers, Peru. *E. haagei,* stem branched at base, covered with matted white silky hairs, flowers white, Peru. *E. lanata,* erect stem, sometimes branching at the top covered with yellowish silky hairs, flowers white, fruit red, Ecuador. *E. melanostele,* dark green stems branching at base, short golden spines, flowers white, Peru.

**Cultivation** A suitable soil mixture is one of a rather light nature to which a sixth part of added sharp sand or other roughage to increase porosity. Repot in April, every three years, or sooner if plants are pot-bound. Place the pots in a very sunny place in the greenhouse. Water the plants from April to September, when a suitable temperature range is 65–80°F (18–27°C), but keep them dry during the winter, at a minimum temperature of 40°F (4°C). Propagation is by seed sown in sandy soil in pans. Place these in a warm position, shade and keep moist. Cuttings may be made from sideshoots when available; dry the cut part before rooting the cutting in sharp sand.